# Methodism

# Methodism

EMPIRE OF THE SPIRIT

David Hempton

*Yale University Press*    *New Haven and London*

Published with assistance from the Annie Burr Lewis Fund.

Designed by James J. Johnson and set in Baskerville & Bulmer types by Keystone
Typesetting, Inc., Orwigsburg, Pennsylvania.
Printed in the United States of America by Edwards Brothers, Ann Arbor, Michigan.

*Library of Congress Cataloging-in-Publication Data*

Hempton, David.
Methodism : empire of the spirit / David Hempton.
        p.     cm.
Includes bibliographical references and index.
ISBN 0–300–10614–9 (alk. paper)
1. Methodism — History — 18th century. 2. Methodism — History — 19th century. I. Title.
BX8231.H46 2005
287′.09′033 — dc22                                              2004024637

A catalogue record for this book is available from the British Library.

10   9   8   7   6   5   4   3   2   1

*To Louanne, Stephen, Jonney, Winnie, and Margaret, with love*

And this blessed gift of venerating love has been given to too many humble craftsmen since the world began, for us to feel any surprise that it should have existed in the soul of a Methodist carpenter half a century ago, while there was yet a lingering after-glow from the time of Wesley and his fellow-labourer fed on the hips and haws of the Cornwall hedges, after exhausting limbs and lungs in carrying a divine message to the poor.

That after-glow has long faded away; and the picture we are apt to make of Methodism in our imagination is not an amphitheatre of green hills, or the deep shade of broad-leaved sycamores, where a crowd of rough men and weary-hearted women drank in a faith which was a rudimentary culture, which linked their thoughts with the past, lifted their imagination above the sordid details of their own narrow lives, and suffused their souls with the sense of a pitying, loving, infinite Presence, sweet as summer to the houseless needy. It is too possible that to some of my readers Methodism may mean nothing more than low-pitched gables up dingy streets, sleek grocers, sponging preachers, and hypocritical jargon — elements which are regarded as an exhaustive analysis of Methodism in many fashionable quarters. That would be a pity.

— GEORGE ELIOT, *Adam Bede* (1859)

# Contents

# Acknowledgments

The admittedly simple idea that a book about the rise of Methodism could not be written without taking into account the full geographical spread of the movement throughout the British Isles, North America, and beyond came to mind a decade ago at a conference on Methodism and the shaping of American culture held at Asbury, Kentucky. Having already absorbed from W. R. Ward the importance of locating Methodist roots among the displaced and persecuted pietist minorities of central Europe, and from John Walsh the importance of viewing Methodism as a significant part of the religious and social history of the British Isles, participants at the conference in Asbury, including Nathan Hatch, Mark Noll, George Rawlyk, Russell Richey, John Wigger, Cathy Brekus, Richard Carwardine, Will Graveley, and Bill Sutton, showed me that Methodism was also a decidedly transatlantic phenomenon. In more recent times, Dana Robert, David Martin, Andrew Walls, and others have shown me that Methodism (and its Holiness and Pentecostal offshoots) was also a truly global phenomenon. To all these colleagues, mentors, and friends I am pleased to record my intellectual indebtedness.

As Methodism crossed the Atlantic, so in 1998 did I. Both the colleagues I left behind in Queen's University Belfast and those who welcomed me in Boston University have contributed ideas, support, and collegiality without which this book could not have been written. I am particularly grateful to the distinguished cast who attended the seminar on religious history at Queen's and those who teach history of Christianity in Boston. I am also grateful to Bill Hutchison and David Hall for their kind invitation to join the American Colloquium at Harvard Divinity School, where faculty and graduate students have helped educate me in the history and historiography of what is still to me a new nation.

All historians have a special fondness for the libraries and librarians who make the otherwise lonely hours companionable. I am particularly grateful to Gareth Lloyd and the staff of the John Rylands Library in Manchester, Raymond Van DeMoortell, Jack Ammerman, and Steve Pentek in Boston University, Bill Kostlevy in Asbury, and the staff at the Bodleian Library in Oxford and the Widener Library in Harvard. Others too numerous to mention on both sides of the Atlantic have generously replied to apparently endless requests for information.

Over the years I have had the pleasure of working with unusually accomplished graduate students without whose interaction my own work would be greatly impoverished. I am particularly grateful to Myrtle Hill, Janice Holmes, Brian Clark, Jonathan Cooney, Billy Francis, Ben Hartley, Yeon-Seung Lee, and Gary VanderPol. My special thanks are to my research assistants. Glen Messer, whose tireless enthusiasm for Methodist archives is matched only by his generosity in serving the work of others, has served mine also, while Eric Baldwin worked heroically on archives relating to Methodism and global mission. Research and scholarship are often portrayed as lonely, isolated, even eccentric pastimes, but the truth is that like other human enterprises they also bring forth community and friendship in which ideas are shared and creativity encouraged. Over the years my chief intellectual debts have been to Richard Carwardine, Sheridan Gilley, Martin Ingram, David Livingstone, Hugh McLeod, Mark Noll, Reg Ward, and John Walsh, who all combine intellectual excellence with a quite remarkable generosity of spirit.

My chief debt as always is to my wife, Louanne, and children, Stephen and Jonathan. Where the Methodists have gone they have uncomplainingly (most of the time) followed, and must now pray that their journeys have come to an end. They confess to be pleased that this book ends before the worldwide expansion of Methodism and Pentecostalism took hold in manifold different locations in the twentieth century. Their spatial stability depended upon it.

When the distinguished Victorian essayist Sir James Stephen penned the preface to the first edition of his collected *Essays in Ecclesiastical Biography,* which first appeared in the *Edinburgh Review,* he helpfully distinguished between corrigible and incorrigible faults. In what follows, I appeal to the same distinction. For those incorrigible faults that are the result of the mere want of learning and ability to do better, I apologize. For those corrigible faults occasioned by dealing with a wildly expansive subject in a restricted space, I earnestly appeal to others in the future to make good the deficiency.

Parts of this book were constructed for, tried out, and presented in a wide variety of settings. I was particularly honored to give the F. D. Maurice Lectures in King's College London in 2000 on "Enlightenment and

Enthusiasm: Popular Christianity in Trans-Atlantic Perspective, c. 1750–2000." I am grateful to the late Colin Gunton and Mark Smith for their hospitality during that occasion. The chapter titled "Money and Power" was first delivered in 1998 at a "Financing American Evangelicalism" conference held under the auspices of Wheaton College's Institute for the Study of American Evangelicals. I am grateful to Oxford University Press for permission to reproduce that chapter from the book *God and Mammon* (2001), edited by Mark Noll. Chapter 1, "Competition and Symbiosis," was first delivered as the Lowell Lecture in Boston in 2001, and some of the ideas in "Consolidation and Decline" were first presented at a conference on secularization held in the University of Amsterdam in 2003. I am grateful for the comments and suggestions of all the participants in those various conversations.

I am honored to have been awarded the quadrennial Jesse Lee Prize of the United Methodist Church's general commission on archives and history, and hope that the published version of the manuscript repays the faith the commission has shown in my work. Finally, I wish to thank Lara Heimert, the editorial staff at Yale University Press, and the anonymous readers of the manuscript for their careful reading and helpful suggestions. This book is very much better for their input. All remaining errors and limitations are of course in the category of incorrigible faults and are my responsibility alone.

# Methodism

# Methods and Methodism

A revealing encounter took place between two eminent Victorians at a public meeting in Oxford in the early 1880s. Hugh Price Hughes, arguably the most influential figure in late-Victorian Methodism, who was then stationed in Oxford, asked the chair of the meeting, Mark Pattison, the distinguished scholar and rector of Lincoln College, why the university had no adequate memorial to John Wesley. Lincoln was of course Wesley's old college, and Pattison, no lover of religious enthusiasts, rankled at Hughes's suggestion that Wesley was one of the "greatest sons" of the university. Pattison, after all, had been one of the seven contributors to *Essays and Reviews* (1861), a controversial volume extolling the free handling of "religious and moral truth." Pattison's essay, "Tendencies of Religious Thought in England, 1688–1750," runs for more than eighty pages, but John Wesley's name is conspicuous by its absence, and Methodism itself is referred to as somewhere near the opposite pole of reasonable religion. Hughes responded that he was astonished by the university's neglect of the founder of a religious movement numbering some 25 million people throughout the world. Pattison interjected that Hughes surely meant to say 25 thousand, not 25 million. Hughes rummaged in his coat pockets for the statistics that would prove his case, but digits alone could not overcome Pattison's display of Oxonian chauvinism.[1]

Hughes was put down in the intellectual heavyweight Pattison's own Oxford ring, but he was in fact correct. When some years later the aptly named Methodist trio of W. J. Townsend, Herbert B. Workman, and George Eayrs produced their *New History of Methodism*, in 1909, they included a table of world Methodist statistics showing that there were in existence some 8.7 million Methodist church members and around 35 million Methodist worshippers spread over six continents. (Historians conventionally multiply Methodist membership figures by between three and five to estimate adherents.) By the end of the nineteenth century a new and formidable empire of the spirit had come into existence. Moreover, if one takes seriously the recent work of historians and sociologists who argue that the explosion of Pentecostalism in the twentieth century (ironically just taking off when Methodism's *New History* appeared) can best be explained as a much-modified continuation of the Methodist holiness tradition, then at least another 250 million religious enthusiasts could be added to the statistical heap. The speed of Pentecostal growth in Africa, South America, and Asia is staggering. Philip Jenkins states, "According to current projections, the number of Pentecostal believers should surpass the one billion mark before 2050." By then there will be almost as many Pentecostals as Hindus, and twice as many as there are Buddhists. Those like Pattison who find the heap of religious enthusiasm too distasteful to contemplate either minimize its size or confine it to the outskirts of their intellectual cities, but its existence still has to be explained.[2]

The problem before us, therefore, is the disarmingly simple one of accounting for the rise of Methodism from its unpromising origins among the flotsam and jetsam of religious societies and quirky personalities in England in the 1730s to a major international religious movement some hundred and fifty years later. During that period Methodism refashioned the old denominational order in the British Isles, became the largest Protestant denomination in the United States on the eve of the Civil War, and gave rise to the most dynamic world missionary movement of the nineteenth century. For all these reasons, there are grounds for stating that the rise of Methodism was the most important Protestant religious development since the Reformation, yet it remains remarkably under-researched, not least because of the problems raised by Methodism's expansion across national boundaries.

Taking Methodism seriously as a transnational religious movement introduces obvious complexities. Even at the beginning of the twentieth century, before the explosion of scholarship fueled by the rise of the modern universities, the editors of Methodism's *New History* stated that "the task is too large, its relations are too numerous and indefinite, for any one mind, however well stored, to appreciate them all," and farmed out their project to an international team of scholars, all of them Methodists, ironically confirming Pattison's statement in *Essays and Reviews* that "we have not yet learnt, in this country, to write our ecclesiastical history on any better footing than that of praising up the party, in or out of the Church, to which we happen to belong." Since the publication of the *New History* single minds have grappled with parts of the problem, usually

# THE
# Oxford Methodists :

Being some ACCOUNT of a

## Society *of* Young Gentlemen

IN

That CITY, so denominated ;

Setting forth their

RISE, VIEWS, *and* DESIGNS.

WITH

Some Occasional REMARKS

ON

A LETTER inserted in *Fog's Journal* of *December* 9th, relating to them.

---

*In a* LETTER *from a Gentleman near* OXFORD, *to his Friend at* LONDON.

---

LONDON:

Printed for J. ROBERTS, at the *Oxford-Arms* in *Warwick-Lane.* 1733.

Title page from *The Oxford Methodists* (1733), the work in which John Wesley's name was first associated with the term "Methodist" (Courtesy of the John Rylands Library, University of Manchester)

within the narrow confines of national historical traditions, but Methodism, as the *New History*'s statistics amply demonstrate, was an international movement. By the end of the nineteenth century fewer than 10
percent of Methodists lived in the British Isles. By then the United States,
with over 75 percent of church members, had emerged as the power-
house of world Methodism. There were, for example, considerably more
African-American Methodists in the United States than the entire Methodist population of Europe, where the movement originated. That fact
alone should be of interest to those seeking to explain the different
secularization trajectories of the United States and western and central
Europe. It is possible to argue, for example, that western Europe's
greater secularism in the twentieth century is at least partly owing to the
comparative failure of populist religious movements in the nineteenth
century. Such a response, of course, only pushes the question of secularization back one stage, but it is at least a more fruitful line of inquiry than
some of the material produced on this subject.[3]

How then is the rise of a great religious movement to be explained,
and what is the approach to be followed in this volume? I should perhaps
start with my own interest in the Methodist movement, which goes back
over a quarter century. It all started, as it did for many people who came
of age in the 1960s, with Edward Thompson's brilliant book *The Making of
the English Working Class* (1963), which sat on the shelves of many a history undergraduate as a kind of status symbol or bookend. That thunder-
ing chapter on Methodism, "The Transforming Power of the Cross," with
its Blakean prose and Muggletonian Marxist ideology, has a fierce intellectual power and stylistic affluence not easily forgotten.[4] Having grown
up in Ulster, where the fusion of religion and politics is intravenously
injected at birth, I chose not to believe Thompson's Marxist/Freudian
portrayal of Methodism and popular politics in England during the industrial revolution. My first book, *Methodism and Politics in British Society,
1750–1850* (London, 1984), was an attempt to show why. The task
seemed to be not too difficult, for Thompson did very little primary
research on Methodism in early industrial England, and graduate students are always eager to tilt at their intellectual superiors. But I later
learned that Thompson had something that I underestimated at the
time: Methodism was in his genes, as it was in some other great Marxist
historians of the twentieth century. "The Transforming Power of the
Cross," whatever its methodological deficiencies, was both genetic and
splenetic, and as such it went much deeper than mere ideology, far beyond the reach of a mere graduate student.

My second book on Methodism, *The Religion of the People: Methodism and Popular Religion, c. 1750–1900* (London, 1996), was a set of exploratory essays seeking fresh ways to look at Methodist growth and experience. By then it had dawned on me that Methodism was not merely an English movement but had roots in European Pietism, spread rapidly for a time in Ireland and Wales, and more significantly crossed the Atlantic to North America where it achieved its greatest nineteenth-century gains. It was clear to me that any account of Methodism that failed to take into account its international dimensions was by definition incomplete, perhaps even dangerous, for it had become fashionable within the academy to think of Methodism as the religious product of a particular national historical tradition. Several other matters had also become clearer. First, Methodism was predominantly a women's movement and needed to be treated as such. Second, it was also a movement of people who claimed a particular kind of religious experience that was difficult for us moderns to understand, but could not be avoided. Third, Methodism's sheer complexity as a religious movement required a wide range of investigative techniques to get somewhere near the heart of it. With varying degrees of success, I experimented with legal history, biography, literature, and various other tools pioneered by exponents of what was then known as "popular religion," and has now been defined somewhat differently, if scarcely more satisfactorily, as "lived religion."[5]

Bearing in mind the three-strikes rule of American baseball and California law enforcement, one should probably have settled for two swings at the target and retired to the dugout. The reason for a third book on Methodism is a strong conviction that there is still something worthwhile to be done that has not been done. This conviction came after circumstances permitted a much deeper acquaintance with Methodism on the American side of the Atlantic. First I had seen Methodism as an English phenomenon, then as a British Isles movement, and now as an international movement. Although I had not self-consciously conceived of it in this way, it has become clear that my Methodist pilgrimage follows closely recent trends in the writing of English history in the early modern period as it slowly expanded to take account of the rest of the British Isles, Europe, North America, and the Empire. It was no accident, therefore, that my first book on Methodism was written largely in Britain, the second in Ireland, and the third in the United States.

Ever-expanding geographical horizons is only one part of the story, however. As the horizon receded so too did the conceptual frameworks within which much of my earlier work had been constructed. It was not just that Methodism moved from place to place and therefore needed to be contextualized, vital though that task is, but that the movement was somehow greater than the sum of its parts, and could not be reconstructed simply by aggregating its regional manifestations. That realization determined the structure of the present book. One way of writing an international history of Methodist expansion is to approach it in the same way as Townsend, Workman, and Eayrs planned their *New History of Methodism* almost a century ago. First they tried to place Methodism in the life and thought of the Christian church, and then they parceled out "Methodism beyond the seas" to an international team of Methodist worthies with resident expertise in particular countries. They produced an excellent institutional history of the Methodist empire, the publication of which coincided with the high-water mark of the British Empire on the eve of the First World War. It would be tempting to reproduce their model a century later by assembling a team of scholars to write on Methodist growth in particular locations, but there are two problems with such an approach. The first is that it would be difficult to improve upon the quality of local, regional, and national histories of Methodism already published, especially those produced within the last twenty years, when historians of Methodism broke free from the partisan ecclesiastical and institutional priorities of their predecessors. The second problem with a team approach is that, however impressive the individual contributions might be, the final product would almost certainly lack a unified conceptual apparatus within which the rise of Methodism as a transnational movement could be located.

When this project was first conceived, therefore, the intention had been to organize the book around the chronology and geography of Methodist expansion, a strategy one might employ, for example, to explain the rise of a political empire. The realization soon dawned that it would be almost impossible to improve upon the highly specialized work already in the field, so that one would have ended up either synthesizing or plagiarizing the work of others. Moreover, the rapacious demands of supplying an appropriately comprehensive geographical coverage would have seriously limited the space available for more penetrating questions about the nature of the entire Methodist project and its relation to the world in which it grew. What follows therefore is an attempt to write a history of Methodism as an international movement—an empire of the spirit—by concentrating on eight important themes, each one designed to get beneath the hard surface of mere institutional expansion. Having neither the genius nor the luxury afforded by artistic license, my evocation of Methodism cannot hope to rival Dickens's portrayal of the dense social fog of early industrial England in *Bleak House* or Conrad's fictional journey in *The Heart of Darkness,* or even George Eliot's biopsy of social tissue in *Middlemarch,* but the same aspiration to penetrate somehow to the heart of something both elusive and important is the motivation for what follows.

Those with even a passing familiarity with Methodism as a religious movement know that it appeared to thrive on the energy unleashed by dialectical friction. It was a movement of discipline and sobriety, but also of ecstasy and enthusiasm. It was a voluntary association of free people, but also specialized in rules, regulations, and books of discipline. It railed against riches, but became inexorably associated with the steady accumulation of wealth. It once prided itself on its appeal to the unlearned, but then founded educational institutions with unparalleled fecundity. With the power of Methodist dialectics in mind, therefore, I have chosen to organize each chapter around parallel or competing concepts.

"Competition and Symbiosis" is an attempt to explore the growth of Methodism across the North Atlantic world by applying a metaphor derived from evolutionary biology. Methodism was a missionary organization that thrived on mobility and expanded in association with the rise of markets and the growth of empire. What gave it its competitive advantage over scores of other populist religious traditions, and why did it grow in some places but not in others? By examining case studies on both sides of the Atlantic the chapter shows how Methodism forged a symbiotic relationship with its host environments. The closer the environmental fit between species and habitat, the faster and more sustained was the growth.

"Enlightenment and Enthusiasm" shows how these apparent extremes on the eighteenth-century religious scale were brought into dialectical tension by a movement that owed more to enlightened thought than its critics were prepared to accept. Methodism was not a product of the Enlightenment in any neat formulaic sense, but both its theology and its ecclesiology owed a great deal to Lockean empiricism and contractualism. Wesley was without doubt an enthusiast, albeit of a particular kind, but he also absorbed, both consciously and unconsciously, some of the characteristic ideas of the Enlightenment. The contents of Methodist archives throughout the world display the trace elements of Methodism's origins in enthusiasm and enlightenment as children carry the genetic codes of their parents.

"The Medium and the Message" is an attempt to get to the heart and center of the Methodist *message* and how it was *heard* and *experienced* in the eighteenth and nineteenth centuries. Too often the Methodist message is reduced to its theology and enters the world through learned discourse with printed texts, but that is not what made the movement fizz. The chapter paints two triptychs, one of birth, life, and death (in Methodist parlance, conversion, sanctification, and holy dying) and another of hymns, sermons, and social gatherings. What was Methodist noise and how was it heard and appropriated by women and men? (Women were almost always the majority.) How did the noise and the experience vary from place to place and even from continent to continent?

"Opposition and Conflict" is based on the idea that opposition to Methodism is revealing both of the kind of movement it was and of its interaction with the communities in which it took root. Vigorous opposition shows that something important is at stake and sensibilities are being offended. In England early Methodism was thought to be disruptive and divisive in families and villages. Methodists were accused of fragmenting communities, disrupting work, stealing money, hosting orgies, inducing madness, and reviving Puritanism. No matter that many of these allegations were contradictory; what mattered is that they were made. In America Methodists were accused of promoting ignorance, enthusiasm, and hypocrisy. The pattern of opposition to Methodism varied with location, changed over time, and became less intense as Methodism became more respectable. Moreover, conflict within Methodism is as revealing as opposition to it. Methodism as a voluntary religious association had a way of transmitting wider social tensions into internal disputes about governance and policy. Discord within Methodism not only was a product of an egalitarian message and an authoritarian ecclesiology but also was suggestive of the stresses and strains affecting the wider society. Methodism acted as a litmus test of social tension.

"Money and Power" is an ecclesiastical version of the Watergate injunction to "follow the money." Being neither a state church nor a federation of gathered congregations, the financing of Methodism in its great age of expansion is a complex and almost completely neglected area of study. It is also profoundly revealing of the kind of movement it was and how power was distributed within the connection. In religious organizations, as in other large corporations, money and power are rarely separated for very long, and so it was with Methodism. The way money was raised in Methodism, the purposes for which it was spent, and how fund-raising changed over time are all deeply illustrative of the wider values of the movement. Comparing and contrasting the financing of British and American Methodism is another way of penetrating to some important differences between the two most significant early traditions of Methodism.

"Boundaries and Margins" attempts to explain why Methodism recruited so prolifically among "the lower orders," women, and African Americans. Some Marxist and some feminist historians find no difficulty interpreting Methodism as a form of social or gender control, but the evidence is never unambiguously supportive of such an interpretation. No doubt Methodism could operate as a form of social control, and no doubt it was appropriated by many as a way of absorbing the shock of social change, but there is compelling evidence also to suggest that women, African Americans, and workers *chose* to be Methodists because it offered them tangible benefits of various kinds. Methodism's sober disciplines and tender pieties were not to everyone's tastes, but they were embraced by people who had opportunities to choose alternative forms of religious affiliation, or none, and chose neither of those options.

"Mapping and Mission" is an attempt to look at Methodism's rise to globalism in the nineteenth century on the back of two expanding civilizations, British and American. Ironically a populist religious movement was the beneficiary of the trappings of power and empire, including military conquest, commercial exploitation, and cultural imperialism. In each new space in different continents Methodism established something of its distinctive religious style. Sometimes the conflicts inherent in such transactions echo earlier controversies within Methodism as it spread throughout the British Isles and then across the Atlantic. Tensions soon arose between denominational planning and individual initiative, between bureaucratic control and personal inspiration, and between cultural conquest and inter-cultural negotiation.

"Consolidation and Decline" looks at the ways in which a populist religious association became a settled denomination and then began to experience declining growth rates. Wesley left his successors in Britain and North America with an unenviable task. Methodism's rambling connectional structure was a nightmare to govern. In the early nineteenth century the problem was less acute in America than in England because the ever-expanding frontier allowed for the possibility of Methodism marching to its old tunes. But sooner or later in every country in which Methodism established a large presence, the problems posed by connectional governance and administration had to be faced. Was Methodism's path to denominational consolidation and decline in the West the inevitable product of its transition from a revival movement to a settled church, or did Methodist leaders fatally embrace wrong strategies? What does the decline of Methodism in the West reveal about wider patterns of secularization as the center of gravity of world Christianity inexorably shifted from the developed northern and western hemispheres to the undeveloped southern and eastern hemispheres? Does the Methodist holiness tradition live on in the worldwide expansion of Pentecostalism, or is it essentially a new movement with different characteristics?

Each of these chapters has an independent claim to reveal something profound about the heart of Methodism, but together they show also the elusive nature of a religious movement that by the end of the nineteenth century had attracted the loyalty of more than 30 million people on six continents. The two things that can be said with certainty about Methodism are that it grew prodigiously from its roots as a tiny religious society within the Church of England in the 1730s to a major worldwide denomination, and that historians will continue to disagree vigorously about why such growth took place and what were its consequences. My aim has been to make a contribution to that debate by examining the rise of Methodism as a transnational movement of ordinary people not easily confined to particular times, places, and institutions.

# CHAPTER ONE

# Competition and Symbiosis

In research the horizon recedes as we advance . . . and research is always incomplete.
— MARK PATTISON, *Essays and Reviews* (1861)

How is the rise of a great religious movement to be explained? As the title suggests, my approach will be to use two concepts from the field of evolutionary biology, competition and symbiosis, to explain how the Methodist species survived, adapted, and expanded. As biologists learn more about the mechanisms of natural selection and genetic mutation, they have come to place more emphasis, not on the relatively well known concept of the survival of the fittest, but on the idea that species survive in a complex symbiotic relationship with one another. Similarly, systems biologists now see the need not only to understand primitive cellular tissue but also to appreciate bigger pictures of organisms and their environments. So it is with Methodism. Much has been written about the movement from an internalist point of view, stressing quite properly the infrastructure of a religious movement built for growth, but Methodist growth did not take place in isolation from other important trends in the new world order of the eighteenth and nineteenth centuries. How were they linked? How did the symbiosis work in practice, not just in theory?[1]

I set out on this discussion with not a little trepidation, because previous attempts have not worn very well. Forty years ago it was fashionable to regard Methodism as expressly a counter-enlightenment and counter-revolutionary movement that helped enslave its members to a new economic order based on factory production and raw capitalism. Much of this interpretation has withered with the Marxist and Weberian ideology that sustained it, but there are still books coming off the presses arguing that Methodism's primary appeal was to a predominantly superstitious popular culture that had been abandoned by more cultivated and rational religious institutions. The implication of all this is that Methodism was essentially a socially regressive movement, either at odds with good modernizing forces or an agent of bad modernizing forces. Those who

"John Wesley Preaching to the Indians in Georgia, c. 1736," an engraving from the early nineteenth century. Since there is no firm evidence that Wesley ever preached to Native Americans, this engraving shows the Methodist propensity for inventing tradition. (Courtesy of the John Rylands Library)

resisted that interpretation, out of good intentions, often replaced it with an unconvincingly urbane kind of Methodism shorn of its raw populism and contributing to a new world order based on liberalism, ecumenism, and freedom of choice. Thus, neither critics nor defenders seemed able to capture the essence of a religious movement with the capacity to grow with explosive energy from very unpromising origins.[2]

Unpromising may be an understatement. Protestant churches, suffering from external threat and internal decay, were at a low ebb in the late seventeenth and early eighteenth centuries in Europe. Under pressure from the cumulative weight of the Counter-Reformation and from vigorous policies of confessional assimilation, Protestant morale was sagging. In the England of Wesley's early manhood there were litanies of woe about the general wickedness of the age, the progress of rationalism and deism, the decline of Church courts, the existence of new proto-industrial populations wild and free from religion, the political corruption of Robert Walpole's brand of whiggery, and, whether imagined or real, the general malaise of the Church of England. European Protestantism seemed to be entering a religious ice age in which old species were more likely to disappear than new ones arise. Yet beneath the surface, vigorous new forms of life were already taking shape. Just at the point when old religious establishments began to creak, new forms of Protestant Christianity, according to W. R. Ward, "exhibited astonishing new vigour by going over wholesale to unconfessional, international, societary means of action, in which the laity paid for and often ran great machines which had no place in the traditional church orders."[3]

One of Protestantism's great post-Reformation deficiencies, therefore, its lack of religious orders, was partly redeemed by the international mobility of pious Protestants from central Europe. The catalysts were the Moravians. An unlikely combination of Moravian and Anglican enthusiasm for mission on the frontier of Britain's new American empire soon opened up a more benign religious version of the infamous triangular trade of slavery and cotton that fueled the economics of empire. This particular religious triangle was between continental Europe, especially Halle and Hernnhut, Britain, especially London and Oxford, and Georgia, especially Savannah. Some of this was facilitated by the existence of the Hanoverian court in London, some of it was generated by the activities of the Society for the Propagation of the Gospel, but most of it was sustained by the remarkable speed and volume of religious communications (both of literature and personnel) in the early eighteenth century. As the expansion of Europe into the New World gathered pace in the eighteenth century, the spoils would go to those who were prepared to be mobile, and who had a powerful religious message to trade.[4]

The message was refined in the Fetter Lane Society in London, a religious pollen factory that performed the same role for Methodism as Azusa Street did later for Pentecostalism. Fetter Lane, strategically situated in the capital city of trade and empire, was a meeting point for German visitors to London, Calvinist evangelicals, Welsh revivalists, French Prophets, London's artisan pietists, and English High Churchmen like the Wesleys. Not all was sweetness and light, however. The Fetter Lane Society was repeatedly rocked by doctrinal, ecclesiological, and semi-political disagreements. Wesley was particularly concerned with potentially dangerous quietist, mystical, and radical opinions such as the obliteration of distinctions between clergy and laity. Those with long memories of the social mayhem attributed to the radical sectaries of the seventeenth century knew well that popular religious enthusiasm, especially when yoked to social or political egalitarianism, was an unstable compound. Of particular importance was the conflict between Wesley and the Moravians. The Moravians brought Wesley's hard-schooled, High Church piety face to face with a heart-warming variety of European pietism with roots deep in classical Lutheranism and Reformation spirituality. But there was a parting of the ways in 1740 over "stillness," which Wesley repudiated as antinomianism, and Christian perfectionism, which Nikolaus Ludwig von Zinzendorf and the Moravians (and most everyone else) regarded as delusional. The dispute, which crystallized over different approaches to the sacrament (Moravians urged avoidance by those without faith, whereas Wesley saw it as a means of grace for all), was no mere theological tiff; at stake, to continue the biological metaphor, was the genetic structure of a new kind of religious species. The particular theological components of this new species, its evangelical Arminianism, its doctrine of assurance, and its quest for entire sanctification, are all well known, but what is not sufficiently appreciated is how these components, working together, created the kind of energetic activism for which Methodism became notorious. Spreading scriptural holiness throughout the land, and indeed the world, was the task; outdoor and itinerant preaching, societary association, and connectionalism were the means; individual assurance, communal discipline and national regeneration were the ends.[5]

All this seems neat and tidy; it was anything but. Unsurprisingly, given his political and religious heritage, Wesley oscillated between seeking to reform the national religious establishment from above and trying to forge new structures from below. This tension between authoritarianism and religious conservatism on the one hand, and something approaching egalitarianism and religious radicalism on the other was evident wher-

"John Wesley Preaching from the Market Cross at Epworth." Outdoor preaching to humble people became a trademark wherever Methodism took root. (Courtesy of the John Rylands Library)

ever Methodism took root. The resulting conflicts were played out as ferociously within the Methodist tradition as they were between the tradition and its surrounding culture. The outcome was nevertheless vital, for what the tables of Methodist growth rates throughout the world clearly reveal is that Methodism did not prosper for very long when yoked to religious establishments with little popular appeal. New species gain nothing by clinging tenaciously to old and declining habitats; but not much of this was clear in England in the 1740s. Early Methodist expansion was spotty, eclectic, and messy. Wesley's much vaunted genius for organization turns out upon closer inspection to have been a ragbag of pragmatic innovations borrowed from Moravians and Quakers, or suggested to him by other free-market itinerant evangelists, most of whom he later fought with.[6] As research moves forward on Wesley's early contemporaries such as John Bennet, Benjamin Ingham, and David Taylor, it becomes clearer that Wesley was not the lonesome genius of Methodist legend. He often reaped where others had sown, and borrowed ideas others had generated. What gave him his preponderance were energy, mobility, perseverance, and sheer force of will. What gave Methodism its preponderance over other early evangelistic associations was its ability to bestow an element of coherence and order on the disparate and often bizarre religiosity it encountered. The surviving diaries of Methodist leaders in the 1740s reveal passionate attempts to impose a degree of religious discipline amid the psychological disturbance, sexual repression, and immediate providentialism that wafted around early Methodist spirituality. Both men and women felt anxiety, shed tears, prayed fervently, saw visions, encountered scoffers, and slowly bowed the knee to Wesley's iron will and charismatic leadership. Bands and classes, hymns and love feasts, and rules and discipline supplied the requisite structures and rituals for reconstituted lives. In short, Methodism evolved with a theology and a structure that enabled it to meet the essential demands of individual assurance and communal discipline in a world order on the brink of very substantial changes. Methodism survived as the fittest of the various brands of evangelical piety in the first half of the eighteenth century, but its future growth depended largely on how well it would adapt to dramatic environmental changes.

The changes from which Methodism stood to gain, or lose, show up in the standard histories of the later eighteenth century: rapid demographic expansion; population mobility, whether compulsory or voluntary, especially to the New World; the development of proto-industrialization, industrialization, and social class; the rise of domestic and international markets; the growth of consumerism; the spread of the British Empire and

therefore of Anglicanism; the beginnings of revolutionary political movements; and the transplanting of old European religious conflicts into new
soil in different parts of the world. These relatively concrete changes,
which can be counted and reproduced in maps and graphs, were accompanied by less utilitarian but equally important changes in thought and
culture involving the spread of enlightenment and religious toleration,
changes in gender relations and family structure, and subtle shifts in the
construction of individual and group identities.[7]

The precise relationship of Methodist expansion to these changes is
infinitely complex, as complex as the relationships between species and
their environments. Faced with such complexity there are a number of
misleading ways to think about the problem of religious growth. The first
is to assume a kind of uniformity of conceptualization that chains Methodist growth to only one or two of these processes. For example, parallels
are frequently drawn between Methodist Arminianism (a free-choice salvation open to all) and the spread of markets and consumerism.[8] Such
explanations, because of their conceptual clarity, are often dispropor-
tionately influential. They also have the advantage of plugging into established discourses in national historiographical traditions. The explanatory power of drawing attention to these symbiotic relationships between
Methodism and its surrounding culture is considerable, but never absolute, because it limits the possibility of other symbioses working just as
influentially, either in the same location or in other places at other times.
Faced with these difficulties it is tempting to shift the focus from the
demand side of the equation to the supply side by attributing Methodist growth solely to its own theological, organizational, and human resources. Such explanations are particularly attractive to those writing
from within religious traditions who assume that species always change
environments, never the reverse. This error is more damaging to the
process of historical explanation than the first, because it generally ignores context, and decontextualized history turns easily into hagiography or institutional reconstruction. The price for such an approach is
often paid by religious traditions when attempting to explain their decline. Having never properly grasped the forces producing their own
growth (the same could be said of some secularization theorists), explanations of decline are similarly naive and attenuated. The one advantage
of this tradition of interpretation, however, is that it usually pays more
attention to religious motivation and human agency than accounts based
on structural or metaphorical symbioses alone.

One solution to the problems posed above is to multiply highly detailed local studies, many of which now exist, but the result can be the

same as a heavy-handed pointillist painting that draws the eye more to the spots than the painting. Georges Seurat's conviction that painting in dots would produce a brighter color than painting in strokes is true of some brilliant local studies of Methodism, but an attempt also has to be made to shape the dots into a recognizable canvas.[9] The approach I want to experiment with here is to outline briefly some of the most important symbiotic processes in Methodist expansion and then select four suggestive case studies, two from each side of the Atlantic, to show how symbiosis worked itself out in particular environments.

The obvious place to start, but ironically the most neglected, is to look at Methodism's relationship to the religious tradition out of which it emerged, Anglicanism. Good books exist on John Wesley's relationship with the Church of England or on the place of Methodism within the broad Anglican tradition, but the way in which Methodism as a growing movement nurtured itself, sometimes parasitically, on its parent is scarcely ever analyzed despite the fact that any number of local studies raise the issue. For example, Methodism gained its toehold in America among high concentrations of settlers of English ancestry in the Delmarva Peninsula in the 1770s. Methodism offered a more enthusiastic religion for Anglicans in an environment unsuitable to liturgical and moralistic refinement. In a tough new cultural frontier Methodism "substituted seriousness for frivolity, cooperation for competition, compassion for brutality and egalitarianism for deference." Similarly, Methodism's early success in Ireland, notwithstanding its exaggerated claims of converting Catholics, came among the predominantly English settlers in Armagh and Fermanagh who needed something more vibrant than traditional Anglicanism to equip them for the increased economic and religious competition of the border counties of southern Ulster at the end of the eighteenth century. The Methodist cause in Canada, after unpropitious starts in Lower Canada (present-day Quebec) and the Maritimes, was given a dramatic boost in Upper Canada (present-day Ontario) in the wake of the American Revolution with the settling of some seventy-five hundred United Empire Loyalists, disbanded British troops, and British immigrants. When the British government tried to recognize this new reality in 1791 by endowing the Church of England, the Methodists offered a powerful religious alternative. As is the way with Methodist cultures, once established, the preponderance of Ontario within Canadian Methodism lasted for a very long time.[10]

Slightly different patterns of parasitical relationships show up in Britain. In Wales, for example, Methodism benefited both from Anglican success and its weakness. By securing the popular base of Welsh-speaking literacy, the circulating schools movement established in the eighteenth century by the Anglican clergyman Griffith Jones laid the foundation for the quite remarkable triumph of Methodism and Evangelical Nonconformity in the nineteenth century. In Wales, as in many parts of England, Anglicanism, through education and catechisms, helped establish a religious market that its own resources could never satisfy. More insidiously, from the Established Church's point of view, the Church of England often ended up on the side of landowners, political conservatives, and social paternalists at precisely the point when all three were coming under popular attack. As much recent work has shown, eighteenth-century Anglicanism was not as corrupt, lazy, and moribund as later evangelical and Anglo-Catholic critics alleged, but it simply found itself on the wrong side of major environmental changes—demographic, political, and economic—which, given its establishmentarian assumptions, it was unable to accommodate. Methodists, like clever parasites, took from the tradition what they needed, including the relative tolerance with which it was treated, and then established an independent existence by embracing the enthusiasm and populism that Anglicans generally despised. Consequently, Methodism spread into most parts of the world opened up by British imperial and Anglican expansion. It never made much headway in areas of traditional Roman Catholic strength in southern Ireland, France, and Quebec, where the patterns of growth are low and broadly the same. Similarly, Methodism never made much impression on the Presbyterian and Calvinist strongholds of Scotland, Ulster, and parts of the American colonies. Eighteenth-century Methodism, throughout the English-speaking world, was essentially a sub-species of Anglicanism, but with a greater capacity to adapt to the changing conditions of a new world order.[11]

The story of species adaptation is yet more complicated. Methodism found it difficult to penetrate areas of long-standing Anglican strength, such as the settled parishes of the southeast of England where the tight social control of squire and parson left little room for Methodist encroachment. Its greatest gains came in the large, dispersed parishes of Wales and the north of England where demographic expansion and pastoral neglect offered new openings for the itinerant foot soldiers of the Methodist army. It was at the Anglican interface with mobility and change that Methodism made its conquests. The means by which this happened were sometimes serendipitous. For example, Laurence Coughlan, a converted Irish Catholic who became a Wesleyan itinerant preacher in England before falling out with Wesley over his controversial ordination by the Greek émigré Bishop Erasmus, served the earliest Methodist societies in Newfoundland in the 1760s. Coughlan was eventually ordained by the Anglican bishops of Lincoln and Chester before setting out in 1766 as a missionary to Newfoundland under the sponsorship of the Anglican Society for the Propagation of the Gospel.[12]

Not many could match Coughlan's checkered career, but his story points up an often neglected part of the rise of Methodism, which thrived among geographically mobile populations in the eighteenth century. A more revealing example is that of Barbara Ruckle Heck, who was part of a colony of German refugees from the Palatinate given land grants in Ireland in the wake of Louis XIV's successive devastations of the Palatinate. She, her husband Paul Heck, and her cousin Philip Embury, like many other European Protestant refugees in eighteenth-century Ireland, were revived by Wesley before moving to New York, where they were instrumental in setting up a Methodist society and building the first Methodist chapel in America. But the story does not end there. Forming Methodist societies along the way, the Hecks later migrated up the Hudson Valley and then, as Empire Loyalists, on to Montreal and later to Augusta township in Upper Canada. Their story of how a European pietist minority, displaced and persecuted as a result of confessional cleansing, came into contact with a new kind of enthusiastic Protestantism in Britain and Ireland, which was then exported to America and Canada, is powerfully emblematic of the awakenings of the eighteenth century. Historians more interested in structural economic symbioses between Methodism and its surrounding culture often ignore these stories, partly because they were later embellished for pious consumption and hagiographical purpose, but that is a mistake. What they show is that in the eighteenth century a combination of confessional cleansing, imperial expansion, cultural fascination with the peripheries of empire, religious revivalism, and the rise of global trade all combined to produce a remarkably mobile population of popular Protestants.

There are yet further dimensions to how this worked. Methodism thrived, for example, among soldiers in barracks and garrisons. A combination of a dangerous occupation and mutual dependence, whether in mines, seaports, or armies, was always good for Methodist recruitment. But armies were particularly useful as a means of transmission because they moved, conquered, and demobilized. For example, Thomas Webb, an English military veteran of the Seven Years' War, demobilized, and then organized Methodist societies with military efficiency in the middle Atlantic colonies in the 1760s. Indeed, wherever one looks at the spread of Methodism in its pioneering phase, soldiers patrolling the empire were often key figures in its transmission. The earliest Methodist societies in South Africa (1806) and Tasmania (1820), for example, were directly the result of military mobility. Before leaving this theme it is important to emphasize that mobility was not the preserve of a sanctified elite among early Methodists, but was endemic to its whole cultural constituency. It is a striking feature of the biographies of early Methodist itinerant and local preachers throughout the English-speaking world how many of them were born in one country and ministered in several others. For example, the first Wesleyan preacher to travel in America, Robert Williams, grew up in Wales and ministered in Ireland before fetching up in the New World. In this way the symbiosis of a Methodist structure that was built for mobility and an international order of unprecedented population movement was a particularly important factor in the rise of Methodism from an English sect to an international movement. From the sugar plantations of the Caribbean islands to the trading routes of the East India Company, and from the southwestern migrations of American slaves to the convict ships bound for Australasia, Methodists exploited the mobile margins of trade and empire by establishing societies as they traveled.[13]

Through its Anglican inheritance, and its capacity to move and expand into new social spaces, Methodism established footholds in surprisingly large parts of the British Isles, the Caribbean islands, and British North America within half a century of its origins, although its future expansion was anything but guaranteed. Environmental conditions were not entirely in its favor. The Anglicanism to which it was still yoked was substantially undermined in North America by the American Revolution, and was also showing distinct signs of wear and tear in the Celtic peripheries of the British Isles and in the new industrial regions of England. The deference, dependency, and patriarchy that helped sustain Anglican culture wherever it had deep roots were eroded by new economic and political forces. Revolutionary political energies, the gospel of free trade, and the spread of populist enlightenment ideas were creating new configurations, the religious implications of which were not always clear to contemporaries. In some respects Methodism looked to be in a parlous position. Wesley, it seemed, had backed all the wrong horses. He vigorously opposed the American revolutionary cause, piously endorsed an economic order that was antithetical to aggressive capitalism, and fiercely attacked most aspects of enlightenment rationalism.[14] Even his much admired opposition to slavery created as many problems for his followers as it did opportunities. If the future world order was to be in the hands of people armed with ideas from the likes of Thomas Jefferson, Tom Paine, and Adam Smith, then Methodism apparently faced a difficult future. What has to be explained, therefore, is how Methodism emerged from the age of democratic and market revolutions in a stronger, not a weaker, position. Although Methodism in its establishmentarian forms, in common with other aspects of the old order in Church and State, showed a dogged capacity to ride out the storm of popular clamor, its great leaps forward did not come from such a determination. Neither the British Wesleyans in Canada nor the Primitive Methodists in Ireland (primitive in the sense of holding on to Wesley's old plan of remaining within the Anglican Church) nor the marginalized Episcopalians in the American South showed electrifying growth rates. Rather, Methodism grew most vigorously in those parts of the English-speaking world where it largely abandoned its species dependency on Anglicanism, and became both the instrument and the beneficiary of the rise of more populist and egalitarian brands of Christianity.

This general proposition about the rise of Methodism in the new world order of the eighteenth and nineteenth centuries requires some refinement and illustration. Although most of the well-known local and regional studies of Methodist growth on both sides of the Atlantic explicitly show that Methodism grew in symbiosis with the decline of religious and political deference and the expansion of markets, there are less well known studies showing that Methodism could still make headway even when these environmental conditions were not operational. For example, it is difficult to conceive of a more traditionally conservative society in the early nineteenth century than Shropshire in the heart of rural England. Shropshire had a well-established landowning class, gave rise to few movements of social and religious protest, and was not characterized by unusual Anglican indifference, yet it still exhibited vigorous movements of Evangelical Nonconformity, including Primitive Methodism.[15] The reason is that in the dispersed settlements of large Anglican parishes, Methodism, through cottage meetings and lay preaching, offered a communal and participatory form of popular religion that Anglicanism, with its singular emphases on church, parson, and parish, could not emulate. A map of a single Shropshire parish would show that Methodism, like a cell changing from its peripheries, grew in linear settlements among new populations farthest away from the parish church, the country house, and the parsonage. The purpose of this illustration is to show that Methodism was not the mere product of social change, as some Marxists once suggested, but was itself an active agent in the transformation of religious culture. Other examples could be cited of how Methodism on both sides of the Atlantic could establish footholds in environments not immediately conducive to populist evangelicalism, and these examples are important for what they reveal about Methodism's internally driven religious energy, but the exceptions do not negate the general rule that Methodism thrived in symbiosis with other changes in the English-speaking world in the late eighteenth and nineteenth centuries. Some case studies, two from each side of the Atlantic and all from the turn of the century, will help illustrate how these processes worked in different locations.

On July 4, 1804, the first formal celebration of the Declaration of Independence in the old Massachusetts shoe-manufacturing town of Lynn was a curiously divisive affair. The town's leading Federalists assembled at the Lynn Hotel and walked to the First Congregational Church, while the Republicans marched in the opposite direction to service in the Methodist church. The marchers' political preferences and ecclesiastical allegiances reflected even deeper divisions in Lynn's occupational structure and social geography. Among the ranks of the Federalists were the town's leading merchants and traders. Mostly residents of West Lynn, these were the wealthiest citizens in town, the controllers of the town's elite private school and members of its oldest religious denominations, the Quakers and Congregationalists. Parading in the other direction were the residents of Woodend: the shoemakers, cordwainers, and mechanics. This social differentiation was based not so much on wealth or access to capital, however, as on closeness to the means of production; Federalists, traders, and old Puritans confronted Republicans, producers, and new Methodists. Not everyone in town fitted into these tidy categories, but surprising numbers did. Mr. Jefferson's Methodist supporters were not new to town, but they were new to Methodism, which had made its debut in Lynn as a result of some powerful anti-Calvinist sermons preached in 1790 by the flamboyant Methodist itinerant Jesse Lee. Anti-predestinarianism and anti-elitism created a harmony of values for Methodist Republicans based on equal rights for all and special privileges for none.[16]

In the first half of the nineteenth century, as Lynn's shoemaking capacity expanded dramatically to meet the needs of a fast-growing domestic market, Methodist anti-elitism was infused with moral discipline through societies formed to promote temperance, frugality, and industry. As the geographical radius of markets expanded beyond eastern Massachusetts to embrace a new continent, rewards went to those who could combine an expansionist ideology with the disciplines of sober piety. In Lynn, "a manufacturing people showed an affinity for an ideology, a religion, a politics, and a morality that prized manual labor, democratized salvation, stressed social egalitarianism, and worshipped sobriety, industry, frugality and temperance."[17] The conditions that shaped the

early growth of Methodism in Lynn played out with variations in countless expanding communities in antebellum America as both Methodism
and markets spread with bewildering speed. What Lynn as a case study
shows, however, is that early Methodists were not so much against markets
as they were against the non-producers who exploited the markets. What
Lynn also reveals is that the history of the early republic — its political
divisions, moral crusades, and economic development — is indissolubly
linked with the spread of populist forms of evangelical religion.

My second illustration of early Methodist growth is from farther south.
In the early nineteenth century, Russian diplomat and painter Pavel
Petrovich Svinin spent several years in Philadelphia where he painted
*Black Methodists Holding a Prayer Meeting,* a caricature of a Methodist religious service. Drawing on contemporary stereotypes of African Americans, the brightly colored painting portrays an audience of black men,
women, and children being addressed by a gesticulating preacher. The
picture is a riot of bodily movement and vigorous interaction. Though
silent and one-dimensional in form, the painting is really a portrayal of
noise and physical social encounters; it shouts at the viewer from the
canvas. However stereotypical in form, Svinin's painting captures the energy of one of Methodism's most remarkable early success stories, its
sweeping gains among African Americans in the half century after the
American Revolution.[18] Essentially a cross-fertilization of European evangelical Pietism and African religious tradition, Methodism spread with
revivalistic speed from Virginia, Maryland, and North Carolina into the
Deep South at the turn of the century. By 1815 there were more than forty
thousand black Methodists in the United States (about one-third of the
total) and another fifteen thousand black Methodists in the Caribbean islands. Among the oppressed black populations of the transatlantic world,
Methodists and Baptists achieved more in a few decades than the older
colonial denominations had managed in a century. How is this to be
explained?

Methodism clearly benefited from its early denunciation of slavery
and from its more radical approach to race relations than the majority
of southern whites was prepared to countenance. But there was more
to it than that. Methodism offered African-American slaves a sense of
community, an extended family, an opportunity to meet neighbors, and a
way of building some kind of ethnic solidarity. To its social function was
added the attractiveness of an alternative value system in which African
Americans could help each other sustain a dignified morality based on
freedom of choice as against the ruthless compulsion and ethical corruption of slavery. But all this still ignores the essentially religious content

of African-American spirituality and its emphasis on revival, conversion, experience, and the Bible. The evidence suggests a particular commitment to the ecstatic rituals of conversion and baptism and, at least for some, an eager aspiration for entire sanctification. After all, nothing could offer a more complete recasting of the slave's sense of diminished humanity than the possibility of Christian perfection on earth as in heaven. The texts of the spiritual and sacred songs sung by African Americans show a close match with enduring aspects of Methodist spirituality.[19] The religious revivals that swept large numbers of slaves and free blacks into the Methodist movement were based upon a practical (not necessarily theological) Arminianism: salvation is open to all, not a select few; the songs are dominated not by feelings of depravity or unworthiness, but of personal worth and affirmation; there is less concentration upon the terrors of hell than on the deliverance of a chosen people; and the emphasis is not so much on escape from this world as on an embattled engagement with it.

Moreover, it is important to appreciate the culture and context of spirituals. They were rhythmical, improvisational, communal, and repetitive. They gave new life to old biblical narratives and treated biblical heroes and antiheroes as personal friends or enemies. The spiritual songs of African Americans not only helped mediate the transition from Africa to America but also built mental bridges between white, populist evangelical enthusiasm and black oppressed humanity. The culture of African-American religiosity was unashamedly oral and physical; shouting, singing, and praying linked emotion and bodily movement with an immediate appreciation of divine power and presence in the context of group interaction.[20] In short, African Americans adopted Methodism because its style and content were easily appropriated by a population under duress and in need of emotionally satisfying vehicles of communal religious expression. There was of course a degree of white resistance to this cultural symbiosis, both inside and outside Methodism, which led eventually to racial separation and the rise of black Methodist traditions. Biracialism within Methodism did not survive for very long, but a vigorous African-American evangelicalism did.

The third case study is from the southwest of England. In early May 1814, Francis Truscott, the author of a pamphlet entitled *Revivals of Religion Vindicated*, wrote to John Benson, the Methodist connectional editor, about some astonishing encounters at revival meetings among miners and laborers in Redruth, Cornwall.[21] Amidst wild scenes of singing, clapping, and shouting, Truscott complained, groups of children were standing on tables and chairs surveying the general pandemonium.

Truscott was writing from the enthusiastic heart of English Methodism during one of those pulses of religious revival that, at the turn of the century, happened in Cornwall about every five or six years. Although Cornish Methodism, described by one contemporary as the "mob of Methodism," gained and lost members with remarkable speed, enough were retained to make it a Methodist stronghold throughout the nineteenth century. By 1824 Methodism had a higher proportion of members in Cornwall (one in nineteen) than any other county in England, and by 1851 the proportion of Cornish churchgoers who were Methodist chapel attenders (64.5 percent) was the highest in the British Isles.[22]

Why was Cornish Methodism so rowdily successful? Part of the explanation has to do with Methodism's early start in the area, back in the 1740s, when Wesley first toured the county. According to Bishop George Lavington's extensive correspondence with Cornish clergymen and magistrates dating from the same period, Cornish Methodism had an early reputation for unconventional behavior, including the holding of outdoor meetings addressed by young, female, and illiterate preachers. Not only was Cornwall far removed from the influence of metropolitan culture, but also its tin and copper mines attracted one of the earliest industrial labor forces in England. The miners and seafarers of west Cornwall sustained a rich tradition of folk superstitions and popular sports, which Methodists redirected into love feasts, watch-nights, hymn singing, and richly embellished providential interventions. According to E. P. Thompson, "Wesleyan superstition matched the indigenous superstitions of tinners and fishermen who, for occupational reasons, were dependent upon chance and luck in their daily lives. The match was so perfect that it consolidated one of the strongest of Methodist congregations."[23]

A symbiosis of different species of superstition, one with its roots in Methodism and the other in folk culture, is an intriguing concept, but it does not in itself explain the timing or the geographical patterns of Cornish revivalism. Timing, for example, had more to do with the rhythmical pulse of growth and decline within Methodist societies. A period of steady growth often culminated in a revivalistic peak initiated by a love feast (the 1814 revival began at a love feast in Camborne), or a watchnight service, or a dramatic incident within a Methodist society, and was then followed by a period of declension before the cycle started all over again. The existence of a Methodist population unequally divided between society members and much larger numbers of less committed adherents supplied the necessary raw material and the inner dialectic of Methodist revivalism. Although primarily an internal rhythm, the clock of Cornish revivals was not unrelated to the world outside. In the 1814 revival, for example, contemporary witnesses drew attention to the boost of confidence supplied by the new Toleration Act of 1812 (rescuing the Methodist itinerancy from legal repression), the defeat of Napoléon and the end of a devastating war, and the rapid decline of wheat prices. In this way revivalism traded on the rise and decline of communal anxieties.

If the clock of Cornish revivals was set primarily, but not exclusively, to the internal rhythms of Methodism, the map of Cornish revivals was primarily of external construction. Methodist revivalism was largely confined to west Cornwall, where rapidly growing mining villages rendered obsolete old parochial boundaries and old patterns of social and political control. By contrast, revivalism made few inroads in rural east Cornwall, where the Anglican parish structure was more robust, despite the fervent labors of the Bible Christians, a revivalistic offshoot of Methodism. What the growth of Methodism in Cornwall reveals, therefore, is a complicated set of symbiotic mechanisms — social, economic, political, and cultural, which all need to be taken into account in any satisfactory explanation of Methodist growth. There are two further dimensions to this story. The first is the growing antagonism between the Cornish Methodist rabble and the bureaucratic managers of Methodism. The correspondence of Jabez Bunting, who ruled the connection with an iron hand in the first half of the nineteenth century, is full of complaints about Cornish enthusiasm.[24] Revivalism and connectional managerialism were always unhappy bedfellows.

A second and less well known feature of Cornish Methodism was its propensity, through emigrants and missionaries, to expand its chapel culture to surprisingly large parts of the world. Wherever miners dug, Cornish Methodists often showed up; but nothing could compare with South Australia's "Little Cornwall," which reproduced in remarkable detail all the trappings of Cornish Methodist culture, including its chapel names and its pulsating pattern of cyclical revivalism. The Methodist revivals of early-nineteenth-century Camborne and Redruth in Cornwall were themselves revived in the Moonta and Wallaroo copper mines of South Australia in the 1860s and '70s. Through emigration, the symbiosis between Methodism and mining culture was first relocated, and then cloned.[25]

The fourth case study is taken from southern counties of the ancient province of Ulster in Ireland at the turn of the eighteenth century. Shortly after the bloody collapse of the Rebellion of the United Irishmen in 1798, Ireland's failed revolution, the English Methodist Conference determined that the time was ripe for an organized mission to the Irish-speaking Roman Catholics. The voluminous correspondence between

the three newly appointed missioners and missionary headquarters between 1799 and 1802, when the total number of Irish Methodists increased from around sixteen thousand to twenty-seven thousand, is really
a narrative history of religious revivalism. The coincidence of the establishment of the mission with the fastest growth rates in the history of Irish
Methodism was lost neither on the missioners themselves nor on the
denominational hagiography inspired by the mission accounts. But the
truth of the matter is that, despite a considerable growth in mission resources during the first half of the nineteenth century, the growth rates of
the period 1799–1802 were never reproduced. Why then did Methodism
grow with such speed in these years? The timing of Irish Methodist revivalism is easier to explain than its geography. The collapse of the Rebellion
of the United Irishmen into a bitter sectarian feud followed by near
famine conditions produced fertile soil for Methodist preachers who "denounced the judgments of heaven against the crimes of a guilty nation."
More clearly here than perhaps anywhere else, Methodism benefited
from what some Marxists have called the psychic processes of counter-
revolution. Although Methodism made some converts from among the
Roman Catholics targeted by its mission, it grew chiefly among the majority Anglican and minority Presbyterian settlers of southern Ulster who
had every reason to be fearful of Roman Catholic resurgence. This helps
explain the geography of the Irish revivals. Methodism grew most rapidly
in those areas of southern Ulster where economic, political, and territorial competition between Catholics and Protestants was most intense.
In this landscape, Methodist conversions, especially the relatively uncommon but much trumpeted conversions of Catholics, supplied tangible
evidence that Protestant Christianity was far from a spent force on the
island of Ireland. Methodism offered both a hotter form of Protestantism
and much needed individual assurance and communal discipline for
people experiencing profound anxiety.[26]

To explain a period of extraordinary growth in this way is not to
negate the importance of other, more regular aspects of the Methodist
mission. The correspondence of the missionaries, for example, speaks of
the importance of outdoor preaching, the catalytic power of love feasts in
stimulating revival, and the ways in which Methodists were able to take
advantage of traditional Irish folk practices. As ever, energy and zeal
produced their own rewards, but explaining the distinctive chronological
and geographical patterns of Methodist expansion requires a specific
social context. For whatever reasons, Methodism in Ireland never again
reached the revivalistic peaks of the years after the Rebellion of the
United Irishmen. Unsurprisingly however, emigrant Irish Methodists car-

ried a vigorous tradition of anti-Catholicism with them wherever they fetched up. When the Irish-born Methodist John McKenny found himself in charge of the Methodist mission in New South Wales in the 1830s, he stated that the real question in Australia was whether the country would become "a protestant or a popish colony." Old animosities died hard; Roman Catholics and Calvinists remained the religious enemies of the Methodists even on the peripheries of empire.[27]

The purpose of these case studies has been to show that as Methodism expanded in the new world order of the eighteenth and nineteenth centuries its patterns of growth cannot be explained solely by internal categories. What links the stories of Lynn shoemakers, African-American slaves, Cornish miners, and the Protestants of southern Ulster is that Methodist growth was symbiotically linked to other social, economic, and political contingencies. To argue thus is not to convey a reductionist interpretation of Methodist growth with the "religious" components left out; rather, the reverse is the case. The fact that Methodism, as a religious species, thrived in some environments and not in others is revealing both of the kind of movement it was and of the kind of changes remodeling the world order in the age of revolutions.

Although all four studies represent the forging of vibrant and fast-growing Methodist communities at the turn of the century, their future prospects were not all the same. In the United States, the populist, egalitarian, and anti-Calvinist sentiments evident in early-nineteenth-century Lynn proved to be portable and expandable. As population and markets grew and moved west, Methodism moved with them. Similarly, the spread of African-American slavery into the South and west, however grim the consequences for the nation as a whole, offered new opportunities for Methodists. In short, Methodism, once established, had the capacity to grow in tandem with the spread of its host environment. The case studies from the British Isles show a different picture. Methodism in Cornwall remained a sturdy plant throughout the nineteenth century, but the culture of the Cornish tin mines was not easily exportable, except exotically to the mines of the New World. It is true that Methodism thrived among other mining communities in nineteenth-century Britain, in Wales and County Durham, but such areas had built-in geographical and chronological boundaries set by economic function, about which Methodism could do nothing.[28] Similarly, the Methodist communities of southern Ulster in the nineteenth century occupied a distinctly narrow ground between a resurgent Roman Catholicism in the south and a stubborn Calvinism in the northeast. Growing space within Ireland was circumscribed by powerful social and political realities which Methodism simply could not change. The emigrant Irish carried Methodism with them on their travels, but home base never fulfilled the promise of the community revivals at the turn of the century. The symbiosis between Methodism and its host environments was a powerful factor in the spread of Methodism throughout the world in the nineteenth century, but it did not operate as naked determinism, for Methodism helped build the environments from which it took its nourishment. The mechanisms by which this took place, as with the evolutionary biology which has served as an extended metaphor in this discussion, are infinitely complex and not always transparent, but they do deserve to be taken seriously.

By the second decade of the nineteenth century, Methodism's empire of the spirit had spread to surprisingly large parts of the world. Methodist expansion was the result not of an evangelistic strategy concocted by elites, but was carried primarily by a mobile laity. Some moved along the trading routes established by the British Empire, others were in military regiments that patrolled it; many, including the migratory Irish and the Cornish tinners, moved in search of a better life in various parts of the New World, others, like southern American blacks and English convicts, moved because they were forced to; some moved out of a self-conscious desire to spread scriptural holiness, others discovered a holiness tradition after they moved. The point is that all this took place *before* the formation of official missionary societies. Methodism had a mobile laity before it had missionaries, it had missionaries before it had a missionary society, and it had locally based missionary societies before it had a national missionary society.[29] When the first great Methodist missionary society was formed in Britain in 1813, the Methodists already had more than a hundred missionaries working in India, West and South Africa, the West Indies, the Canadas and the Canadian Maritimes. More important, Methodism had established self-sustaining and rapidly growing churches in the British Isles and North America, the two most expansionist cultures of the nineteenth and twentieth centuries.

What kind of a spiritual empire were the Methodists building? David Martin has asked a similar question of Pentecostalism, a religious movement that he believes grew directly out of Methodism, and many of his answers, with suitable refinement, apply equally to Methodism. Methodism, like Pentecostalism, was a cultural revolution from below, not a political or ecclesiastical program imposed from above. It grew without external sponsorship and thrived among youthful and mobile populations exploiting the opportunities of new global markets. It was predominantly a movement of women, who formed a clear majority of society

members almost everywhere Methodism took root. It was also a movement in search of a voice, which is why it was so noisy and so devoted to
singing. It became first a transatlantic and then a global phenomenon,
but through acculturation and indigenization it adapted to local cultures
and changed its character from place to place. It was a movement that
emphasized personal experience, but also was infused with a set of personal and communal disciplines as means and ways to a better life. Methodism thrived on the margins and frontiers of race and class, continental
expansion and empire. It was a world-affirming movement, relatively free
from the millenarian fantasies of other populist religious strains, but it
set up clear boundaries of dress, speech, and behavior, marking off the
church from the world.[30]

But there are also significant differences between Methodism and
Pentecostalism (maybe only so far), quite apart from those associated
with Pentecostalism's emphasis on the baptism of the spirit. Methodism
grew out of a religious establishment and never shrugged off some of its
autocratic and establishmentarian inclinations. In England it cozied up
to governments, expelled radicals, and built its gothic chapels, often
more out of a quest for social acceptance and respectability than for any
more noble purpose. In America it first renounced slavery, then accom-
modated it, liberated women and then controlled them. Everywhere,
Methodists began as cultural outsiders, but through work discipline and
an unquenchable passion for education, they remorselessly moved to the
cultural center, sometimes with remarkable speed. The carefully considered step taken by Samuel Povey, a character in Arnold Bennet's *The Old
Wives' Tale*, in which he moves from the rough Primitive Methodist chapel
to its mahogany Wesleyan counterpart as his drapery business prospered,
was a step, metaphorically speaking, taken by thousands of Methodists in
nineteenth-century Britain and North America. This drift to somewhere
near the self-improving, bourgeois center of Western culture is a good
example of a religious species adapting to its environment, and at first it
did not lead to very obvious numerical decline, but Methodism, once
shorn of its populist zeal, could not reproduce growth on anything like
the old pattern. Embourgeoisement and institutionalization did not kill
Methodism as a religious species, but they gradually confined its habitat
to more refined and restricted areas.[31] These areas generally did not
include the lower-class migrants to the fast-growing mega-cities of Western civilization, a lacuna that would over time prove very costly to the
Methodist cause.

# CHAPTER TWO

# Enlightenment and Enthusiasm

Nor is there any character for whom the worldly (or selfish) man feels so
much contemptuous pity, as for an enthusiast, until some undeniably
great result forces him to confess that enthusiasm is a powerful reality.
— FRANCIS W. NEWMAN, *The Soul* (1849)

I cannot pretend that Seth and Dinah were anything else but
Methodists — not indeed of that modern type which reads quarterly reviews and attends in chapels with pillared porticoes; but of a very old-
fashioned kind. They believed in present miracles, in instantaneous conversions, in revelations by dreams and visions; they drew lots and sought
for Divine guidance by opening the Bible at hazard; having a literal way of
interpreting the Scriptures, which is not at all approved by modern commentators; and it is impossible for me to represent their diction as correct,
or their instruction as liberal. Still — if I have read religious aright — faith,
love, and charity have not always been found in a direct ratio with a sensibility to the three concords; and it is possible, thank Heaven! to have very
erroneous theories and very sublime feelings.
— GEORGE ELIOT, *Adam Bede* (1859)

A nyone unfortunate enough to be asked to write a chapter on the
eighteenth century for a survey history of Christianity might, with
justification, choose the words "enlightenment" and "enthusiasm" for its title. Someone writing a history of Methodism who chose the
same title would risk censure, for until recently Methodism was regarded
as a movement located somewhere near the polar opposite of enlightenment. As surely as the enlightened have been the custodians of the
printed word, Methodism has been portrayed as a credulous superstition
not only "of the poor," but also "for the poor."[1] Recent work on both
enthusiasm and enlightenment, however, has opened up the possibility
of a more nuanced interpretation. The aim of this chapter is to convey
something of the essence of Methodism and its impact on the North
Atlantic world in the eighteenth and nineteenth centuries by exploring the apparent antithesis between enlightenment and enthusiasm. Although the principal objective is to shed light on Methodism, much is

revealed along the way about the structures of enlightened thought within which the rise of Methodism was interpreted. Methodism was more than a religious movement; it acted also as a metaphorical construction whereby intellectual superiors analyzed populist forms of religion of which they disapproved.

## Wesley and Enthusiasm

As soon as Methodism emerged from its societary closets into the open spaces of English society in the 1740s, it was immediately condemned for its "enthusiasm." Anglican bishops, who feared a recrudescence of the kind of puritanical populism that destabilized the realm in the 1640s and '50s, were quick to diagnose the problem. Edmund Gibson's *Observations upon the Conduct and Behaviour of a Certain Sect Usually Distinguished by the Name of Methodists* (1744) was a comprehensive indictment of Methodism: by failing to comply with the laws regulating religious practice (the Act of Uniformity, the Conventicle Act, and the Toleration Act), Methodists placed themselves in open defiance of government in Church and State; by engaging in itinerant preaching and extra-parochial communion, Methodists infringed the principles of territorial integrity upon which all established churches depended for their security; and by encouraging the "rabble" to meet out of doors they were inviting, even instigating, social instability. But there was more. In a series of queries for consideration Gibson asked whether the traditional Anglican emphasis on "regular attendance on the publick offices of religion" was not a "better evidence of the co-operation of the Holy Spirit than those sudden Agonies, Roarings and Screamings, Tremblings, Droppings-down, Ravings and Madnesses; into which their [Methodists] Hearers have been cast." Gibson particularly disliked Methodism's tendencies toward extremism, antinomianism, and instantaneous conversionism. For him, a gradual improvement of grace and goodness, along with the disciplined practice of moral duties, offered a better route to spiritual enlightenment than the "Madness and Enthusiasm" into which the English people had been led "during the Times of Anarchy and Confusion." Gibson's juridical and moralist critique of Methodism stood the test of time better than Bishop Lavington's more prurient and banal *Enthusiasm of Methodists and Papists Compar'd,* and set the tone for two centuries of criticism of Methodist enthusiasm.[2]

The story is told with great elegance and some insight by Ronald Knox, who devoted a lifetime of scholarship to the history of religious enthusiasm, in which Methodism plays a leading part. Wesley perplexed and intrigued Knox. Here was an Oxford-trained logician of cold and mechanical disposition who flirted with the raw edges of religious enthusiasm all his life. He never unambiguously welcomed the emotional paroxysms and prostrations that accompanied the preaching of many eighteenth-century revivalists, including himself, but he preferred religious excitement to complete indifference or to the Calvinistic theological canniness he encountered in Scotland. He endorsed claims of Christian perfection, but carefully sifted the evidence, and often found it wanting. He believed in the existence of witches and poltergeists, but chastised others for their religious gullibility. He energetically stirred up religious zeal, but published any number of "Calm addresses." He disparaged the millenarian excesses of some of his followers, but nurtured eschatological excitement through his comments on natural disasters and public events. He fulminated against gambling, but took many a major decision by the casting of lots. He distrusted any claims to prophetic gifts or inner illumination, because he could not embrace anything not subject to argument, but he constructed and defended a high view of religious experience and felt assurance. Knox concluded from all this that Wesley sympathized with enthusiasm, but was never carried away by it; "his pose is one of marble detachment from the passions of his age. He is determined not to be an enthusiast." Whatever his determination, Wesley's *Journal* shows him to be the self-appointed supervising pastor of some seventy thousand souls whose virtues and vices, zeal and zealotry, and conviction and credulity threw up just about every imaginable form of human behavior, from millenarian predictions to infanticide. To his credit, Wesley generally faced down the worst excesses of stupidity or cruelty by using expulsion as the ultimate weapon of ecclesiastical discipline. Wesley, and this is equally true of the movement he founded, generally tempered enthusiasm with discipline, and rugged individualism with communal accountability.[3]

Attacks on Methodist enthusiasm are legion in the anti-Methodist literature of the eighteenth century. Enthusiasm was most commonly defined as a false belief in the inspiration of the Holy Spirit, an irrational attribution of everyday occurrences to divine intervention, a spurious belief in "dreams, visions, fancies, reveries and revelations," a predisposition to hypocrisy and laziness (since the road to heaven was paved with false imaginings), an illusory attachment to ridiculous doctrines such as Christian perfection, and a capricious view of the world that led all too often to insanity. In his mock epic *Methodism Triumphant* (1767), Nathaniel Lancaster points to mania as the Methodist guide:

> O thou celestial Source of Ecstacies.
> Of Visions, Raptures, and converting Dreams.
> Awful Ebriety of New-Birth Grace!
> Thee, MANIA, I invoke my pen to guide
> To fire my soul, and urge my bold career.[4]

Wesley's writings contain more than two hundred references to enthusiasm. Most are carefully argued refutations of charges made against him, but a surprisingly large number are warnings to his own followers who claimed, fancifully in his view, some special divine revelation. Generally speaking Wesley accepted the epithet "enthusiast" if it was meant as a rough synonym for a vigorous and earnest faith, but strenuously repudiated it if it was intended as a synonym for false claims to divine inspiration. The issue at stake in many of Wesley's controversies over enthusiasm is what exactly constituted defensible and indefensible claims to divine inspiration and supernatural agency. The rub of the matter was that Wesley accepted as a general proposition that God regularly and strikingly intervened in the created order to advance his purposes and protect his servants, whereas most of his critics did not, at least not in the same way.[5]

Although most eighteenth-century Anglicans and Presbyterians (except Deists) held that God providentially did shape the course of history, they saw the divine influence as coming more discreetly through secondary causes than John Wesley did.[6] For Wesley, therefore, any particular charge of enthusiasm was not so much reduced to a first-principle issue of theological interpretation, which he regarded as not negotiable, but was tested case by case on the persuasiveness of the evidence. Those cases in which someone claimed some kind of divine illumination above and beyond what was contained in the Bible, such as millenarian predictions or fanciful revelations of special authority, Wesley judged as enthusiasm; those cases where God intervened to quell a multitude, heal a sickness, send a friend, or settle the weather were regarded by Wesley as evidence of God's regular superintending providence of the kind that could be found in page after page of the scriptures. The issue at stake here is not whether Wesley's tightrope marches across the ravines of religious enthusiasm were sustainable or not. Like all logicians with a record to defend, Wesley's writings betray a slippery self-interest and a remarkable verbal dexterity. When it came to splitting hairs to shore up his religious opinions, no one was more creative than Wesley. But the point is that Wesley managed to establish a religious movement that encouraged its adherents to place themselves in the way of God's providential intervention,

"John Wesley, that Excellent Minister of the Gospel, carried by Angels into Abraham's Bosom," colored engraving by an unknown artist published on August 1, 1791, by Robert Sayer of Fleet Street, London (Courtesy of the John Rylands Library)

but generally speaking did not endorse the extra-biblical claims of self-appointed visionaries.

Whatever one makes of Wesley's opinions about enthusiasm, there is a broad consistency of approach throughout his writings. The essence is expressed in a *Journal* entry in May 1752 when Wesley experienced a calming of the wind as he addressed an outdoor meeting in Gateshead. Wesley records rhetorically, "Is it enthusiasm to see God in every benefit we receive?" On other occasions he speaks of "a strange chain of providences" or "a signal instance of God's particular providence over all those who call upon him." In short, Wesley believed that God looked after his followers, not by blazing a trail of miracles (he refused to accept that God's superintending providence over weather and unexpected encounters was miraculous), but by being of necessity the author of every good thing in the life of the believer.[7]

Where then was the dividing line in Wesley's mind between acceptable and unacceptable forms of enthusiasm? Early in his career as an itinerant evangelist Wesley wrote: "I was with two persons, who I doubt are properly enthusiasts. For, first, they think to attain the ends without the means; which is enthusiasm properly so called. Again, they think themselves inspired by God, and are not. But false imagining is enthusiasm. That theirs is only imaginary inspiration appears hence, it contradicts the Law and the Testimony." On other occasions he defined enthusiasts as those "who charged their own imaginations on the will of God," or those with "a religious madness arising from some falsely imagined influence or inspiration of God." In his *Complete English Dictionary* published in 1777, Wesley defined enthusiasm as "religious madness, fancied inspiration," and an enthusiast as "a religious madman, one that fancies himself inspired." In practice Wesley employed a series of tests to identify enthusiasm. Was what was claimed consistent with scripture? Did it have a natural explanation? Was the claimant a reliable witness? Did the claim produce good or bad spiritual fruit, humility or vanity? Was the claim antithetical to sound reason? In this way George Bell's millenarian prophecies were determined to be enthusiasm (Bell created mayhem in the London Methodist society in the early 1760s), while Jeannie Bisson's claim to have experienced entire sanctification was accepted by Wesley, who could not detect in her any "tincture of enthusiasm."[8]

George Bell's case is particularly instructive, not only for what it shows about Wesley's attitude to "enthusiasm," but also for what it reveals about the raw edge of populist enthusiasm in some early Methodist environs. Bell, a former soldier who became a Methodist in the late 1750s and established a substantial following in London, claimed to have experienced

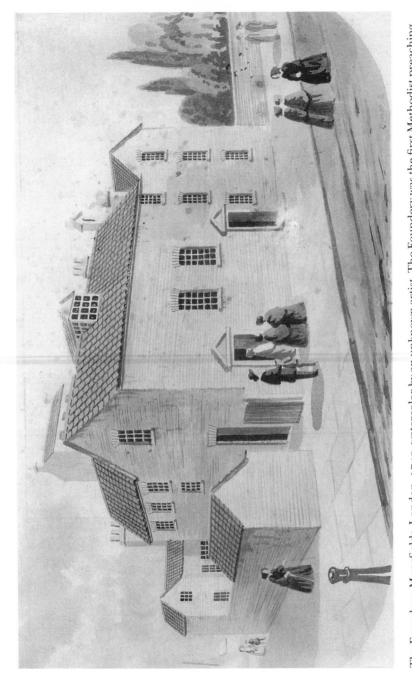

The Foundery, Moorfields, London, 1740, watercolor by an unknown artist. The Foundery was the first Methodist preaching house in London and served as Methodism's headquarters for some forty years. (Courtesy of the John Rylands Library)

Christian perfection and also to have special knowledge about the apoc-
alyptic end of the world, which he dated precisely to February 28, 1763.
The controversial content of Bell's message was matched by his style, well
captured by an eyewitness account of one of his meetings.

> Amidst the crowd, at the farther end of the pulpit, I saw an hand
> waving about & soon found it was Mr Bell giving out the hymn. After
> the hymn he spoke a few minutes to explain the intent of their
> meeting . . . that all might come up to a state of perfection. He next
> prayd, & soon ran into such an extraordinary strain, screaming in
> such a violent manner to compel a blessing upon the present meet-
> ing, that he seemed to be in a rapture & in fact as one raving with
> agony. . . . I cannot but esteem Mr Bell ripe for the most unscrip-
> tural extravagancies. I expect to hear of his prophecying, denounc-
> ing judgements & calling himself one of the witnesses. I hope he is
> honest at heart; but to me he appeared to be acting a part, whether
> out of vanity or mere delusion, I am not able to determine.[9]

Wesley was slow to act on Bell's perfectionist claims (which he did not
accept) and exhortations (which he did not stop), but he became un-
easier with the advance of Bell's millenarian predictions, which eventually
he came to see as entirely without foundation. After hearing Bell speak at
the Foundery (the early headquarters of London and English Methodism) in December 1762, Wesley wrote, "the reproach of Christ I am
willing to bear, but not the reproach of enthusiasm, if I can help it."
Wesley eventually took action to restore order and discipline to the London society, and Bell was thrown into prison by the authorities for "raising
unnecessary fears in the King's subjects, for blasphemy and for holding
meetings in unlicensed places."[10] Bell's case shows just how difficult it was
for Wesley, given his assumptions about the way God acted in the lives of
humble people, to make a judgment between what he considered a legitimate expression of Methodist piety and what was indefensible enthusiasm. His protracted delay in taking action against Bell is not only revealing
in itself but also led to a serious crisis in London Methodism, the ripples of
which extended to other Methodist locations. Perfectionism, millenarian-
ism, illuminism, and emotional manipulation were all present in the London society influenced by Bell. Yet Wesley's tactic was to wait and see the
results of Bell's ministry, which in this case produced greater damage than
would have been the case had he acted more promptly.

The best-documented account of Gorge Bell's pernicious influence
on London Methodism in the early 1760s takes an even more critical view
of Wesley's role in the crisis. Wesley had ample opportunity to view at first
hand what Bell was up to, and received any number of written complaints

about Bell's behavior, but chose to do nothing about it for almost a year. Blinded by his own belief in the possibility of attaining Christian perfection and by a strong conviction that religious excitement, however messy, was preferable to religious dullness and apathy, however orthodox, Wesley was more tolerant of Bell's antics than his bother Charles and many evangelical Anglicans were prepared to be. By the time Bell's millenarian predictions had made him an obvious public liability to the Methodist cause in London and forced Wesley into belated action, Bell had substantially undermined not only London Methodism, which took some twenty-seven years to replenish its lost members, but also Wesley's relations with Anglican evangelicals and the wider Church of England. Even those Anglicans like John Berridge, William Grimshaw, Thomas Haweis, and John Newton, who in general supported the Methodist cause, came to see that Wesley was more dangerously tinctured with enthusiasm than they had supposed. The real object of their concern was Wesley's persistent belief in Christian perfection and his consequent gullibility in processing claims to Christian perfection from sources of dubious credibility. In short, Wesley sat on his hands in the Bell case, not because the evidence was ambivalent, but because Wesley's predilection for religious enthusiasm affected his judgment and slowed his reactions.[11]

There were yet other occasions when Wesley's "tests" delivered no clear answer. A strange encounter with a French Prophet in 1739 left him uncertain about her authenticity, so he resolved to wait and see. Similarly, under repeated attack for the fits and trances reported at Methodist meetings, Wesley responded that some had natural explanations while others had not, and he could not be expected to know which was which on every single occasion.[12] He also grew impatient with the sheer number of allegations of enthusiasm made against him, so much so that he complained it was a word increasingly without a meaning. It was simply a term of abuse, which in his opinion revealed more about the feeble state of Christianity in eighteenth-century England than it did about Methodism. Naturally his critics took a different view.

Wesley, in his own mind, positioned himself and his movement somewhere on a line between faith and credulity. The position was never a fixed point for his followers; it varied subtly according to gender, class, race, and level of education. Wherever Methodism took root in the eighteenth and nineteenth centuries there are stories of special providences and unusual events. Methodists believed that God was with them, not in a general theological sense, but in a set of encounters, which supposedly obeyed no other explanation than that of a proactive divine presence. Deep within every Methodist archive there are bizarre tales of strange occurrences, many of which would not have passed Wesley's own tests of validation.[13] But the important point is that Methodism thrived on the raw edge of religious excitement without capitulating, in the main, to some of the more extreme manifestations of populist religion. While bubbles of religious enthusiasm expanded and burst with ubiquitous regularity in Britain and America in the eighteenth and nineteenth centuries, Methodism had an inner theological and organizational discipline that saved it from the fate of many other contemporary forms of popular religiosity. Wesley's reasonableness, however circumscribed in practice and challenged by opponents, acted as a bulwark against the kind of irrational extremism he tried, and often failed, to eradicate from his own societies. He was, in a peculiar sense, a reasonable enthusiast, but an enthusiast for all that.

## Wesley and Enlightenment

Whatever the complexities of Wesley's relation to enthusiasm, they pale in comparison with his attitudes toward the Enlightenment. It was once common to see Wesley as expressly a counter-enlightenment figure, and this view still commands some respect. No one who believed so passionately in God's immediate supervising providence, and who tried to work this belief into almost everything he wrote about science, nature, and history, could be described as anything other than peripheral to the main currents of enlightened thought. On the other hand, Wesley was deeply influenced by the structure of eighteenth-century thought, which he consumed voraciously in his horseback reading and edited remorselessly for popular consumption. A host of recent studies have drawn attention to Wesley's indebtedness to Lockean empiricism and sensationalist psychology, his endorsement, within limits, of the scientific method, his boyish enthusiasm for all kinds of experimentation, his fundamentally optimistic emphasis on human progress (as against what he saw as the drab fatalism of Calvinism), and his shared assumptions with some of the Enlightenment's most celebrated historians. Moving from thought to practice, Wesley, in his defense of religious toleration, advocacy of slavery abolition, concern for bodily and mental health, and dislike of all persecution and violence, could be regarded more as a product of the Enlightenment than a reaction against it.[14]

Wesley's opposition to slavery is particularly pertinent. Not only was he the first English religious figure of real significance to denounce slavery, but also his principled opposition influenced others and later bore remarkable fruit in Methodism's ubiquitous petitioning against it. Wesley opposed slavery, not on grounds of economic pragmatism, but on a bold assertion of the natural rights of all people to pursue freedom, holiness, and happiness. He believed that life on earth was more than just a vale of tears to be endured patiently in anticipation of eternal life. He was a restless advocate of self-improvement and the improvement of society; in his view "the ideal Christian life was one of ceaseless, cheerful activism."[15] Wesley was a well-read classicist who admired Socratic virtue and reason as the apogee of human wisdom without Christ. In short, Wesley neither disparaged learning nor was at permanent war with the thought of his age. What he most disliked was the religious skepticism of some aspects of the Scottish and French Enlightenments and the religious hetero-doxy that emerged from the English Deists and rational dissenters. But he also disliked Calvinism, which in Wesley's writings is almost always bracketed with antinomianism and with the evil doctrine of reprobation. Wesley's famous, but scarcely original, summary of Calvinism was, "One in twenty (suppose) of mankind are elected; nineteen in twenty are rep-robated. The elect shall be saved, do what they will: The reprobate shall be damned, do what they can." This comment is, in a profound sense, a product of the impact of enlightenment thought on his theological and moral sensibilities. The idea that an angry God could condemn vast num-bers of human beings to eternal punishment without so much as an offer of salvation was as morally offensive to Wesley as it was to the most ad-vanced of the philosophes.

The movement that Wesley founded flirted with the edge of religious enthusiasm, but had some powerful restraining impulses; it came across to outsiders as fundamentally irrational, but it had deep roots in rea-sonableness if not rationality. The point of arguing this way is not to portray Methodism as some kind of much misunderstood paragon of enlightenment rationality, which it was not, but to show how it was that Methodism in its anti-Calvinism and antislavery, its emphasis on disci-plined self-improvement, and its willingness to place itself in the way of special providences was peculiarly well positioned to make advances among the populations of Britain and North America in the eighteenth and nineteenth centuries. If the relationship between enthusiasm and the Enlightenment within Methodism was more complicated than some contemporaries were prepared to admit, the same is true among those with much better enlightenment credentials than Mr. Wesley. The millen-nialist musings of Isaac Newton and Joseph Priestley, for example, have not been welcomed by posterity with any more enthusiasm than Wesley's belief in witches and poltergeists.

For Wesley's dialectical tension between enlightenment and enthusiasm to add up to more than a mere personal transaction, it had to be capable of mass realization. To find out how that happened it is necessary to move outside the narrow confines of Methodism to look at much wider changes in the religious and social structure of late-eighteenth-century Britain and America. The best place to start is with two of the period's most celebrated enlightenment figures, Adam Smith and Thomas Jefferson.

## Methodism's Context: Adam Smith and Thomas Jefferson

Adam Smith, a humble professor of moral philosophy and later a customs official, wrote in *The Wealth of Nations,* published in 1776, the following thoughts on religious establishments.

> The institutions for the instruction of people of all ages are chiefly those for religious instruction. This is a species of instruction of which the object is not so much to render the people good citizens in this world, as to prepare them for another and better world in a life to come. The teachers of the doctrine which contains this instruction, in the same manner as other teachers, may either depend altogether for their subsistence upon the voluntary subscriptions of their hearers; or they may derive it from some other fund to which the law of their country may entitle them; such as a landed estate, a tythe or land tax, an established salary or stipend. Their exertion, their zeal and industry, are likely to be much greater in the former situation than in the latter. In this respect the teachers of new religions have always had a considerable advantage in attacking those ancient and established systems of which the clergy, reposing themselves upon their benefices, had neglected to keep up the fervour and devotion in the great body of the people; and having given themselves up to indolence, were become altogether incapable of making any vigorous defence even of their own establishment. The clergy of an established and well-endowed religion frequently become men of learning and elegance, who possess all the virtues of gentlemen, or which can recommend them to the esteem of gentlemen; but they are apt to lose the qualities, both good and bad, which gave them authority and influence with the inferior ranks of people, and which had perhaps been the original causes of the success and establishment of their religion. Such a clergy when attacked by a set of popular and bold, though perhaps stupid and ignorant enthusiasts, feel themselves as perfectly defenceless as the indolent, effeminate, and full-fed nations of the southern parts of

Asia, when they were invaded by the active, hardy, and hungry tar-
tars of the North. Such a clergy, upon such an emergency, have
commonly no other resource than to call upon the civil magistrate
to persecute, destroy, or drive out their adversaries as disturbers of
the peace.[16]

Smith's *Wealth of Nations* "was more than a book; it was the summary of a
new European consciousness," a legitimizing economic and social philosophy for a dynamic new era of liberal capitalism. But how was religion to
fit into this new world order of open markets, free trade, and minimal
government intervention? Smith's writings on religion display a classic
enlightenment ambiguity. In the above passage he virtually enunciates a
law of religious progress in which old establishments are constantly challenged from below by new populist forms of religion. They in turn eventually seek out the very state sponsorship that they once challenged, but
this destroys their own zeal even more quickly than it destroys their rivals.
Smith further believed that if the state refused to endorse the winners of
these ecclesiastical talent contests the result would be a wild proliferation
of sects, a great explosion of lugubriousness, and an increase of religious
toleration. The latter would be occasioned not by generosity of spirit but
by enlightened self-interest — resulting eventually in the growth of "pure
and rational religion, free from every mixture of absurdity, imposture, or
fanaticism." This ecclesiastical free market, to be sure, would be a bare-
knuckle ride for governments, but if they held their nerve and refused to
intervene, except to keep public order, good would triumph in the ecclesiastical sphere as in every other area of life. The proof of this proposition,
according to Smith, was to be found in the New World, where the radical
sects of mid-seventeenth-century England had survived mayhem to establish in Pennsylvania a new order of "good temper and moderation."[17]

The root of the ambiguity in Smith's thinking, however, is his patent
dislike of popular religious enthusiasm, especially its predilection for
moral austerity. Smith, to be fair, could see the attraction and social utility
of austerity for the common people, who of all social classes had the most
to fear from the consequences of levity, carelessness, and dissipation. For
gentlemen such vices, if vices they be, can be engaging displays of the
privileges of wealth, but for the poor they can be ruinous, or worse than
that — they can be a dangerous source of increased criminality and economic wastefulness in society. Even allowing for this balanced insight,
Smith regarded the moral austerity of religious sects as "disagreeably
rigorous and unsocial."[18] In other words, the religious free market, just
like the economic free market, was not entirely free from the effects of

the stupidity of the poor. It was for that reason that Smith, the apostle of laissez-faire, had a sneaking admiration for the established churches of the Swiss cantons and, unsurprisingly, of his own native Scotland. The established Church of Scotland, according to Smith, had many advantages: it was cheap to run; it was moderated by the patronage of the cultivated gentry; it produced a near uniformity of faith and devotion; it sustained national morals without recourse to sectarian enthusiasm; and, unlike England, it did not keep talented professors like himself out of its universities. Above all, it was a service provided to the state at a value-for-money price. The Scottish Church, with its employees neither underpaid so as to incur ridicule, nor overpaid so as to promote vanity and dissipation, was as close to perfection as any state-supported institution was ever likely to get. Smith's preferred options, then, were either a cheap and efficient established church or an ecclesiastical free market of competing sects. An established church risked collapse into state persecution or the dissipation of valuable economic resources, and a religious free market was prone to superstitious sectarianism or uncultivated austerity.

Writing in the 1770s, Adam Smith anticipated the dilemmas facing states and their churches throughout Christendom in the later eighteenth century. In Europe after the Peace of Westphalia, religion was too important a matter to be left entirely to the churches. Most rulers before the late eighteenth century regarded religious toleration as a sign of state weakness and relied principally on established churches to enforce conformity and order. But the established churches, which had worked so hard for their place in the political sun, soon found themselves in unexpected difficulties. Some rulers coveted their wealth, while the churches themselves struggled, unsuccessfully as it happened, to find sufficient resources to cope with rapidly expanding populations. Disappointed mutual expectations resulted in clashes between religious and secular authorities, which were played out with equal bitterness in many different regions, from the disputes over patronage in Scotland to the almost relentless sniping between French kings and the papacy throughout the period. The inability of established churches to align their resources with their objectives or to eradicate popular "superstition" left them "creaking audibly" in the generation after the Seven Years' War (1756–63). Creaking became groaning in the 1790s, when the revolutionaries summarily dealt with the French church and the English church began slowly to lose the affinity with national sentiment that had once been its crowning glory. While established churches were suffering from accumulated lethargy, more populist forms of Protestant Christianity were showing signs of vigorous new life.[19]

From Methodism to the great missionary societies of the nineteenth century, the voluntary pietism of a mobilized laity achieved remarkable feats of gospel transmission throughout the transatlantic world and beyond. The roots of all this, according to W. R. Ward, are to be found in the pietist revivalism in the Habsburg lands, where pious and persecuted minorities had to achieve quick results or else go under.[20] Often with no time to wait for church renewal, or more likely with no institutional church to renew, Moravians, Silesians, and Salzburgers pioneered new forms of popular Protestantism and exported them to western Europe and then to the New World. Class meetings began with Philipp Jakob Spener in 1670; camp meetings originated with the Swedish army in Silesia in the early eighteenth century; and itinerant preaching developed as a survival strategy for pietist communities with no access to a regular, formal ministry. All was accompanied by a phenomenal increase in hymn writing and by revivals instituted and conducted by children. The money behind the expansion came from the commercial exploitation of medicaments and Bibles and religious literature, and from the availability of Dutch credit at low rates of interest. In this way, populist enlightenment notions of spiritual and bodily health were fused with liberal capitalist methods of fund-raising to produce new kinds of religious organizations. Following the trail of how money was raised and where it was spent is one of the great neglected themes of early modern Christianity.

John Wesley made contact with this new form of popular pietism in the American colonies and constructed a new religious movement that was almost a perfect fit for Adam Smith's paradigm of a religious free market. Methodism was a popular religious association funded by voluntary subscriptions with a strong emphasis on discipline, austerity, and moral earnestness. It grew within the legal protections afforded by a relatively tolerant Established Church, but was remorselessly critical of its lax standards of "scriptural holiness" and pastoral care. It was restlessly energetic in seeking out new hearers and converting them into disciplined members, but was careful not to provoke the civil and ecclesiastical magistrates more than was absolutely necessary for the advance of its cause. Its itinerant preachers were notably more industrious and more mobile than the clergy of the established churches, and they were financed not by tithes or church rates but by voluntary contributions and book sales. Hence they were not caught on the exposed edges of class conflict, legal coercion, and cultural paternalism in all its manifold forms. Smith was shrewd enough to recognize that such a movement might find the going easier in the New World than the old and that a religious free market was in some ways dependent on freer economic and political markets. It would be foolish to conclude from all this that Methodism was merely some sort of religious product obeying the laws of laissez-faire economics, but it would be equally foolish not to notice that Methodism thrived under Smith's economic system.

If Methodism seemed to be flowing with the tide of expanding markets and diminishing established churches in the late eighteenth century, it seemed to be fully against the tide of the religious thought of the Enlightenment, especially in the United States. By the late eighteenth century enlightened thinkers were prone not only to despise the content of popular religious enthusiasm, but also to underestimate its significance. They did so because their rationally conditioned habits of seeing the world triumphed over their empirical peripheral vision, which their enlightenment training might have nourished. Arguably the most representative figure of the European Enlightenment in America, or at least indisputably its most famous offspring, was Thomas Jefferson of Virginia. While recent scholarship has steadily undermined Jefferson's reputation as the embodiment of pure liberal values, especially in regard to his ambivalence over slavery, his use of executive power as president, and his treatment of political opponents, his commitment to enlightenment ideals in the area of religious belief and practice remains relatively unchallenged. As someone who deplored the religious intolerance and sectarian conflict of eighteenth-century European society, Jefferson expected better of his native America. As is well known, Jefferson's tombstone, located in the paradise of natural and architectural beauty of Monticello, states that here was buried the "author of the Declaration of Independence, the Statute of Virginia for religious freedom and the Father of the University of Virginia." The Virginia Statute, described by Martin Marty as "the key moment marking the close of the Age of Constantine and the opening of the modern age," was designed to effect the disestablishment of the Anglican Church and pave the way for the separation of church and state throughout the American colonies. Behind it lay Jefferson's impeccably enlightened view that both state-established and sectarian religion were enemies of human rationality and human brotherhood.[21] The best kind of religion was that which was based on the universal principles of natural religion, moral excellence, and personal freedom. By contrast, the competing claims of Calvinists, Catholics, and partisan enthusiasts offered only conflict and intolerance, which in turn destabilized civil polities and led to social mayhem. As Jefferson looked out over the religious life of the new American Republic he thought he saw a conflict between state-supported religion and voluntarism, and between Calvinism and

Unitarianism. He was in no doubt about which sides would triumph. In a confidential letter to James Smith in 1822, he stated:

> I have to thank you for your pamphlets on the subject of Unitarianism, and to express my gratification with your efforts for the revival of primitive Christianity in your quarter. No historical fact is better established, than that the doctrine of one God, pure and uncompounded, was that of the early ages of Christianity; and was among the most efficacious doctrines which gave it triumph over the polytheism of the ancients, sickened with the absurdities of their own theology. Nor was the unity of the Supreme Being ousted from the Christian creed by the force of reason, but by the sword of civil government, wielded at the will of the fanatic Athanasius. The hocus-pocus phantasm of a God like another Cerberus, with one body and three heads, had its birth and growth in the blood of thousands and thousands of martyrs. And a strong proof of the solidity of the primitive faith, is its restoration, as soon as a nation arises which vindicates to itself the freedom of religious opinion, and its external divorce from the civil authority. The pure and simple unity of the Creator of the universe, is now all but ascendant in the eastern states; it is dawning in the west, and advancing towards the south; and I confidently expect that the present generation will see Unitarianism become the general religion of the United States. The eastern presses are giving us many excellent pieces on the subject, and Priestley's learned writings on it are, or should be, in every hand.[22]

Similarly, in a letter to Benjamin Waterhouse fulminating against the "demoralizing doctrines of Calvinism," Jefferson wrote: "Had the doctrines of Jesus been preached always as pure as they came from his lips, the whole civilized world would now have been Christian. I rejoice that in this blessed country of free inquiry and belief, which has surrendered its creed and conscience to neither Kings nor priests, the genuine doctrine of one only God is reviving, and I trust that there is not a *young man* now living in the United States who will not die a Unitarian."[23]

Even as these letters were signed, the evidence suggests that Jefferson's confidence was entirely misplaced. By the 1820s the fastest growing religious traditions in the United States were not the rational Unitarians and Universalists he so much admired, but the Methodists and Baptists whose credulous evangelical enthusiasm he so much deplored. As is so often the case, predictions based on the most internally consistent of rational arguments turned out to be horribly wrong. The sheer extent of Jefferson's predictive blunder in 1822 was revealed by the unforgiving facts of the official United States census in 1850. The prejudices of enlightenment rationalism were exposed by the cold logic of enlightenment-inspired utilitarian calculations.

The seventh census of the United States, carried out in 1850, conveys the extent of a remarkable shift in religious practice since the American Revolution. There were 38,183 buildings counted as used for purposes of religious worship in the United States, supplying accommodation for 14,270,139 persons, and with a total value, including other church possessions, of some $87,446,371. What are particularly striking about the figures are the denominational proportions. Methodists accounted for just over a third of all churches and the Baptists for about a quarter. Thus, the combined numbers of Methodist and Baptist churches comfortably outstripped all the other churches put together. Even allowing for the fact that Presbyterian, Congregational, Episcopal, and Roman Catholic churches were mostly larger than their more humble Methodist and Baptist counterparts, the figures are still remarkable. Even in terms of church accommodation, as distinct from church buildings, Methodists comprised just under a third of the total, and Methodists and Baptists supplied more than half of the available capacity for worshippers. Far from the triumph of Unitarian universalism that Jefferson confidently predicted, by 1850 probably more than three-fifths of American church attenders were worshipping at temples devoted to some brand of popular evangelical enthusiasm.

The 1851 religious census in Britain indicated a similar surge of non-Anglican religion of a predominantly evangelical kind. The surge was not as dramatic as in the United States, the chief reason for which was the greater strength of the Established Church in Britain, and the consequent weakness of Evangelical Nonconformity in the south and east of the country. Indeed the closest comparison of numbers and the speed of transformation is between England and New England, and between Wales and the southern states of the United States. The preexistent strength of established churches and the amount of free cultural and social space available for competitors account for much of the difference between these patterns.


## Experience, Consent, and Evidence


The argument presented so far is that Wesley's Methodism occupied a position of creative tension between the apparent polar opposites of enlightenment and enthusiasm and that such a position was well adapted to broader intellectual, economic, and social changes in the North Atlantic world at the turn of the century. But how do ordinary rank-and-file Methodists fit into this tidy picture? How were the respective poles of enlightenment and enthusiasm played out within the hearts and minds of Methodist individuals and communities?

It is wise to admit in advance that answers to these questions are heavily dependent on what one judges to be enlightenment and enthusiasm, and that those are wide and hotly debated categories. Much of the recent work on the Enlightenment, for example, has gone the same way as other historical constructs. It is now widely assumed that in the eighteenth century there were many different kinds of enlightenment in many different places at different times, and that context shapes thought as decidedly as the reverse.[24] The danger here then is that one selects out of personal preference what one regards as "enlightened" or "progressive" or, even worse, "modern" and then shapes the argument to suit the premise. Something like that has been done to Methodism on any number of occasions, both by admirers and by critics. Yet the questions are too important to leave alone. One way out of the dilemma is to select some aspects of the Enlightenment that are uncontentiously central and to see how they played out with Wesley and his movement.

Frederick Dreyer, in a perceptive chapter on Methodism and the Enlightenment, suggests two areas worthy of consideration: Wesley's indebtedness to Lockean empiricism and his appropriation of enlightenment notions of natural jurisprudence.[25] In the first case Wesley followed Locke's rejection of Descartes' view that real knowledge was to be obtained by the operation of reason working on ideas innate to all, believing instead that "all the knowledge we naturally have is originally derived from our senses." It followed from that proposition that in all areas of thought, from medicine to theology and from natural philosophy to theories of knowledge, Wesley was "the champion of experience and the opponent of speculation."[26] Dreyer shows that although Wesley's sensible empiricism derived ultimately from Locke he was influenced by an even more extreme view of empiricism in Peter Browne's *Procedure, Extent, and Limits of Human Understanding*. From these works and his own experience Wesley declared that matters of speculative theology were of little concern to him, that what mattered was the perceptibility of faith in the experience of the believer. In this way faith was knowable and could therefore deliver assurance to those who had it. For Wesley it was impossible for anyone to be filled with the fruits of faith and the fruits of the spirit without knowing it. Religious conversion was therefore a sensible experience that ought to result in assurance of sins forgiven.

The second point of contact between the Enlightenment and the Methodist revival identified by Dreyer is based on the principle of consent in natural jurisprudence. Wesley's conception of the church was based not upon apostolic authority, confessional orthodoxy, or state coercion, but rather on the free consent of equals to form a voluntary association. The radical implications of such a view are far reaching. Wesley accepted that nonbelievers could contract into such an association and that the only basis of admission or expulsion was the member's willingness to consent to the rules of the association. Hence ejection from a Methodist society was based not so much on a theological determination as on whether or not someone disobeying the rules had broken the contract of membership. John Wesley, the inveterate rule maker, made rules not only out of autocratic tendencies (though surely that as well), but also because it was the only way to construct a voluntary association that acknowledged no other authority than that of the consent of its members. Some of Wesley's most controversial actions stemmed from such a belief. He took an essentially pragmatic view of priesthood, a completely functional view of the sacraments, and an infinitely expansive view of lay ministry. "Against the claim of church authority," Dreyer writes, "Wesley asserted a right of private judgment that was absolute and uncompromising."

> Every man living, as a man, has a right to this, as he is a rational creature. The Creator gave him this right when he endowed him with understanding. And every man must judge for himself, because every man must give an account of himself to God. Consequently this is an indefeasible right; it is inseparable from humanity. And God did never give authority to any man, or number of men, to deprive any child of man thereof, under any colour or pretense whatever.[27]

It is difficult to overestimate the importance to the future development of Methodism throughout the English-speaking world in the eighteenth and nineteenth centuries of its debts to these twin components of enlightenment thought, one based on a theory of knowledge and the other on a principle of association. Associations were of course not a brand new feature of the social landscape in the eighteenth century, as any student of medieval fraternities and early modern clubs and societies will attest, but they positively flowered in the eighteenth and nineteenth centuries. Peter Clark has estimated that there were as many as 25,000 different clubs and societies meeting in the English-speaking world in the eighteenth century and that there were over 130 different types of society operating in the British Isles.[28] At a time when increased religious and political pluralism led to a greater use of public social space by clubs and societies, Methodism was a religious association coming to fruition in the age of associations.

Twenty-five years of sifting Methodist archives in six countries have persuaded me that much of what one sees in them stems from Methodism's roots in enthusiasm and enlightenment. The journals, diaries, memoirs, recorded experiences, and autobiographies that line the shelves are proof positive of the enduring importance of recounting spiritual experience as the heart and center of the Methodist movement. These ubiquitous materials can be parsed for gender, color, class, upbringing, personality, and place of birth, but they all want to tell about sensible experience, however unconventional much of it seems to modern taste. The characteristic features of Methodist spirituality — its tendency to morbid introspection, its ruthless self-examination, and its compulsion to share and tell — are all products of its Lockean emphasis on sensible experience.

Methodism's second debt to the Enlightenment, an ecclesiology based on the principle of association, has also left ubiquitous archival traces. The immaculately kept lists of members and financial contributions, the almost obsessional preoccupation with rules, books of discipline, and trials of members, the recurrent feuding about rights and the location of authority within the connection, and the complex debates about what was legitimate and illegitimate social praxis for members are all characteristics of a voluntary association based on rules, contracts, and ubiquitous membership tickets. Even during Wesley's lifetime, but more commonly afterward in both Britain and America, there were fierce debates within Methodism about who had the right to make the rules, what the rules should be, and how they should be enforced. These are essentially the preoccupations of a voluntary association, not of a confessional church with its apparatus of clerical authority, historic confessions of faith, and hallowed traditions. Over time, as Methodism slid toward the confessional model (at a faster speed in the Old World than the new), it invented tradition to suit the current needs of the inventors, whether they be English preachers in search of a high doctrine of the pastoral office, or American "croakers" eager to establish their reputations as the builders of the movement. In this way invented traditions came to be hallowed traditions.

This chapter has sought to demonstrate that Methodism operated in a dialectical tension between enthusiasm and enlightenment that had enormous consequences for the sort of movement it became. Read any substantial collection of Methodist manuscripts, whether composed by

Assorted Methodist class tickets (Reproduced with permission of the Boston University School of Theology library)

preachers or the laity, men or women, black or white, and this theme is endlessly repeated. It shows up in a disciplined commitment to self-improvement combined with a fervent belief in divine intervention in daily life. It helps explain the lives of men like David Niles Bently, who was converted in a dream inspired by Lorenzo Dow and then, "being of a mechanical turn," went on to forge a formidable business empire that became a family dynasty.[29] It helps account for Methodism's infatuation with education and the cultivation of the mind, and the willingness of its members to put stock in visions, dreams, and trances. In characteristic enlightenment fashion, Methodists believed in gospel transmission by means, not by millennial fiat. Although Methodism was not free from eschatological immediacy, especially in times of social crisis, it did not capitulate to a pessimistic resignation to events beyond its power of influence. In America its declared aim was to reform a continent, not wait for Jesus in the clouds as with any number of millennialist sects who believed primarily in ends not means. In short, most of the paradoxes of Methodism and most of the ambiguities of its distinctive kind of spirituality go back to the fact that it was a movement of religious enthusiasts coming of age in the era of the Enlightenment.

# CHAPTER THREE

# The Medium and the Message

O ye Methodists, hear the word of the Lord! I have a message from God to
all men, but to you above all. For above forty years I have been a servant to
you and to your fathers. And I have not been as a reed shaken with the
wind: I have not varied in my testimony. I have testified to you the very
same thing, from the first day even until now. But "who hath believed our
report?" I fear, not many rich.

—JOHN WESLEY, *Sermons*, "The Danger of Riches"

W hat was the Methodist message, how was it transmitted, and
how was it heard among the diverse transatlantic populations
of the eighteenth and nineteenth centuries are not easy questions to answer. One is reminded of E. P. Thompson's astute observation
penned some forty years ago: "Too much writing on Methodism com-
mences with the assumption that we all know what Methodism was, and
gets on with discussing its growth rates or its organizational structures.
But we cannot deduce the quality of the Methodist experience from this
kind of evidence."[1] How then can it be done?

One suggestive route is to borrow from James Secord's book *Victorian
Sensation*, an experimental biblio-biography of Robert Chambers's *Vestiges
of the Natural History of Creation*, published anonymously in 1844.[2] Secord
brilliantly shows how Chambers's book was first a product of its author's
own complex biography, then became a production item shaped by all
sorts of technological changes in the construction and distribution of
print as a commodity, and then had a history of consumption as variegated as the social spaces in which it was read. Readers read it differently
according to their social class, religious disposition, institutional loyalty,
personal network, and geographical location. Secord also shows how
individual readers had their personal identities and worldviews shaped by
a fresh encounter with a powerful interpretation of how nature worked.
The point is that if a single material object can have such a complex
history of construction, dissemination, and consumption, how much
more is it the case for a religious movement attracting thousands of
people in different places at different times?

A second problem in getting to the heart of the Methodist message arises from the fact that Methodism was largely an oral movement, but its history has been constructed mostly from written sources. Of course sermons were printed, hymnbooks published, denominational magazines distributed, and letters exchanged, but the living voices of an oral culture are not easily extracted from such materials. In a creative attempt to come to terms with this problem Leigh Eric Schmidt appeals to the historian to become a kind of necromancer, or a ventriloquist, "for the voices of the past are especially lost to us. The world of unrecorded sounds is irreclaimable, so the disjunctions that separate our ears from what people heard in the past are doubly profound." Not only has hearing lost status against seeing in the modern proliferation of print culture, but also our post-enlightenment acoustical antennae are simply not adjusted to hearing the religious sounds of the past the way they were heard at the time. Moreover, religious insiders and outsiders heard noise differently. The phrase "all nonsense and noise" was a favorite of critics of Methodist revival meetings, but for those enraptured attendees at love feasts or camp meetings there was nothing nonsensical about the noise. Schmidt has shown how many Methodists who were immersed in the scriptures and traditions of mystical spirituality claimed to hear all sorts of sounds, from the direct call of God to the playing of heavenly music. Schmidt quite properly presses his analysis of these phenomena beyond what he calls "the safer terrain of social explanation" within which they have been interpreted into "the liminal space where the spirit and the flesh were under constant negotiation." Here was a place where "noises were silent yet heard, external yet internal, transient yet deathless, in the body yet beyond the body."[3] How that space is mapped within the hearts and minds of individual Methodists and in the broader life of the Methodist community is obviously controversial territory, but what can be stated with confidence is that the Methodist message was inexorably bound up with the medium of oral culture. Itinerants preached, exhorters exhorted, class members confessed, hymns were sung, prayers were spoken, testimonies were delivered, and revival meetings throbbed with exclamatory noise.

In coming to terms with the Methodist message (as with Chambers's *Vestiges*) it is obviously important to have a grasp of Wesley's own biography, his patterns of thought, and the breadth of his theological influences. He read and was influenced by a bewildering array of Christian traditions: the church fathers, monastic piety, and ancient liturgies; continental mystics such as Jeanne-Marie Guyon, François Fénelon, Claude Fleury, Marquis de Renty, Brother Lawrence, and Antoinette Bourignon; Byzantine traditions of spirituality approached through Macarius and Gregory of Nyssa; the English and Scottish Puritan divines; the Moravians and other channels of central European Pietism; his mother and through her to Pascal; classics of devotional spirituality including Thomas à Kempis, Jeremy Taylor, and William Law; and the canon of Anglican writers from Hooker to the seventeenth- and eighteenth-century High Churchmen. Writers on each of these traditions are prone to compete for the preeminent influence over Wesley, but the truth of the matter is that Wesley's eclecticism is itself preeminent. Similarly, the attempt to boil Wesley's theology down to a simple formula, such as the much-peddled quadrilateral of scripture, reason, tradition, and experience, spectacularly misses the point. A forensic appeal to geometrical precision, of all the approaches to Wesley's theology, is the one least likely to capture its essence. If Wesley's theology must be reduced to a model, one that offers better explanatory power than the quadrilateral is to see it more as a moving vortex, fueled by scripture and divine love, shaped by experience, reason, and tradition, and moving dynamically toward holiness or Christian perfection. Any model that lacks dynamic movement toward holiness and its growth within individuals and its dissemination throughout the world is clearly inadequate.

Another approach to Wesley's theology is to consider what he cared passionately about, so passionately that he was prepared to risk friendship or incur abuse and ridicule. Of course some of his theological spats were occasioned by his ego or his desire for control, but the fiercest ones were over issues he thought were nonnegotiable. Three stand out. The first was his controversy with the Moravians over their quietism and his emphasis on the discipline of an active spirituality as the means and the way to practical holiness. The second was his repudiation of Calvinism and all its supporting apparatus from predestination to limited atonement, and from eternal perseverance of the saints to the reprobation of the wicked. The third was his conflict with just about every other Christian tradition over the issue of entire sanctification or Christian perfection. Of course Wesley fought over other things with representatives of other Christian traditions, including Roman Catholics, Quakers, Deists, and Anglican latitudinarians, but if they were his battles, his wars were with Calvinists, Moravians, and opponents of perfection. What does this tell us about Wesley's theological priorities and about the nature of the Methodist message?

The row with the Calvinists was really over the character of God and the nature of human responsibility. Wesley could not conceive of a God who had determined everything in advance or of human spirituality that was mere acquiescence. The argument with the Moravians was really about the path to scriptural holiness and Wesley's profound conviction that works of benevolence and holy charity were essential components of true spirituality. Finally, his disagreement with all those opposed to Christian perfection was fought from the conviction that scriptural injunctions to "be perfect" meant exactly what they said. It would be a mistake to conclude from these emphases on human responsibility and inherent righteousness that Wesley had a weak theology of grace or that he was a closet Pelagian, for he laid great stress on human dependence on grace in all its manifestations — prevenient, justifying, sanctifying, sacramental, and universal. What is distinctive about Methodist spirituality, however, is its remorseless emphasis on scriptural holiness and on the need for human beings to take control of their spiritual destinies, not as passive respondents to the iron will of God, but as active agents in "working out our own salvation," or what one scholar has aptly called "responsible grace."[4]

It is important to recognize that a discussion of Wesley's theology is no mere rhetorical exercise in the history of Protestant thought, but rather is foundational to understanding the kind of movement he created. The whole ecclesiastical superstructure of Methodism, its itinerant and local preachers, its bands and classes, its love feasts and camp meetings, and its hymns and publications were all designed to promote scriptural holiness and guard against laxity or levity. The activism and agency explicit in the message were explicit also in the mediums of transmission. Methodism was restless and energetic, introspective and expansionist, emotional and earnest. It was an unsettling movement led by unsettled people. But how was it appropriated? How did the populations of the North Atlantic world in the eighteenth and nineteenth centuries consume it?

One way into this complex problem is to look at John Wesley's distribution of cheap print for the consumption of rank-and-file Methodists. Indeed, one of the most striking features of Methodism is the extent to which Wesley tried to secure control over the discourse of the movement by remorselessly selecting, editing, publishing, and disseminating print. He commissioned and published biographies and autobiographies as exemplary lives for the edification of his followers. He selected and published books for a Christian Library to be used by his preachers. He edited hymnbooks, published tracts, and distributed a connectional magazine. An inventory of the books owned by Wesley's press in 1791 contains a formidable list of biographies, hymnals, commentaries, sermons, guides, thoughts, addresses, magazines, death narratives, and tracts.[5] Moreover, Wesley refused to allow his preachers to publish works independent of his control. He literally tried to supervise the entire spiritual literacy of his connection by establishing a sort of Wesleyan canon beyond which his followers were encouraged not to go. Here was an attempt to control information, memory, and tradition in a remarkable way. To be fair to Wesley, he was prepared to select material from outside the narrow confines of a single spiritual tradition, and he strenuously denied charges of "miserable bigotry," but he was undoubtedly attempting to define a new tradition whose boundaries of print and access to information were drawn largely by himself. The extent to which Wesley was actually success-ful in inventing and controlling Methodist tradition through print is a matter of contention, and would be difficult to prove conclusively, but what is not in dispute is the seriousness of the attempt, and the energy with which it was pursued. Wesley aimed to produce print for all sorts of different occasions and for use in different spaces, private, communal, and institutional. However the Methodist message is to be defined, it is impossible to ignore the sheer audacity of Wesley's attempt to propa-gandize his own followers through the medium of print. As Methodists learned to read, sing, emulate, understand, and process, they were follow-ing paths carefully chosen by their leader. What was the path they were urged to follow?

Methodists were urged to contemplate Thomas à Kempis's *Imitation of Christ* and William Law's *A Serious Call to a Holy Life*, to emulate David Brainerd's heroic evangelism, to appropriate John Janeway's example of holy dying, and to develop spirituality after the fashion of Marquis de Renty and Gregory Lopez. Revealingly, neither Wesley nor his nineteenth-century followers reproduced lives of the eighteenth-century Calvinistic evangelicals. In this corpus there is no George Whitefield, Augustus Top-lady, or John Newton. The little "advice" tracts of Wesley's corpus are earnest and straightforward, with little of the sentimental sensationalism of the most ubiquitous of evangelical tract writers, Hannah More. Taken as a whole, spiritual zeal, moral earnestness, and serious Christian living characterized the collection of circulating Wesleyan print. Right down to the *Instructions for Children*, the Wesleyan set of prescriptions for the life of scriptural holiness left no room for levity or carelessness. The very energy with which Wesley propagated print was itself a model of disciplined activism for those whose reading was but a vehicle for holy living and dying.

Establishing what Wesley selected for his followers to read is no easy task, but estimating how much was read, how much was appropriated, and how much was applied to daily life is even more difficult. With our present state of knowledge, there is no easy way of dealing with these questions. Methodism not only appealed to host populations of very different so-cial and economic characteristics, but as with all religious traditions it occasioned manifold different levels of commitment from its constituents. Yet it would be a mistake to run from them, for anyone who has spent much time in a Methodist archive sifting diaries, memoirs, and letters swiftly gains an impression of a kind of Methodist style. The personalities and the social contexts change from place to place and vary according to gender, color, social class, and educational background, but the style is still discernible. One way of approaching Methodism's essence is to paint two triptychs, the first dealing with birth, life, and death within the Methodist movement and the second dealing with hymns, sermons, and meetings as means of transmission.

## Triptych One: Birth, Life, and Death

Birth, life, and death, or to Methodize these natural processes, conversion, sanctification, and holy dying, were at the heart of Methodist spirituality. The preaching careers of most early Methodist itinerant and local preachers, as with the spiritual lives of most members of Methodist societies, began with keenly remembered conversion experiences. Indeed, the conversion narrative is a common Methodist genre in which is stressed the drama of the second birth as a means of escaping a world of sin and licentiousness, and of entering a world of faith and godly discipline. One typical example, which can serve for others, is the narrative of John Edwards Risley, who was converted in Middletown, Connecticut, in 1820.[6] Common elements represented in his narrative include the influence of Methodist preachers, the support of prayer and class meetings, the awareness of sensible experience, the desire for assurance, the quest for a subsequent blessing of entire sanctification, the fear of backsliding, and the desire to become a useful instrument of God's grace in the world. The conversion experience was so central to the lives of early Methodists that they are embellished by memory and presented as cosmic dramas. In this case Risley presents his own conversion as a transition from a world of Sabbath breaking, novel reading, and alehouse frequenting to one of prayer, faith, and Bible reading. The episode is remembered as both a social and a psychological event. He recalls the piercing eyes of the preacher and the social pressures to conform either to the jocular, mocking presence of his rakish friends or to the life of the church community with its mechanisms of corporate insistence. His divided mind is presented as part of a divided society and then as part of a divided cosmology of good and evil, God and Satan. At stake in the transaction is nothing less than his temporal happiness and his eternal destiny. Fear of death

"The Conversion of John Edwards Risley (1820)," from an original painting by Glen Messer (Courtesy of the artist)

and the implied fear of eternal woe are powerful psychological induce-
ments to come down on the side of the believers against the scoffers, and
yet the narrative is presented more as a voluntary submission to the offer
of a new life than as an escape from a world of threats and torments.

Once the decision is made, there are the customary doubts and epi-
sodes of self-examination. It is at this point that the Methodist machinery
of class meetings and prayer groups offers crucial community support.
In addition, another preoccupation soon supersedes Risley's conversion
dialectic, the desire for the blessing of Christian perfection as against the
ever-present fear of backsliding to the world left behind. Out of the heat
of dialectical friction emerges his desire to *tell* the story to others and to
*work* for the triumph of his new principles. Out of the drama of Methodist
conversion experiences comes the remarkable energy of the movement.
Risley's subsequent career as preacher, revivalist, city missioner, and pa-
tron of dying Methodist causes is a remarkable tribute to the enduring
power of the message he first embraced as a teenager. His claim to have
relayed the message to more than thirty thousand people and to have
been involved in the conversions of many hundreds is a vivid illustration
in itself of how and why the Methodist cause prospered over the course of
the nineteenth century.

Risley's narrative of his life's work is not without its tales of hardships
and disappointments, but what is striking about it is how a set of experiences in his late teens set a course from which he never appears to have
deviated and seems never to have regretted. It is not surprising, therefore, that in trying to tell the story of his own life, he devotes over a fifth of
the narrative to only a few weeks. The memory of those events, simultaneously disturbing and liberating, became the organizing principle of his
entire life.

A similar pattern emerges from the conversion narrative of Fanny
Newell, who was born in Kennebec, Maine, in 1793. Her childhood was
punctuated with experiences of death, separation, and intense anxiety,
some of it inspired by religious parents warning her of the reality of hell.
Although she described her life as part of "the giddy multitude," her
diary is anything but lighthearted. A combination of Methodist sermons,
Bible reading, and morbid introspection brought her to a period of crisis
when she was fifteen years old. "Filled with sorrow," she wrote, "I went
mourning day after day, night after night, and month after month. While
everything around, wherever I turned my eye, seemed to be dressed in
mourning on my account." She wasted away, contemplated suicide, and
had a series of disturbing visions in which she was pitched in a tug of war
between Jesus and Satan. The denouement came at a Methodist meeting

where, after the sermon, the assembled congregation prayed for her. She describes her conversion in visionary language: "Through the cloud of darkness that surrounded me, I saw a small ray of light, and my eyes seemed fixed upon it. This light increased, until at length it appeared as large as the blaze of a candle, only differing in color. Then I saw the appearance of a man, and then the darkness which had surrounded me withdrew and stood in a body before me, which I thought to be my sins. They appeared like mountains piled on mountains; and the man who presented himself to my view seemed to be Christ." Throughout this dark trial of the soul Newell interpreted her experience through a fund of biblical stories and snippets of sacred verse. Once the decision was made, everything seemed better: sleep came easily, breakfast tasted sweeter, nature appeared lovelier, family shone more radiantly, and her snippets of religious verse changed from doom and gloom to rhapsodies of joy and redemption. After the joy of the decision came the joy of telling and the joy of being received into the Methodist fellowship of the faithful. Fanny's release from despair opened up a new terrain of visionary ecstasy, for "that which I cannot comprehend when awake, he revealeth to me when deep sleep locks up the bodily senses." Fanny's early pilgrimage was not without its difficulties. Sometimes her exuberance and sense of drama occasioned unwelcome cautions. A year later she attended a camp meeting at Monmouth, where she recounts an even more dramatic experience of entire sanctification in terms of being "caught up to the third heaven." A year later she married an itinerant preacher, whom she accompanied as a full partner in ministry, including public preaching, for the rest of her life. Once again, a fiercely intense experience as a teenager established a pattern of "telling" that continued until death.[7]

The experiences of Risley and Newell are but two well-documented examples of many hundreds of recorded conversion narratives and many thousands of unrecorded memories in the Methodist tradition. What is the historian to make of them? It is possible to detect a number of common themes. Most occurred during teenage years; most betray some sense of deep psychological distress; most contain within them an explicit or implicit fear of death; many seem to take place in communities experiencing rapid change or an unusual degree of social dislocation; and most converts had some preexisting religious knowledge. Just as captivity narratives do, conversion narratives form a literary genre the conventions of which need to be taken seriously by any investigator.[8] They are meant to be good stories fit for the telling as well as honest accounts of states of mind. How these documents are decoded will in large measure determine the kind of interpretation of Methodist growth that emerges from them.

Whether pitched as the products of social anomie, psychosexual repression, economic dislocation, or religious fervor (by no means exclusive categories), no history of Methodist expansion can afford to ignore them.

Conversion was the entry into a life of faith, the intensity of which occasioned both admiration and criticism among contemporaries and among interpreters of the Methodist tradition. There is a ubiquitous literature of anti-Methodist publications drawing attention to the extremism, narrowness, and hypocrisy of Methodist spirituality. In his influential attempt to get to the heart of the Methodist experience, E. P. Thompson regarded the violent recasting of personalities under the "promiscuous opportunism of Methodist theology" as one of the most unpleasant features of the English industrial revolution. Thompson's view was that the uncertainty principle in the salvation theology of Arminian Methodism combined with a psychic compulsion to adapt to new economic environments produced a manic spirituality driven by fear of backsliding and craven acquiescence in the work discipline of industrial capitalism. Neither the theology nor the economics of this interpretation quite fits the facts, but Thompson was on to something in his attempt to get at the apparent extremism of Methodist piety. What was the inner driving force and how did it work? Consider for a moment the richly documented life of Hannah Syng Bunting, which is suggestive of wider patterns that show up in many of the diaries, memoirs, and letters of Methodists in the eighteenth and nineteenth centuries.

Hannah Bunting grew up in Philadelphia in the early nineteenth century and was converted to Methodism under the influence of family members at the age of sixteen. "I have this night openly professed to be on the Lord's *side,*" she writes. "Angels and men have witnessed my *solemn vows.* Much is now required of me: numerous obstacles surround me." Her conversion leads to a greater, not lesser, awareness of "the monster sin," and the next few years of her life are dominated by struggles and temptations punctuated by bouts of assurance and joy (mostly experienced at love feasts or at prayer and camp meetings). She longs for entire sanctification, takes instruction from Methodist preachers, and reads the standard accounts of Christian perfection by Wesley and John W. Fletcher. Some particularly intense experiences of "the awful presence of Jehovah" almost persuaded her that entire sanctification had come to her, but the denouement comes over six years after her conversion. "Since my last date I have felt my desires after purity of heart and entire holiness of life much increased. My views of sanctification are so high, that I seem scarcely at the threshold." The final struggle for perfect love, predictably, comes in the context of a camp meeting where she is urged to believe it. "With a mighty effort of faith I resolved in hope against hope, self desperate, to believe, and leave the event with God. Immediately heaven-born peace and love took possession of my heart." Recording the moment in her diary and speaking about it to others confirmed its reality. Even so, her struggles against impatience, testiness, and melancholia did not end, for Methodist perfection was perfectible. Bunting lived only for another eight years, and they were not easy ones. Consumptive illness and attendance at any number of deathbed scenes convinced her that life was indeed a vale of tears. After a lengthy and emotional description of the death of her sister, Bunting writes: "This is the triumph of our holy faith. The saddest, most dreary, and most heart-rending moments of life are occasions of the most Divine consolation and support." Later she wrote: "How has the luster of the world faded in my view, and its fascinations been broken by bodily and mental anguish. It is all of grace that I am what I am. Death is certain."[9]

As her own death approaches she communes in dreams with her dead sister and looks forward with eagerness to a new life altogether. Bunting's diaries and letters to her female correspondents with whom she met for prayer and mutual support are written with a remarkable intensity. Clearly an ardent spirit, with or without Methodism, Bunting's quest for conversion, then for entire sanctification, then for a deeper knowledge of God, and then for a holy death meant there was no letup until death itself. But what drove her was not so much fear of backsliding and loss of faith, as in Thompson's paradigm of Methodist spirituality, so much as an eager search for peace and purity. Although each one of the thousands of Methodist memoirs and diaries is unique, there are consistent themes. Usually conversion came early, in the teenage years, and was often vivid and somewhat frightening. The struggle for entire sanctification was usually protracted and rarely resulted in the perfect peace that was unrealistically anticipated. Close experiences of suffering or death persuaded the believer of the transience of earthly life and the vanity of its fleeting pleasures. Most were reinforced and kept on track by bands, classes, sermons, love feasts, and camp meetings. Many are punctuated with quotes from scripture or from hymns or spiritual songs—little aphorisms that kept up morale in difficult times. All operated with the dreadful certainty of suffering and death.

If conversion started the Methodist pilgrimage, and the pursuit of entire sanctification moved it along, death was its consummation. Much insight into the distinctive nature of Methodist spirituality can be gleaned from the attitudes to death portrayed in Methodist print and in the recorded experience of individual Methodists. It has been shown, for example, that the Methodist *Arminian Magazine* carried far more accounts of

"Death of the Rev. John Wesley," from a color engraving by R. Owen of London. This illustrates not only Wesley's patriarchal status but also the importance of holy dying in the Methodist tradition. (Courtesy of the John Rylands Library)

deathbed scenes than its Calvinist rival, *The Gospel Magazine*.[10] With characteristic emphases on experience, assurance, and community, deathbed
scenes in Methodism were portrayed with something of the same theatrical largesse as conversion narratives. The approach of death, that twilight
zone between life and eternity, was the final testing point of Methodist
spirituality. To die a good and holy death, free from anguish and uncertainty, was the aspiration placed before the Methodist faithful in the
pages of the *Arminian Magazine*, a periodical read by as many as a hundred thousand people by the end of the eighteenth century. Like conversion narratives, accounts of deathbed scenes have a defined pattern, and
increasingly moved from edited description to even more edited prescription over the years. As with conversion narratives, the experience of
death is recounted in language replete with metaphors, this time of slum-
ber, surrender, flight, departure, and rest in the arms of Jesus. Also present is resistance to Satan and his evil legions. In death evil is resisted and
defeated, eternity is welcomed and embraced. Women, as well as men,
had their experiences recounted, but for them metaphors of a heavenly
embrace were more common than the surrender of the will in men.
Children also had their stories told, in pious laments not too dissimilar
from those in high-grade and, more commonly, in low-grade Victorian
fiction. As in the wider Euro-American tradition of revivalism, the testimony of pious infants facing death was thought to have particular power
of emotional persuasion.

The deathbed scenes of the Methodist faithful popularized through
print were melodramatic, ritualistic, and paradigmatic. Above all they
were meant to show to the immediate family, the wider Methodist community, and thousands of readers that the faith of the Methodists worked
unto death itself. Here were stories of earthly renunciation and heavenly
anticipation in which lives well spent in disciplined holiness were given
the ultimate reward of triumphant glory. No wonder Wesley, a consummate religious marketer, saw the potential of these accounts earlier than
some of his competitors. Although both the published and unpublished
accounts of Methodist deaths are highly formulaic in language and structure, and a trifle too melancholic and self-absorbed for modern sensibilities, there is no denying that death was the final litmus test of the
claims of the Methodist message. Conversion and death were points on
the linear scale at the beginning and the end of the Methodist life; everything in between had its real meaning within those coordinates. If Methodists of all people could not die well, then what had been the point of it
all? For those who had invested in, and sacrificed for, the Methodist
message, a holy and peaceful death not only was an authentication of the

way they spent their lives but was also a powerful and final evangelistic gesture. As in life, Methodists used the deathbed to admonish, reform, warn, and persuade. There was no more appropriate place from which to preach the Methodist message of fleeing from the wrath to come than the attended deathbed. It was entirely characteristic of Methodism that these stories were first collected and edited by Wesley, then turned into print and proclamation, and finally circulated as a means of prescription and persuasion.

## Triptych Two: Hymns, Sermons, and Gatherings

It has long been recognized that the most distinctive, characteristic, and ubiquitous feature of the Methodist message, indeed of the entire Methodist revival, was its transmission by means of hymns and hymn singing. If one were to choose one single artifact of Methodism somehow to capture its essence, the most defensible choice probably would be the *Collection of Hymns for the Use of the People Called Methodists* of 1780. For a movement that attracted far more literary abuse than praise, the *Collection of Hymns* has commanded almost universal admiration. Bernard Manning described it as "a work of supreme devotional art by a religious genius"; Rodney Flew called it "a liturgical miracle"; Ernest Rattenbury considered it "a Methodist manifesto, . . . a splendid summary of Methodist devotion"; and Carlton Young viewed it as a beautiful piece of "lyrical theology."[11]

Suppose for a moment that one were able to subject the *Collection of Hymns* to Secord's biblio-biographical method, what picture of the Wesley brothers and their movement would emerge from it? Such a venture would require a lifetime of scholarship, but Franz Hildebrandt and Oliver Beckerlegge have already supplied some of the raw materials in their standard edition of the text for the new Bicentennial Edition of John Wesley's *Works*. They show that Wesley was an inveterate collector and publisher of hymns, beginning with *A Collection of Psalms and Hymns*, published in 1737 for the use of the infant colony in Georgia. Wesley had been influenced by his mother's psalm singing, his father's parish choir, the hymns of Isaac Watts, and the Moravians' *Singstunde* (singing hour). This edition contained approximately seventy hymns, mostly by Watts, and was printed in Charleston by Lewis Timothy, a French Protestant refugee who learned the printing trade in Holland and then in Philadelphia in the employment of Benjamin Franklin. Wesley's first venture into hymnbook publishing was not a spectacular success, but it was important nevertheless. It was the first Methodist hymnbook, the first Anglican hymnbook, and quite possibly the first hymnbook published in America for use in public worship. It also showed Wesley's enthusiasm for hymnody, his willingness to alter texts to suit his own purposes, his ability to organize hymns into a wider liturgical framework, and his capacity to fuse German and English works of popular devotion into a new synthesis. A worldwide singing movement was born in what Frederick Gill has called "a wretched outpost of empire."[12]

Over the next fifty years the Wesley brothers issued some thirty hymnbooks: some with tunes and some without; some intended for special occasions, some for more general consumption; and some intended for all "real Christians," some only for Methodists. John was the selector, organizer, editor, and publisher; Charles was the prolific poet, writer, and lyricist. It is estimated that he composed some nine thousand hymns and sacred poems, some of which are classics of devotional literature. Many are easily forgettable. The point is that, well before the *Collection of Hymns* in 1780, Methodism was a movement distinguished by its devotion to sacred songs. Why was there such a mania for singing? What was sung? Where were hymns sung and by whom? How were they sung and what effects did they have on the singers? The *Collection of Hymns* offers a way into these questions. John Wesley's preface is instructive. After carefully delineating the market objectives for the new volume ("a collection neither too large, that it may be cheap and portable, nor too small, that it may contain a sufficient variety for all ordinary occasions"), Wesley stated that the volume contained "all the important truths of our most holy religion, whether speculative or practical; yea to illustrate them all, and to prove them both by Scripture and reason. And this is done in a regular order. The hymns are not carelessly jumbled together, but carefully ranged under proper heads according to the experience of real Christians. So that this book is in effect a little body of experimental and practical divinity."[13] In Wesley's words, poetry was to be "the handmaid of piety" in quickening devotion, confirming faith, enlivening hope, and kindling or increasing the Christian's love of God and humankind.

As the contents page shows, Wesley was correct to state that the volume was not casually organized. Part one was an exhortation to return to God by describing the pleasantness of religion, the goodness of God, death, judgment, heaven and hell. Although the last four sections seem superficially morose and threatening, Rattenbury is correct to state that these hymns strike a "wooing note." The dominant themes are invitational ("Come sinners to the Gospel feast; / Let every soul be Jesu's guest" [2]); celebratory ("Happy the man that finds the grace, / The blessing of God's chosen race, / The wisdom coming from above, / The faith that sweetly works by love" [14]); and anticipatory ("I long to behold him arrayed / With glory and light from above, / The King in his beauty displayed, / His beauty of holiest love" [68]). In these hymns the reality of death, judgment, and hell are all declared, sometimes in strikingly morbid tones, but the main focus is on the "pleasantness of religion" and the "goodness of God." These are expressed not with cloying sentimentality or with banal platitudes, but with a poetic love of the invited life of faith in a harsh world. Part two of the *Collection* describes the difference between formal and informal religion; part three contains prayers for repentance and recovery from backsliding; part four envisages the believer rejoicing, fighting, praying, watching, working, suffering, groaning for full redemption, and interceding for the world; part five includes hymns of corporate life, celebrations of Methodist community. What is striking about the hymns as a body is their relative absence of doctrine (though hymns on the trinity, the church, the incarnation, and the eucharist appear in other editions), and their concentration instead on the Christian life as a pilgrimage, a journey from earthly despair to heavenly blessing. They are filled with personal pronouns, active verbs, and intense struggles. They aim to persuade, to convince, and to plead. They are more winning than threatening, more appealing than damning.

The literary characteristics of the hymns, the great bulk of which were written by Charles Wesley, have been subjected to careful examination. Commentators pay tribute to influences from Milton and Dryden, but above all to the Scriptures. There is general agreement that Charles had a particular mastery of meter, rhyme, and language, but that he wrote too quickly, descending more often to cliché and repetition than is evident from a perusal only of his great hymns. Similarly, there have been criticisms of John's sometimes crude appropriation of tunes, especially in the early days when his boldness was not matched by his expertise. The Wesleys, in hymnody as in many other aspects of their lives, appeared to operate in a twilight world between elite and popular culture, sometimes creatively mediating, sometimes falling between stools. John was nervous of sophisticated anthems or singing in parts, preferring tunes that were "singable, teachable, memorable, functional and accessible to all."[14] Tunes were taken from a wide range of sources from Georg Friedrich Handel, Henry Purcell, and Johann F. Lampe to folk melodies from England, Scotland, and Ireland. John also had strong views about the way hymns should be sung. He urged Methodists to learn the tunes, sing the exact words, sing lustily, modestly, and in time, and above all to sing spiritually so that they would not be carried away by the sound. Again characteristically, the Wesleys valued passion and sincerity, even some emotion, but they feared excess or lack of self-control. John, always inquisitive if not always insightful, thought about the power of music on animals and on his followers. His "Thoughts on the Power of Music" written in 1779 show that he was aware of the potential of music to "raise various passions in the human mind." He thought the ancient Greeks were masters of musical manipulation of human passion, but that moderns, despite having access to more sophisticated instruments, traded melody for harmony, simplicity for complexity, and as a result produced "delicate, unmeaning sound" with no capacity to excite the passions. Wesley perforce wanted spiritual passions excited by music, and understood the power of it as a means of transmission.

How then was Wesleyan hymnody consumed by Methodists? "Hymns played an important part in all the additional means of grace developed by the Methodist societies," including bands, classes, love feasts, watch-nights, prayer meetings, covenant services, outdoor preaching services, and camp meetings.[15] Almost every Methodist gathering began and ended with a hymn. Sometimes participants wanted to sing more often than Wesley deemed prudent, and said so. The hymns designated for society meetings and love feasts in part five of the *Collection of Hymns* resonate with themes of mutuality, partnership and encouragement. "Help us to help each other, Lord / Each other's cross to bear; / Let each his friendly aid afford, / And feel his brother's care. / Help us build each other up, / Our little stocks improve; / Increase our faith, confirm our hope, / And perfect us in love" (489). Hymns were not only sung on public occasions, they were sung privately or memorized. Wherever one looks in Methodist archives, from the recorded experiences of itinerant preachers to the diaries of the Methodist faithful, hymns are used for expression, consolation, anticipation, and interpretation. Methodists absorbed their faith through the words of their hymns and sacred verse.

The *Collection of Hymns,* first published in 1780, was issued in many editions and served as the backbone for manifold new books of Methodist hymns in Britain and America. As Methodism expanded so too did the number of hymns in the standard Methodist hymnodies, from 525 in the 1780 edition to 1,026 in 1876. Editions might change and grow larger, but hymn singing as a devotional practice remained a consistently vital part of the movement throughout its period of rapid growth in the eighteenth and nineteenth centuries. The Wesley brothers, Charles as composer and poetic genius, John as collector and editor, were keenly aware of the power of hymns in achieving manifold objectives: they transmitted complex theological ideas in accessible language; they reached deep into

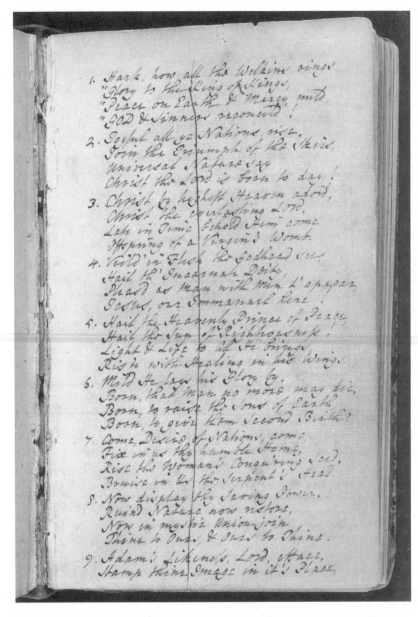

Charles Wesley, autograph of the hymn "Hark, the Herald Angels Sing." Hymns became a powerful medium for communicating the Methodist message. (Courtesy of the John Rylands Library)

the will and the emotions of believers through meter, rhyme, and melody; they made connections with the wider culture through the appropriation of popular tunes; they were easily memorized (more so than the biblical verses that inspired them) and used by individual believers in the crisis moments of their lives; they helped build communal solidarity and collective devotion; they enlivened meetings of all kinds that otherwise would have run into the ground of emotional sterility; they inspired the imagination, mediated biblical metaphors, and helped build a system of symbols; they defined for Methodism a religious content and style of a more vibrant and populist kind than was available through confessions of faith or chanted liturgies; in short, they supplied a poetic music of the heart for a religion of the heart. The medium and the message were in perfect harmony.

What was clear to the Wesleys is only now becoming clear to historians of "popular religion" who are beginning to subject hymnody to a more systematic analysis. James Obelkevich considers hymns to have a better claim than anything else to be at the emotional heart and center of British popular religiosity. Stephen Marini similarly states that "the hymns of evangelical Protestantism are the most widely used spiritual texts in American history," transmitting the evangelical worldview across regions, denominations, and time. Following Clifford Geertz, he sees hymnody as supplying a major ingredient in religion as an extensive cultural system. "From that perspective," he writes, "hymnody may be considered a medium of evangelical culture, a complex symbolic form comprised of poems and music, physical acts and psychological effects, texts and techniques, group behavior and ritual gesture that expresses virtually the entire range of religious meanings available to participants in evangelical religion."[16] In a systematic attempt to find out what early American evangelicals sang or did not sing, Marini constructed a database of the most frequently published hymns in the period 1737–1860. What surprised him about the content of these hymns was the lack of emphasis on the church, worship, doctrine, and eschatology, which are often regarded as evangelical preoccupations. The emphases are rather on atonement, invitation, salvation, sanctification, witness, perseverance, death, and heaven. The hymns redact the gospel narrative and draw the believer into that narrative. As with all the classics of Protestant spirituality, from Milton to Bunyan, the emphasis is on the believer's participation in the journey of faith from gospel invitation to heavenly celebration. In this narrative Marini detects more mystery, awe, and uncertainty than is customarily associated with evangelical hymnody.

Some of Marini's methods and conclusions need to be treated with caution. His method of database selection may have the effect of editing out the omissions he finds surprising, and what was most commonly published was not necessarily what was most commonly sung by the great mass of the people associated with evangelical Christianity of all stripes. Nevertheless, his general emphasis on the cultural power of hymnody as a means of religious transmission and his insight into the pilgrimage mentality of many of the hymns fits the Methodist branch of popular evangelicalism. Revealingly, the Wesleys chose hymns expressing the life of faith, from invitation to heavenly joy, for their more generic publishing ventures, while producing any number of niche collections for special purposes. Whatever the enduring value of Marini's creative attempt to place evangelical hymnody at the center of "American popular religion," there can be no doubt that hymnody was somewhere near the heart and center of Methodist popular religion. Hymn singing was an expression of individual and corporate affirmation, an aid to memory, a trigger of religious emotion, and a creator of spiritual identity. It was the message set to music.

A close competitor for that accolade is the sermon. A veritable army of itinerant and local preachers and exhorters, of both sexes, preached millions of sermons in different kinds of social spaces throughout the North Atlantic world in the eighteenth and nineteenth centuries. So ubiquitous was the sermon, so variable was the educational background of preachers, and so different were their target audiences that it is difficult to make general statements of universal applicability. Nevertheless, most Methodist sermons were based on a selected biblical text; most were delivered extemporarily or from a loose structure of notes; most were preached many times and were refined on the move according to reception; most were designed to evoke a response, whether of conversion, sanctification, or a warmed-up spirituality; most were delivered in plain language and enlivened by illustration, anecdote, or humor; most operated within the accepted "canon" of Wesleyan theology, sometimes guaranteed by use of Wesley's notes on the New Testament or by other established sources of connectional orthodoxy; most were delivered in a particular kind of social space that shaped content and style of delivery; most were measured by fruitfulness, however determined, not by eloquence; most were attempts at communication from the heart and to the heart, not bypassing the mind, but not aimed directly at it; most accepted the authority of scripture at face value; most assumed that what was being declared was the plain truth untainted by sophisticated apologetics or hermeneutics; most were preached by preachers of a roughly similar social status to their listeners. In the period before increasing connectional bureaucracy offered alternatives, the road to wider influence and power within Methodism was through preaching. Only a fraction of Methodist sermons were ever published, especially in the early days before anniversary, funeral, and special occasion sermons were printed for more general consumption.

Special insights into the nature of the Methodist message and its means of transmission are to be found in the manuscript sermon books of the itinerant preachers and their accounts of classes and camp meetings. Although the sermon was the ubiquitous means of Methodist proclamation, scholars, for obvious reasons, have paid more attention to the printed sermons of the learned than to the spidery sermon outlines of the itinerant foot soldiers. Based upon a survey of several hundred such sermons, my preliminary conclusion is that the Methodist message, to quote George Eliot, focused more often on "the blessings of faith than upon the accursedness of infidelity."[17] The preoccupation with hell-fire preaching and scare tactics, the interpretation conveyed by satirical prints and anti-Methodist literature, is not as common as one might suppose. In fact, the predominant themes of most Methodist sermons are grace, godliness, repentance, temporal and eternal joy, perseverance, vigilance, and assurance. One good example, which can stand for many, is taken from the sermon book of Daniel Webb, a Massachusetts itinerant preacher, in 1806.

Rom. 8.28. "And we know"

I. Make some remarks on the purpose of God. This phrase frequently occurs in the scriptures. Eph. 3:11, 2 Tim. 1:9. See extract from Wesley's notes on this passage. For the most part when the words purpose, ordain, predestinate, with their derivatives, are used in the word of God they refer to his grand design of saving lost men by the merit of the death of his Son, on the conditions he himself has specified. He has given his son to die for us, he calleth after us, he offereth us mercy, he hath promised, and we have full assurance of it, that the obedient shall be called his people and that all things shall work together for their good.

II. Describe the character to whom the gracious privilege belongs of having all things work for their good.

    1. By their Christian affection "they love God" for what he is and for what he does. This love implies a high estimation of him, delight in him, desires after him, and earnest longings for the full fruition and enjoyment of him.

    2. By their effectual vocation "they are called," outwardly by his works, providences and gospel, and inwardly by conscience and the holy spirit — out of darkness into light, from bondage to liberty, from sin to holiness, and from hatred to love.

III. That things work together for good to such persons.
   1. Not sin or sins of any kind.
   2. Prosperity or adversity, riches or poverty, health or sickness, liberty or captivity, persecution or toleration, temptation or freedom from it, means or want of means, life or death. They shall all work for good, not separately apart, but as coadjutors and mutual helps. But in what respects shall their good be furthered? Answer, their spiritual and eternal good.
IV. The certainty of this proposition and assertion. It is not built upon conjecture and mere probability, but upon certain knowledge. "We know."
   1. From divine revelation. God has told us so.
   2. From experience. We find it so.[18]

Here, pithily expressed, are the common centerpieces of the Methodist message. Delivered in a popular style to plain people, Webb's sermon emphasizes the authority of scripture and of Wesley's interpretation of it, the gracious offer of divine mercy, the assurance of divine goodness, the enjoyment and delight of the believer in God, the importance of religious experience, the notion that Methodists are those called out of darkness to light (literally enlightenment), a sense of vocation, and finally, "certain knowledge." The power of the voluntary request, thus exemplified, was held to be a more powerful persuader than the coercion of established churches or the terrors of eternal punishment.

Some of the itinerant preachers, including the most often cited such as Lorenzo Dow in America, Gideon Ouseley in Ireland, and Billy Bray in Cornwall, were characters larger than life, but most itinerant and local preachers were more pedestrian, if scarcely less zealous. Thomas Marcy, a New Englander of no great distinction born in 1813, was converted in 1826, licensed to exhort in 1834, licensed to preach as a local preacher and admitted to conference in 1835, ordained deacon in 1837, and then elder in 1839. Each step was typical for itinerant preachers and had to be navigated by endurance and fruitfulness. "We had but few meeting-houses at that time," he writes, "and they were small and rude, we more generally met in school-houses, private dwellings, barns, and in the warm season of the year often in the open air. We usually preached three times on the Sabbath and twice or three times in week time: in 1836 my second year in the ministry I averaged six sermons per week, and only in two instances did I stay two nights in succession in the same house."[19] All was accomplished on a salary of around a hundred dollars a year (any surplus was given back to meet the deficiency of others), a fraction of that enjoyed by ministers in more established denominations.

A typical description of the kind of preaching that was on offer from these itinerants has been provided by Ralph Willard Allen on the career of Ira Bidwell: "His ordinary preaching, while it showed a want of study & careful preparation, was scriptural, practical, convincing, & the truth was presented in a manner to make a deep impression on his hearers." Enoch Mudge (1776–1850) wrote his sermon outlines on long strips of paper about three inches wide, with four sermons to every folded column. Most were taken from the New Testament, but there was also a sprinkling from the Old Testament, with Psalms and Proverbs the most popular. Once again the themes were largely directed at "the requirements of a holy life," including endurance, self-denial, obedience, and diligence. The narrative structure of the believer's life was to be conformed to the narrative structure of the New Testament itself, with a strong sense of being able to reproduce many of those experiences in the present. George Steele, reflecting on the contribution of preachers to a century of Methodist growth in the United States, stated: "One secret of their success was in their ability to speak to the intuitions of men. . . . They attacked the old orthodox dogmas with resolution and energy, and it was the intellectual stock in trade of many a circuit rider of those times—a collection of arguments supposed to demolish the whole Calvinistic structure. I'm afraid the reasoning would not always have stood the tests of simple logic, and its effectiveness, I apprehend, did not so much lie in the dialectic power displayed as in what I have just alluded to as the appeal to the intuitions of the common people."

Sermons preached were sermons consumed. Few approached the devotion of Sarah Murch, who kept a little book of sermon texts and titles that she heard preached in Boston from 1817 to 1835 as an aide-mémoire, but very few of the diaries, memoirs, and recollections of Methodist lives in the nineteenth century come without a meaningful engagement with a Methodist sermon. Sermons as much as hymns were the currency of Methodist transmission. Mark Noll's ingenious calculations have shown that by the 1850s the Methodists had constructed almost as many churches as there were post offices in the United States and employed almost as many ministers as there were postal workers. "Considered together," he writes, "the evangelical churches employed nearly double the personnel, maintained nearly twice as many facilities, and raised at least three times the money as the post office. Moreover the churches delivered their message to more people than the postal service delivered letters and newspapers."[20]

What is striking about Methodist hymns and sermons, taken together, is the close fit between theology, practice, and style. The communication media, the communicators, and the content of the message displayed a harmony of values well adapted to its mobile mission to the common people. Its emphases on invitation to a new life, freedom of choice, and the journey to holiness, combined with its fusion of preached word and sung verse, offered an obvious appeal to populations breaking free from the more static and emotionally restrained worldviews of Established churchmen, Calvinists, and Deists. Methodism marched on its message.

How that message was heard and appropriated by Methodists depended both on the kinds of social spaces in which it was propagated (mostly within Methodist control) and on the economic, political, and social conditions of the regions in which it took root (mostly outside Methodist control). The Methodist ecclesiological structure of bands, classes, societies, circuits, and conferences, what John Wigger has helpfully called "the social principle," was a riot of association in the age of associations. The basic unit was the class, which commenced in Bristol in the early 1740s, initially as a financial expedient to support the ministry and relieve the poor. Originally classes were groups of about twelve meeting in a particular geographical area under a specified leader. Entry was based on a desire to "flee from the wrath to come" and the aim was to nurture godly language, temperance, honesty, plainness, seriousness, frugality, diligence, charity, and economic loyalty within the connection. The issue of the much-prized quarterly membership tickets cultivated a sense of membership and identity. For those who were decidedly Christian believers pursuing sanctification, the smaller bands, divided by gender and marital status, were places of confession, or "mutual inquisition," as Robert Southey described it. The aims of these little Methodist associations were to finance the movement's expansion, exercise spiritual discipline (unrepentant backsliders were ejected), pursue scriptural holiness, nurture fellowship, and train future leaders. Opponents of Methodism criticized classes as popish (for their confessional element) and divisive (for raising the bar of spiritual devotion). Wesley acknowledged the experimental nature of the whole system and stated that everyone had "an equal liberty of speaking."[21]

Almost all membership surveys of Methodist classes show a preponderance of women on a ratio of almost three to two.[22] The early records of American Methodism show that classes were the most important building blocks of the movement. Generally speaking, classes grew in size to around twenty-five to thirty-five people, and displayed various patterns of gender and color separation or integration according to time and place. Although classes also varied in terms of emotional intensity and noisiness, their sheer ubiquity in the surviving records of Methodism show them to be places where members were assimilated, voices were found, spiritual experiences were shared, and communities of faith were built. Much would obviously depend on the personalities and diligence of class leaders and members, but at their best they were the spaces in which the message became flesh. Fanny Bartlett wrote of one of her "fathers in the gospel," Timothy Merritt:

> Holiness was the great business he loved to promote. . . . Some are still living who with me remembered how he "laboured night and day with tears," from house to house urging individuals to attend class & prayer meetings . . . in the hope of benefiting some soul athirst for salvation, or for urging its importance on the half-hearted professor, who would appoint a *watch meeting*, and gather a room full, some of whom being strong in faith, with their heavenly minded pastor struggled in constant prayer until the Holy Ghost descended as in the days of the apostles when "they were all with one accord in one place." Frequently at the meetings souls received the witness of perfect love, and if, as our father often observed, one sanctified Christian can do more good than ten unsanctified, what must have been the result of his pious work in that wicked city [Boston]. He organized *band meetings* according to the discipline of our church, these met weekly apart, and once in two or three weeks, they came together for a general band meeting. Every one had perfect liberty to express his or her view in regard to holiness, while our pastor stood like an almost super-human being urging us on to perfection. He would say "be not satisfied with spending moments, but be willing to spend hours in wrestling for the blessing."[23]

Even allowing for the spiritual hyperbole, this letter demonstrates the close connection between the message of entire sanctification and the media of band, class, and watch meetings. Such were the places, par excellence, where the Methodist message moved from print to voice, from individualism to community, from cognition to emotion, and from private to public. They were the message transmitters of the movement.

If bands, classes, and societies exemplify the principle of association within Methodism, love feasts, quarterly meetings, and camp meetings demonstrated a principle of celebration. Love feasts, initially revived by the Moravians, were simple fellowship meals for the Methodist faithful; quarterly meetings transacted Methodist business, enforced discipline, and spilled over into celebration; and camp meetings were prolonged outdoor revivalistic extravaganzas. Each had a different theatrical style and contributed something distinctive. Love feasts were admittance by ticket only and built up notions of separation (from a hostile world), cohesion (the shared meal), and adoration (the offered praise of a loving community). Quarterly meetings brought church administration and ecclesiastical discipline (typically for Sabbath breaking, sexual immorality, drunkenness, or debt) out of the closet of private bureaucracy, where many churches had confined it, into a more public arena, and by doing so nurtured a sense of participation and collective responsibility. Revealingly, in Britain quarterly meetings gradually became the law courts of Methodism, in which preachers with inflated views of their pastoral office laid down the law for the connection, whereas in America quarterly meetings often ran over into "seasons of blessing" when routines shaded into revivals.[24]

Similarly, in England camp meetings were resisted by the main branch of Methodism, becoming the grounds of secession for the Primitive Methodists, whereas in America they became a normal part of the Methodist experience, as much on the eastern seaboard as on the expanding frontier.[25] Camp meetings, described variously as Christian versions of the old Jewish feast of the Tabernacles, as modern equivalents of medieval pilgrimages, and as religious embodiments of community fairs, were highly ritualized gatherings, which often resulted in large numbers of conversions or of commitments renewed. It is remarkable how often they show up in the reminiscences of the Methodist faithful as emotionally charged memories of life-changing encounters. Outdoor festivals organized around common collective purposes, and enriched by affecting music and ritualized behavior, are literally sensory and sensible experiences for those in search of sociability, entertainment, and community.

The Methodist message was subtly altered by the social spaces in which it was expressed, as different aspects of it were emphasized according to personality, function, and context. Context is the tricky part of the story, for since so much Methodist history has been written within either national or regional historical traditions, thereby militating against comparison, the assumption is often made that Methodism is much the same kind of plant wherever it takes root. But Methodism changed and was changed by contexts. The language of classes, societies, love feasts, and conferences might remain similar, but the experiences they describe are not. It has been shown, for example, that Wesley's evangelistic strategy, if as such it can be described, varied with time and geographical location. Until the early 1750s his declared aim was to "reform the nation, more particularly the Church; to spread scriptural holiness over the land." To achieve this he allied himself with a clutch of country Tories and Jacobites who hoped to propel themselves into positions of national influence through the reversionary politics of the Prince of Wales at Leicester

House. They hoped to reform the Established Church from above by having input into episcopal appointments. That strategy collapsed with the tennis ball that killed the prince, but what was the alternative?

In England Wesley set about creating an institution from his mission to the poor that could survive outside the episcopal discipline of the Established Church without necessarily attacking it. In Scotland, he flirted with the General Assembly of the Church of Scotland, routinely ridiculed Calvinists, and got nowhere very fast. In Ireland he tagged alongside the Protestant Ascendancy, appealed to European Protestant minorities, endorsed the cultural superiority of Protestant Ulster over the rest of the country, and not surprisingly made little headway among the nation's majority Catholic population. In America something more creative was accomplished largely without Wesley's input, though the sending of Francis Asbury turned out to be an inspired choice. But there is more to it than that. Ward writes that American Methodism "inherited the 'language of Canaan,' that common language of European Pietism, which in America had been made a folk idiom by the First Great Awakening in the 'forties. It was natural to them to talk of the Spirit 'falling' upon a meeting, for people to have 'melting experiences,' and to 'find great freedom,' to be knit together in 'love,' to call each other 'brother,' and 'rejoice in the prosperity of Zion.' "[26]

In short, despite the fact that American Methodism adopted an episcopal structure and drew its ecclesiological language from English Methodism, its real language of common spiritual discourse was more radically pietist than its British antecedents. That made it easier for it to operate in creative engagement with the egalitarian republican language of its new national context. Ward's point is that English Methodism grew up under the shadow of that "most grossly-overrated incubus of European Christianity, a Catholic church order which affected even those who resolved to do without it," whereas American Methodism was freed from the burden of having to operate within the parameters of religious establishments.[27] That freedom was more than just a structural transaction, which is the way it is commonly written about, but it affected Methodist language, ritual, experience, and energy. At first sight the American branch of Methodism seemed to have roughly the same ecclesiological, ritualistic, and experiential characteristics as its British counterpart — that is, the message was essentially the same — but the content of each of these categories was so modified by context that even its language was different. In short, whatever one says about the heart of the Methodist message, and the superficial similarity of its methods of transmission, it was *spoken* and *heard* differently in different national and regional contexts. It was also heard differently, as a later chapter will show, according to age, gender, race, and social class. To say this is not to collapse Methodism into some kind of postmodern morass where its content is reduced merely to a set of power relationships, or to say that it is meaningless to talk about Methodism as a supranational religious movement with defined characteristics, but rather to show that Methodism altered and was altered by the social contexts in which it grew. Here is an interface worth exploring, especially for Methodism in America, where Methodist gains were the most striking.

One way of exploring that interface is to look at the liturgical development of American Methodism from its common origin in the four "guides" supplied by John Wesley in 1784: his *Sunday Service,* his letter to the American brethren (giving permission to worship "according to scripture-guided conscience and Spirit-inspired piety"), the Large Minutes (1780), and the minutes of the conversations with the preachers. This combination of Wesleyan form and popular freedom allowed American Methodism to adapt to its host culture. Karen Westerfield Tucker has shown how in the first third of the nineteenth century American Methodists "peppered their preaching, their prayers, and their polity with the Americanized language of liberty of conscience and personal responsibility before God." Nevertheless, Methodism still retained its boundaries with the world in the distinctive ways it administered baptism and the Lord's Supper, performed marriages, and preached funeral sermons (all to believers). If Methodists were adapting to the values of a new nation, they were also in a profound sense a distinctive people. But from midcentury onward Methodist liturgical texts, architectural spaces, and ritual forms all showed signs of Methodism's greater stake in the values of progress and refinement articulated by the larger society. "The acculturation of Methodist liturgy," according to Tucker, was probably inevitable; "as nation and denomination grew up together, each contributed to the development and identity of the other. Once the trajectory of Americanization had begun, Methodism relished its status as both prophet and patriot, and strove to keep pace with the increasing complexity of American life under the banner of progress."[28]

If the development of liturgy and public expression is one way of penetrating to the heart of Methodism's encounter with culture, another is to look at personal experience and internal piety. Recent spates of high-quality books on Methodism have all tried to come to terms with the relationship between the internal drama of Methodist experience and the external characteristics of Methodist expansion. Focusing primarily on the greater Middle Atlantic region in the period from 1760 to 1800,

Dee Andrews has shown how "the making of a Methodist" (whatever the individual filters of generation, gender, and race) ultimately dissolved traditional social boundaries and opened the way for a fierce missionary drive to reclaim a continent. Methodism offered a plain gospel to a plain people who, in the mass, were unwilling to embrace either the grim selectivity of Calvinism or the unemotional urbanity of Universalism. By offering a powerful religious alternative to republican civic culture, Methodism harnessed and organized the energies of a restless American people. Andrews refuses to reduce Methodism to a kind of millennial sect or a refuge for the ignorant and the defeated; for her, Methodists are instrumental and purposeful, seeking to spread "scriptural holiness" across the continent. Lynn Lyerly, writing of southern Methodism in the same period, shows that out of the "marrow of the Methodist self" emerged a Methodist style of emotionalism, mysticism, asceticism, enthusiasm, and evangelism.[29] So powerful was it that it temporarily broke the dams holding in place the white male honor codes of the South, based on greed, gratification, and slavery. Women and African Americans flocked into Methodism in great numbers, but ultimately Methodism made an unhappy peace with its surroundings and opened the way for a tawdry reconciliation between Methodism and the culture of slavery.

Similar tales of how "the making of the Methodist self" resulted in vigorous challenges to surrounding cultures have been told in the British Isles. Rural Methodists in nineteenth-century England set themselves against the culture of Anglican paternalism and landowner dependency. Urban Methodists in northern manufacturing towns set themselves against the whole political structure of class hegemony, at least until Methodist leaders told them that neither their politics nor their methods would be tolerated within the connection. Methodists in Wales organized in liberal hordes against the Established Church, landowners, and other forms of unwelcome Anglicization. Irish Methodists with fierce zeal tried to occupy the narrow ground of opposition to Roman Catholicism, Ulster-Scots Presbyterianism, and Anglican elitism. Immigration and assimilation eventually tempered their zeal. What is striking about each of these examples is that reconstituted Methodist selves had to live and bear witness in different cultural settings, and in the process their message was shaped by those settings.[30] Predictably, the evidence (initially at any rate) shows up not so much in the patterns of how selves are reconstituted internally and privately as much as in the rhetoric of public engagement, as Methodists organized and spoke to meet their various foes. Only slowly does the latter begin to inform the former, often with devastating effects for the Methodist mission.

What this chapter has sought to demonstrate is that the Methodist message was not the same thing as its theology, though theology is no doubt an important component of the message. As Methodism expanded and migrated across the Atlantic it carried the Wesleyan message and subtly adapted it to new conditions. American Methodists initially imported their theology from England in the shape of Wesley's *Sermons* and *Notes on the New Testament,* Fletcher's works against Calvinists and in favor of perfection, and Richard Watson's standard work *Theological Institutes* (1821–29). Not surprisingly, the first stabs at theology by American Methodists were attempts to explain the scripture way of salvation in plain language for plain people, but soon more sophisticated voices, such as those of Nathan Bangs and Wilbur Fisk, emerged to stake a place for the Methodists in a more scholarly theological discourse. Bangs, like Jabez Bunting in England, viewed theological endeavor as a way of getting the attention and earning the respect of other Christian denominations. By the 1840s American Methodists had their own denominational quarterly (the *Methodist Quarterly Review,* founded in 1841), their own colleges and seminaries, and even their own systematic theology, written by Thomas Neely Ralston, whose *Elements of Divinity* appeared in 1847. The distinctive Methodist theology that emerged in America owed much to its roots in English Wesleyanism and its populist polemical encounters in the New World. According to Brooks Holifield, American Methodists "largely ignored Wesley's Anglican admiration for patristic sources, his sacramentalism, and his liturgical piety; they appropriated his anti-Calvinism, his revivalism, and his perfectionism, and they reshaped even that by filtering it through the lens of Scottish philosophy, mental science, and the free-wheeling denominational polemics of American popular Christianity."[31]

Much Methodist theology emerged out of its field encounters with Calvinists, Universalists, and populist millenarians. As such, Methodists defended divine love and justice, emphasized human agency and choice, rejected universal salvation but not universal atonement, and insisted on human depravity while opening up the possibility of entire sanctification. Generally speaking Methodist theology was too biblicist to be entirely consistent, too optimistic to be much preoccupied by speculations of millennial woe, too concerned with human experience to engage in metaphysical abstractions, and too populist to establish a position of genuine respect within the academy. As with other aspects of its mission, Methodism's theology shaped and was shaped by its environment. Holifield has shown that over the course of the nineteenth century American Methodism absorbed influences from Scottish common sense philosophy, including its emphases on evidences and natural theology, defended the authority of scripture in increasingly literalist ways, and found virtually unlimited ways of talking about the role of the spirit in the pursuit of entire sanctification. In the first half of the century the most influential formulations of perfectionist teaching came from Timothy Merritt, who like Fletcher before him associated entire sanctification with the baptism of the spirit, and Phoebe Palmer, who relied more on what she saw as biblical promises than on sensible experience and feelings.[32] Disputes over the ways and means to entire sanctification in the light of human experience and biblical interpretation troubled Methodism throughout its history and led inexorably to the separation of Holiness movements from the main tradition in the second half of the nineteenth century. If the desire for entire sanctification has been one of the defining elements of Methodist spiritual energy, lack of consensus on how it was to be achieved has proved to be one of its most divisive features.

To understand how theology came to be embedded in a message spoken and heard by quite humble people has been the aim of this chapter. As with Secord's experiment with biblio-biography, the method here has been to look at how the message emerged, how it was propagated, how it was appropriated, and how it was consumed. Unfortunately, as Schmidt has reminded us, this message can no longer be heard; it has to be reconstructed from materials that do not speak, or sing, or groan. For all religious movements that deficiency is a serious hurdle to overcome, but for Methodism, which thrived on noise, the deficiency is yet more serious. By looking at the respective triptychs of birth, life, and death (conversion, sanctification, and holy dying) and hymns, sermons, and gatherings, the aim has been to catch something of the flavor of the Methodist message for individuals and their communities. But this message was no more spoken and heard with universal templates of perfect reproduction than any book is read the same through different pairs of eyes. In fact the issue is yet more complex than it is for print. Robert Chambers's *Vestiges of the Natural History of Creation* was read differently according to social class, religious affiliation, and geographical location, but the print remained the same. The argument presented here is that the Methodist message was subtly altered by its multi-varied locations and that those alterations had profound consequences, not only for how the message was contextualized, but also for the nature of the message itself. Exploring those fine adjustments and how individuals and communities appropriated them is an inexhaustible process. In the meantime all that can be done is try to construct a basic "map" of the content and means of transmission of the message, and try to hear it through the layered testimonies of those who actually did hear it.

# CHAPTER FOUR

# Opposition and Conflict

If Christians are free citizens of Zion, they should prize those liberties,
seeing they were purchased with the precious blood of Christ.
— JAMES O'KELLY, *The Author's Apology for Protesting Against the
Episcopal Church Government* (1798)

Our people are still ruled without being consulted. They have no voice in
the choice of their own officers, the formation of their own laws, or the dis-
bursement of what they give to carry on the work.
— ALEXANDER KILHAM, *An Appeal to the Methodist Societies of the
Alnwick Circuit* (1796)

In *Middlemarch,* by George Eliot, the author's residual evangelical earnestness, together with her deep belief in the moral importance of all
human action, led her to construct scenes in which the making of
hard choices defined the characters of the novel's main protagonists.[1]
According to Eliot, each human choice not only revealed the essence of
character but also helped determine the pattern for all subsequent human choices. Those who make morally shabby choices today are more
likely to opt for equally shabby choices tomorrow; the reverse is also the
case. In the tough choices Eliot forces her characters to make there is
often a mental and spiritual tug of war between altruism and egotism, between service to self and service to the wider community. The point of
decision thus becomes the point of self-revelation, whether conscious or
not. Eliot's emphasis on key moments of choice as particularly revealing
of the nature of human character might, with some poetic license, be
applied to religious movements. The aim of this chapter, therefore, is to
discover something of the character of Methodism as a movement by looking at some of its key moments of conflict and opposition. These have a
way of distilling the essence of Methodism, both in its relations with the
communities in which it took root and in its internal struggles. As with a
silhouetted caricature, a proper appreciation of the issues at stake in
conflict and opposition makes it possible to trace the hard edges of a
movement that otherwise get lost in social and organizational complexity.

## Opposition

Methodism was born into a culture of hostility.[2] Elite and popular opposition to the new movement was ubiquitous throughout the British Isles in the period 1740–70. Part of the problem was the uncertainty of Methodism's legal status, since it was neither subject to Anglican ecclesiastical discipline nor willing to avail itself of the limited toleration afforded to Protestant trinitarian dissenters by the Toleration Act of 1689. By urging his followers conscientiously to pay tithes and church rates, and by refusing to seek relief under the Toleration Act, Wesley hoped to preserve Methodism's status as a society within the Church of England. It soon became obvious, however, that Methodism's attempt to shelter under the legal umbrella of the Established Church was welcomed neither by churchmen nor by local justices of the peace who were required to administer the statutes against deviant religion enacted during the reign of Charles II. The issue was forced into the open when local mobs, persuaded that there was no law for the Methodists and they were therefore indemnified against prosecution, costs, and damages, attacked Methodist preachers and their followers. Methodism's vulnerable legal status offered little protection, but that in itself does not explain why Methodism was so frequently the target of violent mobs in eighteenth-century Britain and Ireland. Why then did Methodism occasion such opposition?

Early Methodists were looked upon as "disturbers of the world," the new Levellers, and were thus victims of surviving memories of the English Civil Wars when antecedent forms of popular religious enthusiasm led, or so it was thought, to the collapse of political, religious, and social stability. In its new Methodist guise religious enthusiasm appeared to undermine traditional authority by criticizing the vices of social superiors and the worldliness of the parish clergy. The Methodist propensity to use itinerant, lay, and female preachers crossed traditional social boundaries of hierarchy, law, gender, age, wealth, education, and religious vocation. Moreover, Methodism's unregulated nationwide organization cut across the parish, diocesan, and county borders upon which English local government and the administration of the law depended. This lack of official control was exacerbated by the fact that Methodism often took strongest root in marginal areas, scattered settlements, and new industrial and mining environments where the traditional social cement was weakest. Anti-Methodist rioting from one perspective, therefore, acted as an instrument of social control as mobs were often led by the clergy, local government officers, and men in livery.[3]

"The Mobbing of John Wesley at Wednesbury," in 1743. Methodism was frequently the object of mob attacks, especially within the first few years of its appearance in any given location. (Courtesy of the John Rylands Library)

It would be a mistake to conclude from all this that anti-Methodist disturbances were uniformly instituted from above as an elite-driven exercise in social manipulation, for the evidence suggests that Methodism, especially in the first phase of its growth, was genuinely unpopular among some sections of the population.[4] The most frequent criticisms of early Methodism that surfaced in English localities were that it encouraged sexual license, disrupted traditional patterns of work, undermined participation in village sports and festivals, split families and communities, induced madness and displays of paranormal behavior, extorted money for corrupt purposes, and transformed religion from an inclusive emphasis on community solidarity to an exclusive preserve of "the saved." As is commonly the way with new religious movements, criticisms of Methodism concentrated mostly on issues surrounding sexuality, money, secrecy, hypocrisy, novelty, loyalty, family, and community. Allegations could often be mutually contradictory and were heightened during periods of social instability or foreign warfare, when communities had particular reasons for fearing new and disruptive movements. At such times Methodists were often accused of being Jacobites or Papists. On the eve of the Seven Years' War against France, for example, William Williamson, an evangelical Anglican in York, was accused of resorting to the "night revels of the Methodist meeting," which was described as:

> A place of bad fame and Reputation and the practices therein are said to be profane and superstitious, great numbers of persons of both sexes being frequently assembled there at very unreasonable hours in the night, the doors for the most part being locked, barred and bolted, in such private assemblies none being admitted without tickets with Popish pictures and devices upon them as of the Virgin Mary, a Crucifix, or a Lamb, porters being usually placed at the door of the meeting house to hinder admittance to and to thrust such persons back as are not known to be of their sect.[5]

In this way Methodists were associated with every possible offense from revelry to crypto-Catholicism and from secrecy to superstition. Generally speaking, opposition to Methodism, whether measured in rumors or actual intimidation, declined as it became more established and as its legal status became more defined. Most, but not all, of the violence directed against the Methodists was designed to promote humiliation and ridicule rather than to inflict serious injury to persons or property. Itinerant preachers were rolled in mud, doused in ponds, stripped of layers of clothing, and subjected to various forms of ritualistic abuse meant to undermine their authority and their manliness.

Although opposition to Methodism was ubiquitous across the North Atlantic in its first century, its occasion, causes, and consequences were regionally and chronologically distinctive. Some of the same themes appear again and again, for example Methodism's alleged promotion of sexual misconduct among its hearers, but opposition was also revelatory of the assumptions and prejudices of those doing the opposing. The aim of the following three case studies, chosen primarily for their rich documentation and their regional and chronological coverage, is to expose what precisely was at stake in the conflicts between Methodists and those who wished they would go away.

### The Pendle Forest Riots

In the late summer of 1748 John Bennet, one of early Methodism's most influential lay preachers, recorded in his journal this account of an anti-Methodist disturbance in the north of England.

> The rush cart [went] down while we were singing. It was dressed with Flowers and Garlands. The Drum Beat, the Musick played, and they fired their guns which caused the valley below us to echo, as tho' the Hills had fallen. What with the Drum, Musick Guns firing and shouting on one side of a little Croft, and we singing on the other you wo'd have really thought the English and the French armys were engaged in Battle — we gained ye field and kept it about 4 Hours, the enemies fled, making a retreat into the valley . . . no sooner was we dispersed but the rabble began a shouting upon the Hill as tho' the Highlanders were near approaching.[6]

Bennet's account of the "war" between Methodists and the mob is set within a broader context of warfare between the English and the French, the Jacobite Highlanders and Hanoverians, and, as the rest of his journal makes plain, between God and the devil. The pageantry he describes is typical of the highly ritualistic violence directed against Methodists in the Pendle Forest region of England throughout the summer of 1748. Both the date and the place are important. The forest of Pendle was located in east Lancashire near the border with the West Riding of Yorkshire.[7] The area was dominated by a cottage-based textile industry, the population of which had been subjected to an unprecedented wave of evangelical preaching by Moravians, Methodists, and Anglicans throughout the 1740s. Informal evangelical penetration was regularized in 1747 when the Methodists and the Moravians established a formal preaching plan for the area. A centuries-old tradition of sturdy independence (forest areas were notoriously undergoverned) and rough devotion to Anglicanism was coming under pressure from new economic, social, and religious forces. Methodists, by publicly preaching against the revelry associated with Anglican feasts and village sports and by appearing to flaunt established traditions of ecclesiastical and statute law, seemed to be riding roughshod over local sensibilities in a region notorious for its record of resisting religious innovations.

Moreover, Methodist conversionism, especially among women, servants, and children, seemed to threaten an established patriarchal conception of social order. The mobs that were raised against the Methodists throughout the summer of 1748, therefore, were partly endorsed by social superiors (including a particularly controversial Anglican clergyman named George White), partly encouraged by a sense of legal indemnity, and partly an expression of a profound sense of local antagonism against a new and socially subversive religious movement. Their chosen methods were militaristic intimidation, ritual humiliation, and low-grade violence designed more to deter than to punish. Described by one historian as "distinctly popular in character and conservative in tenor, the local men and women who joined the anti-Methodist crowd were concerned to protect their Church, their king, their families, their livelihoods and the integrity of their communities."[8] Many of them were also ruffians emboldened by drink, the support of their social superiors, and the knowledge that they could act without fear of prosecution. It was the latter point that particularly outraged John Wesley, who was both observer and victim of mob attacks in the Pendle Forest in 1748.

By holding local magistrates to a strict accountability and by using his metropolitan legal contacts to take some cases to the court of King's Bench, Wesley attempted to take the sting out of popular protest by demonstrating that even Methodists were entitled to protection under English law. Once it was established that legal indemnity was not an automatic benefit of joining anti-Methodist mobs, the pace and ferocity of attacks gradually diminished. Anti-Methodist disturbances did not end in the 1740s, but they seldom reached the intensity of the Pendle Forest riots in 1748 and the even more violent Cork City riots in Ireland a year later. The riots in Cork were particularly protracted because there was no restraining authority from social and ecclesiastical elites, who did not want the precarious stability of the Protestant ascendancy disturbed by mindless Methodist enthusiasts. Even the local Baptists who were broadly sympathetic to Methodism's godly zeal accused the Methodists of organizing "wild promiscuous assemblies," interrupting work and family responsibilities, grabbing after money, and attempting to build an empire (by publicly claiming to be a nondenominational religious society, but all the time behaving as covert denominational recruiters).[9]

The riots against Methodists throughout the British Isles in the 1740s and '50s show how a new religious movement outraged the sensibilities of both social elites and popular constituencies. That Methodism was not crushed within a generation of making its appearance is due to the determination of its early adherents, the lack of sustained and systematic persecution by leaders in Church and State, and the fact that the Methodist leadership was able to appeal to traditions of English common law until its own legal status became more accepted. Anti-Methodist rioting was thus a phase in the early history of Methodism, not its nemesis. Methodism not only survived the onslaught against it in east Lancashire and west Yorkshire in the mid-eighteenth century, but also was able to transform the region into one of its most enduring strongholds. The same pattern was true of Cornwall. Whatever the intentions of anti-Methodist rioters, therefore, Methodism, it seems, thrived on opposition.

## Revolutionary Opposition

In the winter of 1776, Captain Thomas Webb, a colorful military veteran of the Seven Years' War and the man behind the building of the first Methodist chapel in North America, found himself in New Jersey passing on military intelligence about Washington's troop movements to the British authorities in the unruly colonies. Webb was eventually arrested and brought before the Continental Congress on charges of spying. He was then sent as a prisoner of war to the Moravian settlement at Bethlehem, Pennsylvania, before being allowed to return to Britain in 1778. Webb's strange career is emblematic of a much wider set of problems facing the tiny Methodist movement in North America on the eve of the Revolutionary War. Trusted neither by Anglicans because of their enthusiasm and irregularities nor by American patriots because of Wesley's well-publicized writings against the American colonial cause, American Methodists seemed to be a species in danger of extinction. By the spring of 1778 less than half of the preachers who had joined the connection since 1773 were still traveling, and of all the "Wesleyan licensed itinerant preachers, just one — Francis Asbury — remained in patriot territory. By all appearances, the Wesleyan connection had ceased to exist in America."[10]

A new generation of predominantly native-born preachers, however, mostly from the Middle Atlantic states, gave the movement surprising impetus in the most unpromising of circumstances. During the war Methodist itinerant and local preachers were constantly under surveillance and were subject to official and popular harassment. Some were arrested and imprisoned for noncompliance with militia drafts; others were imprisoned or fined for refusing to take oaths of allegiance to newly formed state legislatures. Preachers were beaten, roughed up, tarred and feathered, and jeered for being unpatriotic and cowardly. To make matters worse, they were often defended by women, which did not help their growing reputation for lacking manliness and patriotic courage. Southerners were particularly worried about Methodism's antislavery stance, which seemed to brand the movement as an enemy to slaveholding republicanism and to white honor codes.[11] In short, the Methodist mission, deprived of leadership, exposed to ridicule, branded as unpatriotic, portrayed as unmanly, and hounded by officials, ought to have emerged from the war in a similarly weakened position as the Episcopal Church from which it came. Yet something approaching the reverse was the case. The number of Methodist members enrolled in societies almost doubled, from around six thousand in 1778 to around twelve thousand near the end of the war in 1782.

Unexpectedly the Methodists had turned the war to their advantage by exploiting the opportunities afforded by a more militarized society, including preaching to gatherings of soldiers or those protected by soldiers. "In a conflict that bore many features of a civil war," states Dee Andrews, "with patriots pitted against loyalists, radical activists against religious sectarians, and slaves against masters, a new dynamic force led by a remarkably resilient band of young preachers" made striking gains. Revivals became more common than battles. Moreover, once the war was over Methodists showed themselves to be skillful inventors of tradition, as they laid claim to a noble enterprise of nation building and heroic self-sacrifice. Southern evangelical preachers, with Methodists in the vanguard, reinvented themselves as courageous crusaders of the gospel that required "not only a gambler's nerves and a dancer's endurance but also the cunning of a hunter and the courage of a soldier."[12] A generation of nervous apologists, made so by their founder's opposition to their country's cause and by his advocacy of passive nonresistance, emerged from the war determined to conquer a continent. The Revolutionary War, far from being the nemesis of Methodism, led to its empowerment. Francis Asbury, who had refused to take the Maryland loyalty oath and who spent part of the war cooped up in depressed isolation, remained in America while others fled home, and reaped his reward in a remarkable period of postwar church building. The Christmas Conference that launched the new American Methodist Church in Baltimore in 1784 was not only a powerful symbol of survival for a movement that might have been crushed by the war, but also freed the Methodist movement from its filial obedience to Wesley. If the Revolutionary War freed America from British control, it also cleansed Methodism from the trace elements of Anglican paternalism that would have hampered its progress in the New World. Not for the first time, opposition and conflict proved to be angels in devils' clothing.

## The Fall River Outrage

On a cold December morning in 1832, the body of Sarah Cornell, a worker in a local factory, was discovered hanging from a pole propping up a haystack on the outskirts of Fall River, Massachusetts. The woman was pregnant. Before her death she claimed that she had been seduced at a Methodist camp meeting by a Methodist minister named Ephraim Kingsbury Avery. Anonymous letters, allegedly written by Avery and discovered in her trunk, seemed to corroborate her story. Was she indeed seduced by Avery? Did he kill her to keep her quiet, or did she commit suicide out of humiliation and despair? These were the questions at issue in a long and expensive trial that has been brilliantly reconstructed by the anthropologist David Kasserman. Given the nature of the surviving evidence and the fact that Avery's alibi could be neither corroborated nor rejected, determining guilt or innocence proved almost impossible. This twilight zone of uncertainty was bad for justice, but good for the historian, because it gave rise to a feast of rumor and popular print that reveals much about how Methodism was perceived in early-nineteenth-century America.[13]

The trial operated on many different levels. At its most basic it was a legal conflict between prosecutors and defense lawyers about the ambiguous nature of the surviving evidence. It was also a clash between a religious man of seemingly high repute and a woman of supposedly loose morals. On yet another level it was a struggle between two expanding institutions in early American culture. On one hand the mill owners, as representatives of the new manufacturing interest, were keen to defend the esteem of the early industrial workforce entrusted to their care, while on the other the Methodist Church was protecting its reputation as a respectable new religion on the American landscape.[14] In addition, local sensibilities were outraged by a salacious crime foisted upon the good name of Fall River by two outsiders. All was reported in gruesome detail by the popular press, which spread details of the case throughout much of the territory of the early republic.

For the Methodists, the Avery case posed special problems. Avery was

a prickly character whose previous career had not been without controversy, but he had somehow survived without official ecclesiastical censure.
The Methodist Church was therefore in the unenviable position of either
abandoning to his fate one of its licensed preachers in good standing with
the church, or defending him in a public trial that would attract the most
unwelcome publicity. The church chose to defend him. Avery was subse-
quently acquitted both by the trial jury in Fall River and later by a Methodist tribunal of seven ministers chaired by Wilbur Fisk, the first president of Wesleyan University. But Avery's triumph was short lived, and his
peaceful reentry into local ministry proved impossible. During and after
his trial Avery was subjected to every kind of ritual humiliation: a coffin
bearing his name was discovered floating in the river at Providence; ef-
figies of him were hung in the streets and then paraded in riotous processions; oil paintings of him committing the crime appeared in public;
bawdy and declamatory songs and ballads were written and sung; and
journalists and writers had a field day discussing his trial and acquittal.[15]

In response the Methodists cranked up their own propaganda apparatus, but in cases like this almost no publicity is good publicity. Predictably,
attacks on Avery soon widened into more general attacks on Methodism
as a degraded religious system. "Aristides," a frequent polemical con-
tributor to the *Republican Herald,* wrote that Methodism employed a despotic and hierarchical system of church government that was inimical to
the interests of the people. The writer and novelist Catharine Read Arnold Williams, echoing long-standing criticisms of Methodism, wrote that
Sarah Cornell had been the victim of manipulative preachers, emotionally charged camp meetings, and shameful sexual exploitation. According to her, Methodism, by contrast with the solid industrial habits nurtured by the mills, was a weak-minded religion designed to rob young
women of their chastity and respectability.[16]

Williams's account of the Fall River episode, topped and tailed as it is
with a preface about the baneful nature of Methodist religion and an
appendix with her own sharply observed eyewitness account of an early
Methodist camp meeting, is particularly revealing of standard criticisms
of Methodism in Jacksonian America. Writing from the standpoint of a
middle-class Episcopalian with conventional religious opinions, Williams
chides Methodism for its egocentric and exploitative itinerant preachers,
its religious competitiveness, and its claim to "superior devotedness" and
"over zealousness," which unsettles the minds of young women. "And is
this counterbalanced by any inward advantage? Does religion thrive in
noise and tumult? Does the heart become better, the imagination purer,
the temper more placid? Can that God, who is worshipped only in spirit

"Methodist Camp Meeting," engraving by E. W. Clay published in New York by H. R. Robinson, 1836 (Reproduced with permission from the Methodist Collections of Drew University)

and truth, be only honored in a crowd?"[17] Williams's opinions about Methodism had largely been formed by a visit to a four-day camp meeting in Smithfield, Rhode Island, in the early 1820s. "I was lost in admiration: a holy calm took possession of my soul," she writes of her first sight of the cleared ground. She was deeply moved by the "fine grove within an impenetrable wood," the sea of "snowy tents," and the plain dress and sober habits of the assembling crowd. It reminded her of the children of Israel making their way to the promised land.[18] But the calm of the sun-speckled landscape did not last long. There soon arrived an army of hangers-on — professional gamblers, horse jockies, liquor sellers, and local louts in search of entertainment. Then the meetings began. The atmosphere soon changed from calm sobriety to emotional excess. Rough sermons were preached by rough people, men and women began to cry aloud for mercy, women fell in hysteric fits and trances, men began to prey upon the women, "there was a good deal of joggling, pinching, and looking under bonnets," and soon the whole atmosphere had changed to one of "uncivil amusement." Williams returned to the camp on three successive days, each one more disturbing than the one before. The onset of darkness changed the atmosphere yet again. "The disposal of the lights" and the constant noise and movement flooded the senses:

> There was a preacher on the stump speaking loudly and vehemently; a black man also on the stand, and nobody attending to either; the noise could not have been exceeded by the confusion of Babel. I could not compose my mind to realize it was a place of worship, although the songs of praise and the voice of exhortation mingled with the groans of despair, and blending in strange confusion with the various dialogues going on, rose each moment on the ear. Prayer meetings had commenced in the different tents, yet there was a continual traveling from place to place — nobody except the immediate actors in the scene seemed stationary for a moment at a time; crowds of people passing and repassing all the time. One woman flew past, throwing her arms abroad, and shouting "there are grapes here and they are good, heavenly times! Heavenly times!"[19]

Williams took her final leave of the camp meeting with the bodily stench of four days of outdoor living in her nostrils and a strong sense of the dislocation of the human mind and spirit. Abraham's tents had given way to Sodom and Gomorrah. Ten years later, therefore, it came as no surprise to Catharine Williams that Sarah Cornell had allegedly been seduced by a lascivious Methodist preacher at a camp meeting. She believed Avery was undeniably guilty, but understood that the civil jury in

Fall River did not convict because of the inconclusiveness of the evidence. What she could not forgive was the Methodist Church's exoneration of Avery's character and its attempt to reinstate him in local ministry. The Methodist Church's vigorous defense of one of its own preachers against the consensus of an outraged community merely drew attention to its unappealing self-righteousness.

In the wake of the Avery trial, therefore, Methodism was portrayed both as an authoritarian enemy of American civic republicanism and as a corruptor of the new nation's morals. The strange death of Sarah Cornell did not create anti-Methodist sentiment ex nihilo; rather, it supplied a focal point for common accusations against a movement regarded by many as ecclesiastically strong and morally and psychologically weak. The Methodist Church's decision to defend Avery, whatever its legal merits, was costly in terms of money and reputation.[20] Despite his acquittal, Avery's reputation never recovered and he was unable to resume his ministry in New England. By settling on an Ohio farm, Avery spared the denomination further embarrassment, and he finally embraced a way of life he had entered the Methodist ministry to avoid. The gruesome death of a poor pregnant factory worker, whatever its cause, did little to interrupt the progress of Methodism, manufacturing, and markets in early-nineteenth-century America, but the Fall River episode occasioned an unusually luxuriant outburst of anti-Methodist sentiment. Most of that sentiment focused on Methodism's undemocratic ecclesiology, its ecstatic emotionalism, and its ability to corrupt human sensibility. Such opposition says something about Methodism, but it also says something about the values of the wider society. Ironically, those aspects of Methodism that many early-nineteenth-century Americans found most appealing, its religious egalitarianism and its capacity to inculcate personal and social discipline, were the very qualities found wanting by its Fall River opponents.

Most of the opposition directed against Methodists in the first century of the movement's existence was limited both in scale and in the level of violence. Methodist preachers were subjected to dipping, mud-rolling, tarring and feathering, stone throwing, and name calling—torments that were designed to inflict humiliation more than actual bodily harm. In some locations, usually for quite specific local reasons, the violence became more ugly and protracted. More threatening than ritual humiliations were the occasions when it looked as if national emergencies were going to result in state-sponsored repression. That nearly happened in the American colonies during the Revolutionary War and nearly happened in England during the war against France from 1791 to 1815.[21]

On both occasions the Methodist itinerancy, the engine of the movement's expansion, came perilously close to extinction, but it survived. In
short, Methodism experienced enough episodic opposition from below
to persuade its loyal supporters that the Lord's work was costly and the
"devil's" hostility inevitable, but not enough sustained opposition from
above to threaten the viability of the whole enterprise. Opposition was as
much enabler as it was destroyer of the Methodist cause.

## Conflict

Methodism was a revolutionary religious movement coming of age in an
era of political revolutions across the North Atlantic region. The precise
relationship between these two frameworks, one religious and the other
political, has occasioned an enormous amount of print, not a little of
which has been driven by the ideological agendas of later periods.[22] One
way of approaching the problem is through the conflicts generated *within*
Methodism over ecclesiastical governance, especially in the last decade of
the eighteenth century, when the English movement was deprived of
Wesley's authoritarian leadership and the American movement had to
forge its own post-revolutionary identity. Not surprisingly, vigorous debates over power, authority, and representation surfaced on both sides of
the Atlantic, resulting in two major secessions. These have been largely
downplayed in Methodist history because the seceding movements, the
Methodist New Connexion in England and the Republican Methodist
Church in the United States, never achieved anything like the numerical
strength of the parent movements, but numbers alone do not do justice
to the importance of the issues at stake. An investigation of these issues
not only reveals a great deal about the kind of movement Methodism had
become by the 1790s, but also illustrates some of the similarities and
dissimilarities between the British and American branches of the Methodist tradition.

At the head of each secession was a powerful personality, James
O'Kelly in America and Alexander Kilham in England, and both were
well schooled in the rhetoric of late-eighteenth-century popular political
discourse. Kilham was variously branded by his enemies as a Paineite, a
Leveller, and a Methodist Jacobin, and he was undoubtedly sympathetic
to a range of popular democratic causes in the later eighteenth century. Within Methodism he advocated a greater role for the laity in connectional governance, sacramental autonomy, and separation from the
Church of England. He emerged as an early critic of the clerical cabals

forming within Methodism to plan connectional governance after Wesley's death, arguing instead for greater lay representation. He criticized the hierarchical structure of Methodism, the financial corruption of its preachers, the inquisitorial nature of its discipline, and the legal coercion of its courts.[23] His criticism of Methodism was in almost every respect a perfect mirror image of the wider radical critique of the English constitution. His polemical pamphlets resonate with the rhetoric of John Wilkes, Tom Paine, Major Cartwright, Thomas Hardy, and Horne Tooke. In the context of Britain's war with the armies of the French Revolution, Kilham was perceived as a dangerous man both inside and outside the Methodist connection. Although some preachers privately admitted the force of some of his criticisms, especially those relating to the movement's finances, he was duly expelled from the connection by the Methodist Conference in 1796 and led a secession movement that never attracted more than 5 percent of English Methodists.

James O'Kelly, an Irish-born itinerant preacher and veteran of the Revolutionary War, emerged in the late 1780s as a thorn in Asbury's flesh. Antislavery, anti-British, and anti-episcopal, O'Kelly focused his attack on the Methodist episcopacy and its self-proclaimed power to appoint preachers to circuits without their consent. Like Kilham, he appropriated the rhetoric of the British Commonwealthman and radical Whig traditions for an attack on consolidated power within the Methodist episcopate. Like Kilham, he considered the government of his own religious connection to be a species of popery in which hierarchy trumped egalitarianism. Having fought a war against the British in defense of representative principles, O'Kelly was in no mood to take orders from an English-born Methodist bishop, Francis Asbury, in his own country and in his own religious connection. He resigned in 1792 and formed the Republican Methodist Church, which soon built up a substantial following in southern Virginia and North Carolina.[24]

The Kilhamite and O'Kelly schisms were about more than the mere defections of a couple of ecclesiastical malcontents. At stake in these disputes was the issue of whether Methodism would emerge from the revolutionary period as a popular religious movement with a democratic government or with an authoritarian government. The latter was the chosen route in both Britain and America, but the grounds and consequences of the choice played out differently in each place. In Britain, Kilham was expelled because he represented the Methodist face of a wider radical movement that seemed to threaten the British constitution, the successful prosecution of the war against the principles of the French Revolution, and the collective power of the preachers within the Methodist system. After his expulsion, the English Methodist leadership penned any number of loyalty addresses to king and country, vigorously defended the rights of the "pastoral office" within Wesleyanism, and set about ridding the movement of disaffected members.[25] In the contest with Kilham, and later with ranters and revivalists, the English Methodist leadership self-consciously steered a course against populist causes because they were deemed unsafe. In that sense Buntingism (a shorthand description of an emerging Methodist clerical bureaucracy) was born before Bunting came to power within the connection.

By contrast, in America there was no need for loyalty addresses and no immediate desire to crank up the ideology of a pastoral office within the Methodist itinerancy. Asbury defended episcopacy, not on the grounds of hierarchical privilege, but because it offered the best form of government for achieving the missionary objectives of the church. As Andrews has shown, Asbury and Thomas Coke defended the Methodist structure on the grounds that the itinerancy was an equal opportunity career for any Methodist prepared to accept its rigors. Asbury further undermined the validity of opposition attacks by showing that his model of episcopal leadership was not to reside in a dignified palace issuing pastoral addresses, but to accept the hardships of an evangelizing itinerancy with even greater alacrity than most of his charges. In so doing Asbury achieved something that otherwise might have seemed impossible. "The Methodist experience," writes Mark Noll, "shows that it was entirely possible for a traditional Christian message that had *not* been adjusted to the norms of American ideology to flourish in the new American nation."[26]

It is one of the ironies of Methodist history that O'Kelly's republican language, with its recurrent terms of "virtue, liberty, corruption, tyranny, republic, rights, and reason," was eventually adopted into the center, first of Protestant ideology, and then, by midcentury, of Methodism itself. Methodism thus entered the mainstream of American religious and political culture on the foundations of an ideology it largely repudiated at the end of the eighteenth century. What this discussion of the respective trajectories of British and American Methodism indicates is that both movements were rocked hard by the inner contradictions of an egalitarian religious message propagated by an inegalitarian institution. Although both movements suffered painful secessions, Asbury's resolution of the contradiction by essentially making the purpose (missionary expansion) subservient to the structure (episcopal hierarchy) was, at least in terms of church growth, more successful than the British solution, which, increasingly, was to allow the structure to define the purpose.[27]

The O'Kelly and Kilhamite secessions were but the first salvos in a half century of bitter conflicts within Methodism on both sides of the Atlantic, culminating in the serious rifts of the 1840s and '50s, when the Flysheets controversies in England and the slavery issue in America led to major schisms from which Methodism never fully recovered. Differing national, regional, and urban contexts determined the shape and resolution of these conflicts, but underpinning many of them were the old issues of power and representation in a populist religious movement with an authoritarian ecclesiology. In England, before the Kilhamite disturbances had a chance to settle down a whole raft of new challenges was thrown up by problems of control posed by Sunday schools, religious revivalism, and financial crises. Problems of control within Methodism were exacerbated by wider political, economic, and social changes. Government pressure on itinerant preaching during the wartime emergency, the rise of political radicalism in Methodist environments in the aftermath of the war against France, changes in the means of production as domestic industry slowly gave way to factory production, and bitter class conflict (both urban and rural) placed additional stress and strain on the Methodist polity. Moreover, internal and external conflicts were not unrelated, for Methodists did not lead lives separated into tidy religious and secular categories. On the whole, those most attracted to populist political and economic causes were those most critical of clericalism, authoritarianism, and conservatism within their own denomination. The way these tensions were played out from place to place are infinitely complex and are not easily amenable to the crude application of Marxist or Durkheimian ideas about the social function of religion, but they do show how the Methodist polity acted both as a lightning rod and as a theater of conflict for much wider stresses in early industrial society.[28]

Although the most significant conflicts in America operated around issues of race and slavery, while those in Britain operated more around class, there is sometimes an eerie similarity between the two. Compare, for example, the conflicts that emerged in the 1820s over the apparently minor issue of ecclesiastical refurbishments in the John Street Church in New York City and Brunswick Chapel in Leeds. In New York the conflict in the city's oldest and most important Methodist church erupted over the proposal to add a carpeted altar and other expensive renovations to the old building. According to William Sutton, "at issue, beyond ownership and control of the property, was the future cultural trajectory of the Methodist Church in New York City." As is the way with such disputes, the two sides represented not only differences in architectural taste but also profound differences in style, status, and strategy within Methodism. The "modernizers," comprising trustees, itinerant preachers, and their Conference supporters, were confronted by "traditionalists" who included some itinerants and black and white lay members. Neither the New York Conference, which supported the modernizers, nor the state legislature could resolve the problem, which resulted eventually in separation. William Stilwell, a fearless advocate for populist causes within Methodism and a supporter of other radical causes in New York City, helped organize the new Methodist Society in the City of New York, whose articles of association read like an egalitarian tract. The African Americans who withdrew, with Stilwell's blessing, went on to form the African Methodist Episcopal Zion Church. Sutton has shown how this contretemps in New York City was part of a much wider evangelical producerist revolt in eastern seaboard cities against acquisitive capitalism and Wesleyan authoritarianism, especially in Baltimore, which had the largest percentage of Methodist members. After a decade of agitation and conflict, the dissident congregations were organized first as Associated Reformers and then as Methodist Protestants, with a membership of some thirty thousand by 1835. "The predominant issue for populist evangelicals," states Sutton, "was accessibility to power. When they were denied access to congregational control, political direction, cultural formation, or socio-economic opportunity, they reacted strongly against what they perceived to be illegitimate authority."[29] Ironically, as soon as autonomy was granted and basic principles of representation were in place, much of the radical economic philosophy of dissident egalitarians simply melted away.

At the same time as Methodism in the eastern seaboard cities of the United States was agitated over issues of power, representation, and cultural style, similar issues were disturbing cities in the north of England. They came to the surface over the proposal of the New Brunswick chapel trustees in Leeds to install a new organ. The Leeds organ, as with the New York City altar, resonated with overtones of wealth, ritualism, and formalism, and persuaded those with more serious grievances to make a stand. The Leeds organ case was superimposed on older conflicts in the industrial cities of the north of England between advocates of Sunday schools (which taught writing as well as reading), manifold radical causes, and lay rights within Methodism, against itinerant preachers, chapel trustees, and the Wesleyan Conference. With characteristic acerbity Jabez Bunting stated: "The organ is the *mere pretext* among the *heads* of the schism . . . the root of it lies much deeper. There was a *radical* faction there, whose meetings had assumed all the fearful characters of a *Methodistical Luddism* (*secret vows or bonds,* etc., included) and of whom it was indispensable to the permanent peace of the Society that it should be forthwith purged."[30] Bunting not only persuaded a Conference committee to overrule the anti-organ verdict of a local Leaders' Meeting, but also summoned a Special District Meeting that expelled large numbers of Leeds Methodists from the Wesleyan connection. The resultant secession split the Leeds circuit in two, along the lines of wealth and ecclesiastical power, and sent shockwaves through the connectional system, causing further trouble in Liverpool, Sheffield, and London.

The burning embers of the Leeds organ case had barely cooled before they were fanned into life by virtually the same issues in response to the establishment of a theological college, unsurprisingly with Bunting as its first president, for the education of preachers. The result was the secession of the Wesleyan Methodist Association and the rise of "Free Methodism" in the Lancashire industrial towns of Manchester, Liverpool, and Rochdale. The social constituency and political preferences of "Free Methodists" show, as with previous secessions, that there was more at stake than a disagreement about how Methodist preachers should be theologically educated. In each city the Free Methodists attracted those who were fed up with the political and social conservatism of the Wesleyan tradition and used their freedom to espouse a number of liberal and radical causes, from support of the Anti-Corn Law League to campaigns against the financial exactions of the Church of England.[31]

With Bunting now in firm control and acting ever more provocatively as "the Methodist Pope," it was only a matter of time before a more substantial controversy rocked British Methodism. The catalyst was supplied by a series of anonymous Flysheets attacking Bunting's whole system of Methodist government. James Everett, the most likely author of the Flysheets, and his two closest supporters, William Griffith and Samuel Dunn, were expelled from the Methodist ministry by their peers at the Annual Conference of 1849.[32] After almost a decade of agitation, the result was the formation of the United Methodist Free Churches in 1857, which siphoned off more than fifty thousand members. More serious even than the loss of members was the battering the whole episode gave to connectional morale. Wesleyan Methodist numbers did not recover until 1875, and Methodism as a whole never again grew as fast as the English population. The series of crippling secessions that afflicted English Methodism in the sixty years after Wesley's death turned ultimately on power, control, and representation within the Wesleyan polity. But these internalist squabbles were deeply affected by wider political, economic, and social strains in early industrial England. It would be a mistake to reduce the complexity of Methodist secessions to a single cause, class conflict, but it would be an even bigger mistake not to acknowledge that class conflict in its multiple variations helped expose some of the inner contradictions of Wesley's ambiguous ecclesiological legacy.

What class did for English Methodism, or conflict with Roman Catholicism did for Irish Methodism, race and slavery did for American Methodism. The rise of the independent black Methodist traditions, essentially because of entrenched discrimination and cultural separation, is already well known.[33] Richard Allen, an African-American local preacher and a member of St. George's Church in Philadelphia, left St. George's over the issues of segregation and discrimination and, in 1794, established Bethel, an independent black church within the Methodist Episcopal family. In 1816 Allen gathered a number of African-American churches to found the African Methodist Episcopal Church and became its first bishop. Two other African-American Methodist denominations were organized in the early nineteenth century. The Union Church of Africans, led by Peter Spencer, split from the Methodist Episcopal Church in Wilmington, Delaware, in 1813, and the African Methodist Episcopal Zion Church, with James Varrick as the church's first bishop, was organized from members in the New York and Philadelphia areas. Although most African Americans remained within the Methodist Episcopal Church, issues of race and racism repeatedly bubbled to the surface.

One of the most insightful accounts of the issues at stake comes from the pen of Frederick Douglass, who escaped from bondage in 1838 and with the help of the Underground Railroad made his way to New Bedford, where he attended the Elm Street Methodist Church. During the public worship service Douglass was forced to take his seat with other African Americans at the back of the gallery, out of sight of white worshippers. Since he regarded this as possibly a necessary concession to unconverted whites in the congregation, he bore the indignity with equanimity, feeling certain that once the unbelievers had left, the Methodist community of believers, black and white, would unite for "the Lord's Supper, that most sacred of all the ordinances of the Christian Church." Douglass states,

> Mr. Bonney had preached a very solemn and searching discourse, which really proved him to be acquainted with the utmost secrets of the human heart. At the close of his discourse the congregation was dismissed and the church remained to partake of the sacrament. I remained to see, as I thought, this holy sacrament celebrated in the spirit of its great Founder. There were only about a half dozen colored members attached to the Elm Street church at this time. After the congregation was dismissed, these descended from the gallery and took a seat against the wall most distant from the altar.

Brother Bonney was very animated and sung very sweetly, "Salvation tis a joyful sound," and soon began to administer the sacrament.
I was anxious to observe the bearing of the colored members, and
the result was most humiliating. During the whole ceremony, they
looked like sheep without a shepherd. The white members went
forward to the altar by the bench full; and when it was evident that all
the whites had been served with the bread and wine, Brother Bonney after a long pause, as if inquiring whether all the white members
had been served, and fully answering himself on that important
point, then raised his voice to an unnatural pitch, and looking to the
corner where his black sheep seemed penned, beckoned with his
hand, exclaiming, "Come forward, colored friends! Come forward!
You too have an interest in the blood of Christ. God is no respecter of
persons. Come forward and take this holy sacrament to your comfort." The colored members — poor, slavish souls — went forward as
invited. I went out and have never been in that church since, though
I honestly went with a view of joining that body.[34]

Douglass gave up his short experiment in biracial Methodism and joined
a small group of black Zion Methodists. The layers of paternalism, social
segregation, and liturgical discrimination so evident in Douglass's narrative proved impossible to bear for many African Americans who thought
they were part of a movement of spiritual and social egalitarianism, only
to discover the manifold restrictions in the kinds of role they could perform in predominantly white congregations. It is important to note, however, that separation from a white-dominated Methodist movement rarely
resulted in withdrawal from the Methodist tradition altogether. Racial
separation did not carry with it repudiation of Methodist practices, and
separated African-American Methodists, by and large, remained Methodists and kept the Methodist name in their separated traditions.

Such divisions were disastrous for the cause of racial integration
within Methodism, but if anything they further facilitated the surging
growth of African-American Methodism. What they did not do was solve
the problem of slavery, which ate away at the Methodist system in much
the same way as it ate away at federal unity in the wider spheres of politics
and government. The denouement came in 1844, when a majority of
delegates at the General Conference in New York called on Bishop James
O. Andrew, a slaveholder by inheritance and marriage, to cease exercis-
ing episcopal oversight while he owned slaves. The debates surrounding
the controversy and the resultant Plan of Separation between the Methodist Episcopal Church and the Methodist Episcopal Church, South, are
well known, but less well known is what happened in the ensuing decade

Bishop Richard Allen (1760–1831), engraving published by P. S. Duval, Philadelphia, ca. 1830 (Reproduced with permission from the Methodist Collections of Drew University)

as northern and southern Methodists squabbled over the ownership of church buildings in the borderlands and the central assets of the church, especially the Book Concern, which was worth over a million dollars. Fierce competition for church property, according to Richard Carwardine, "prevented a clean break and ensured that the persisting mistrust, suspicion and abrasions between the two halves of Methodism contributed more than their fair share to the broader sectional alienation." As Methodists vilified each other with unparalleled ferocity, the church that did as much as any to build national unity in the early republic contributed more than most to the inexorable process of sectional polarization in the 1840s and '50s.[35] Ironically Methodists, who had been charged by their founder to eschew political excitement and who had largely steered clear of the language of civic republicanism in the late eighteenth and early nineteenth centuries, had by 1850 become enmeshed in the divisive politics of sectional conflict. Methodism's integration into the mainstream of political discourse in both Britain and America came at an unexpectedly high price.

Methodism's internal conflicts in the North Atlantic region from 1790 to 1860 were partly thrown up by its own ecclesiological ambiguities and partly absorbed by the movement from its surroundings. Some of the divisions were small and geographically restricted, some others led to the unleashing of creative new energies, but the largest ones in both Britain and America in the 1840s and '50s so unsettled the movement that they were difficult to recover from. Methodism could cope with small secessions and vigorous new traditions,[36] but it could not easily absorb the shock of protracted hostilities on a grand scale that disturbed the peace of the connection and inexorably slowed its momentum. Opposition and persecution sometimes acted as stimulants, but internecine feuds acted inevitably as depressants.

# CHAPTER FIVE

# Money and Power

And numbers are all we have to boast of, for our money matters are little improved.
— MILES MARTINDALE TO JABEZ BUNTING, July 9, 1816

When it was objected "that we spoke for hire;" it was answered, "No — it was only for a passing support."
— FRANCIS ASBURY, September 22, 1783

Two very different kinds of facts and figures can be brought to bear on Methodism's great era of expansion throughout the English-speaking world and beyond in the generation after the American and French Revolutions. The first are membership statistics, which reveal spectacular gains right across the North Atlantic world. In England membership in Methodist societies of all stripes expanded from 55,705 in 1790 to 285,530 in 1830. In the same period Irish Methodist membership almost doubled and Scottish Methodist membership trebled. Even more dramatically, Methodist membership in Wales increased by a factor of twenty. But the most dramatic growth of all occurred in America, which had fewer than a thousand members in 1770 and more than 250,000 only fifty years later. By 1850 the Methodist share of the religious market in the United States had increased to 34 percent of the national total. In addition, Methodism was in the process of becoming a genuinely international religious movement following the founding of the two main Methodist missionary societies, in England in 1813 (formally known as the Wesleyan Methodist Missionary Society) and in America in 1820 (the Missionary Society of the Methodist Episcopal Church). By any standards these figures represent a quite remarkable religious revolution, the causes of which were discussed in the first chapter.[1]

A second set of facts and figures, those more familiar to the accountant than the demographer, suggests a much gloomier picture, for throughout this period Methodism was racked by serious financial problems, which both reflected and exacerbated deep-seated structural deficiencies in the Methodist organization. Religious movements, as with big businesses, can,

up to a point, thrive on deficit finance in periods of expansion, but in
religious organizations the great disadvantage is that there is generally no
access to liquid capital beyond that which is voluntarily granted by their
members or raised by their supporters. Hence, financial problems in
churches, as with families, are never confined to the account books and
are rarely about money alone. Financial stresses and strains within Methodism exposed manifold layers of other conflicts endemic in the wider
society. Money was not only a sufficiently important commodity to be
worth fighting over, but it also served as a scorecard for even more important contests. Both for those who raised the money and for those who
spent it, balance sheets reveal as much about personal and religious priorities as they do about profit and loss. Where money is, the heart is also.

John Wesley's early experimentation with the primitive church's practice of the community of goods did not long survive its encounter with
basic human acquisitiveness, which, disappointingly for him, proved to
be a stronger force in Methodist societies than the social expression of
perfect love. Although Wesley abandoned the experiment, he never lost
his deep-seated distrust of the corrupting power of money on the spiritual life. While he remained in charge, however, money was regarded not
only as a threat to spiritual progress but also as an opportunity to fund
ministry, poor relief, and fellowship in an expanding Methodist connection. His example of rigorous keeping of accounts (see his own account
book) was passed on to his followers in a quite remarkable way. The
records of the Methodist Church in all parts of the world are full of neat
rows of figures constructed by circuit stewards, chapel committees, and
mission secretaries. Behind the accounts lay the principle of accountability, to God and to men, for Wesley recognized that his movement was
vulnerable to all kinds of accusations, from sexual immorality to material
exploitation. Although Wesley's Methodism was by no means free from
allegations of financial corruption, the fate of all new religious movements, it was largely free from corruption itself. Not only did Wesley set a
powerful personal example of frugality and financial discipline, but also
it was well known that the Methodist itinerant ministry was scarcely a bed
of roses for those who devoted their lives to it.[2]

After Wesley's death a combination of unseemly jockeying for power
and influence among the senior preachers, and the crippling economic
depressions of the 1790s, revived older allegations of financial malpractice, only this time from within the ranks of Methodists themselves. The
literature arising from the first secession from the parent connection, led
by Alexander Kilham in 1797, is positively riddled with allegations of
preachers lording it over a starving people.[3] The essence of Kilham's

allegations was that a combination of secrecy, extravagance, and chica-
nery had undermined the people's confidence in the Methodist preachers, whom he accused of behaving like "begging friars; and whining cant-
ing Jesuits." In this way the campaign for lay rights within Methodism was
fueled, at least in part, by a lack of confidence in the financial probity of
the Methodist leadership. Nor was that particularly surprising. By devolving responsibility for Methodist fund-raising and accounting to the laity in
the localities, and by insisting that preachers should both itinerate and
take their orders from above, the Wesleyan system was a recipe for financial discord. What largely held conflict in check was the belief that itinerant preaching was a holy calling and the fact that in the early stages of the
movement preachers were expected to forswear the emotional and material comforts of the settled life. The ideal, therefore, was that spiritually
enlivened preachers would have their needs met by a grateful laity, and in
addition, deficiencies in one part of the country would be made good by
surpluses in another. All was to be held together by bonds of affection.
What put the system under stress and strain in the early nineteenth century, however, was the unpleasant reality that Methodist fund-raising always fell short of Methodist aspirations. Equally problematic was the fact
that the original ideal of a celibate, self-sacrificing, and ascetic brotherhood of preachers proved to be as unrealizable among the second generation of Methodists as had Wesley's earlier experiment with the community
of goods among the first generation. Where money was concerned, Christian perfection, as the Calvinists had always contended, was easier to talk
about than to achieve in practice.

Squabbles about money may be bad news for religious movements,
but they supply excellent sources for religious historians, for they shed
light on deeper structural tensions in religious communities. The aim of
this chapter, then, is to use money as a device to explore the tensions
within Methodism in two different locations, England and New England,
in the generation after Wesley's death. A comparative approach exposes
both the similarities and the dissimilarities of the two Methodist traditions on each side of the Atlantic, and also points up some significant
differences in their social and cultural contexts.

## Methodism in England

The second decade of the nineteenth century was the most crucial period in the financial history of English Methodism, for it was during that
time that a combination of the rising social aspirations of Methodist

preachers and the postwar price deflation exposed serious structural
problems in the Methodist organization. A convenient place to start to
unravel the social dynamics of the relationship between Methodism and
money is with a letter written to Jabez Bunting by a Methodist preacher,
Miles Martindale, from a northern English city in the midst of the economic depression at the end of the Napoleonic Wars.

> You throw out some hints as if this Collection [the annual July
> congregational collection] was to become *permanent*—not advert-
> ing to the number of Collections already established among us,
> which I can prove to be not less than 155 every year. Was there ever
> such a begging system in existence before? Almost *every other day* we
> have our hands in the pockets of our people. You have often main-
> tained in Conference that 450 members are sufficient for the sup-
> port of a married and single preacher. Theoretically this may do on
> paper; but the uniform practice invalidates the system and I can
> prove that neither 450, nor 500 members either do or can pay their
> way, generally speaking. You have 306 circuits and out of these only
> 76 are clear; and a great number of those who have upwards of 500
> members are paupers.
>     You speak of *prudent retrenchment of expenditure*—where will you
> begin? You have 181,710 members—736 preachers, 400 wives =
> 1137 persons besides children to provide for: so that you have
> 159 members to each person, which at one penny per week &c. is
> £66.5.0. Here then is the *core* of your embarrassments, and I main-
> tain that you ought to have either 50,000 more members, or 50
> preachers and 50 wives less: but as the latter is impracticable, and to
> realise the former is a work of time; we must remain in *statu quo,* till
> the *decrease* of preachers and the *increase* of members come to a sort
> of par.[4]

Put crudely, the expansion of Methodist membership, though dramatic, was not fast enough to keep up with the financial demands of its
increasing number of married preachers, their wives, and their children.[5]
Moreover, according to Bunting's correspondent the problems were exacerbated by the propensity of poor circuits to invite eminent preachers
from distant circuits on all-expenses-paid preaching trips. A gravy train,
not unlike the modern lecturing circuit, was eroding Methodist capital.
Still worse, according to the letter writer, was the impact of new demands
to finance home and foreign missions.

> Another cause of our debts has been the *Home Missions,* a system
> that ought never to have been tolerated among us, and which origi-
> nated to cover *lazy* preachers. We were all missionaries once — *Thirty*

*years* ago I used to preach *ten times a week,* and travel many miles, I did so fifteen years ago. I do so now, even the *last week*—And if you will keep your circuits large enough, let them contain a sufficient number of members, say 600 or upwards, and let your preachers labour as we used to do, and as I do yet, and you will not have so many demands, the people will be more joyful to see you, and you will close the mouths of some idle talkers to whom our begging system gives but too much occasion.[6]

To continue with a business metaphor, the expansion of the Methodist enterprise at home and abroad depended on a careful balancing of its income and expenditure, circuit by circuit, at a time when rising overheads, in the shape of increased numbers of married preachers with families, stretched its resources. Two possible solutions were either to increase the church's membership faster than its unit preaching costs or to recruit richer members. Bunting's correspondent was pessimistic about the possibility of achieving either of these options, especially in a period of rising social tension and incipient class conflict.

I suppose you have heard of our revival in this circuit, as it has been trumpetted around the nation: if your Cornish and other revivals are as mechanically produced and carried on as this has been they will neither be any credit nor lasting good to the connexion. When Nelson came here we had not a single seat to let in our chapel, and though we are building a new chapel, and have added 1100 new members in the City and Circuit, yet last Sunday evening I had to read the advertisement of 6 whole pews and many single seats for which there is no application, nor one seat in the new chapel ever enquired after, while the Calvinist Chapel tho' not as forward as ours, have all their seats engaged! The fact is, the noise and nonsense has produced a number of the lowest order, and driven many respectable people from our chapel.[7]

Financial exigencies, styles of evangelism, and contested expressions of social class and culture were inextricably linked together in the cash crisis of early-nineteenth-century Methodism.

The nub of the problem was that the expenses of the connection had increased dramatically at a time of severe economic stress and strain. According to W. R. Ward, the Methodist connection in those years had come to "resemble a modern cut-price motor-car insurance company tempted or deluded by a large cash flow into prodigal disregard for its future liabilities." Financial demands were legion: money was required to fund home missions and convert the Irish and the Welsh, to build new chapels and extend old ones, to retire chapel debts and fund interest payments, to build schools and supply educational materials, to bail out poor country circuits and distant villages, to meet the expenses of the itinerant preachers and their increasing numbers of dependents, to supply the needs of infirm preachers and societies in distressed districts, and to pay for foreign missions. In essence, the burgeoning costs of chapels, preachers, and missions virtually rendered obsolete the old pattern of Methodist fund-raising based on voluntary class subscriptions. Moreover, as Methodism became a powerful new force in the world, the material expectations of its itinerant foot soldiers also began to rise.[8]

Itinerancy, as a system of ministry, was remarkably cheap and effective in pioneering mode, but it became less so as circuits grew more established. A new generation of preachers began to discriminate between good and bad hospitality and between "easy" and "hard" circuits. Bunting, who increasingly took on responsibility for administering the system, had his ears bent by a bewildering range of requests for more comfortable lodgings, better educational facilities for children, and accommodation of a suitable standard for newly married preachers. One preacher even had the audacity to make known his new bride's requests and preferences. Besides the ordinary costs of itinerancy, attendance at Conferences, expensive removals every three years (a costly consequence of the circuit system), and, where necessary, horse maintenance expenses, all had to be paid for.[9] Where was the money to come from?

There was general agreement among the senior preachers in the connection that "a permanent plan of finance" was better than the "temporary expedients" of special collections, which both irritated the laity and failed to supply a recurrent income. In a response to yet another request for a new subscription Bunting outlined the traditional Methodist approach to fund-raising.

> Could they [Methodists] be brought uniformly to contribute 1d per week, & 1s. per quarter, those *deficiencies,* to which you allude, would have no existence. Without Yearly Collection, & the profits of the books, we could then bid defiance to *want*. . . . In many circuits of the South, indeed, & in some of the North, the present rules are more than *kept,* they are considerably exceeded. Now how can we press the people of such Circuits to a new & *permanent* subscription, in order to make up for the indolence & covetousness of their neighbours?[10]

In theory the one penny a week was to help supply the "weekly wants of the preachers, first in the place or society where it is made, and then in the Circuit at large," while the quarterly monies were to meet the more general expenses of the itinerant system. The delicious simplicity of the old Methodist plan, combining as it did piety and payment, commitment and contributions, and savings and sanctification, had one fatal flaw — it simply could not be made to work. Devised as a system for bringing together societies and preachers in bonds of affection and mutual dependency, the old Methodist plan had also the capacity to generate financial conflicts that undermined the goodwill upon which the whole system depended. Once the lubricant of adequate revenue dried up, the moving parts simply ground together and generated heat and friction. The preachers blamed circuit stewards and class leaders for poor performance of duties, while the laity, especially in periods of economic hardship, blamed the preachers for unrealistic expectations. Preachers laboring mostly in poorer circuits accused those in wealthier circuits of a lack of commitment to genuine equality in the sharing of connectional resources. More substantially, the system was cumbersome to administer and set up tensions between poorer and richer Methodists. In some districts the more affluent congregants preferred to settle up quarterly at the renewal of class tickets, often in excess of what was nominally required, while the poorer members, who had also lost the weekly habit, could not make good the deficiency at the end of the quarter. Moreover, many Methodist chapelgoers were "hearers" only, not society members, and were therefore under no obligation to pay their dues to receive their class tickets. Some no doubt kept clear of membership to escape not only the discipline but also the costs and the fear of eviction for debt. What is clear from the private correspondence of the preachers is that the old Methodist plan was not working properly and that it was difficult for *them* to solve it, since they were both its beneficiaries and its custodians. Either the system needed to be cranked up more assiduously to maximize contributions from class members or the number of preachers and their families would have to be scaled down to bring profit and loss into due balance. While some of the preachers retained confidence both in the spiritual potential of the old system and in its capacity to deliver the goods, others favored retrenchment or fresh initiatives for tapping into new wealth.[11]

Meeting the day-to-day running costs of the connection would have stretched Methodist resources even without the added burdens of chapel building and foreign missions. Although the great new urban chapels were ferociously expensive, there were at least established ways and means of raising the capital. Subscriptions from "our leading friends" (a recurring Methodist phrase), special collections (openings, anniversaries, and interest repayments), pew rents, and borrowed money all played their part.[12] Debts were sometimes crippling, especially during the postwar price deflation, when interest payments became artificially inflated, but the system chugged along reasonably well with the help of new wealth and frequent collections. Indeed, in some cases chapel fund-raising was so successful that there were calls to divert chapel surpluses into the financing of the preachers, a plan that would have brought Methodism closer to the dissenting model of congregational independence. Bunting, predictably, held the line against suggestions that would have undermined the integrity of the pastoral office, and insisted on chapel surpluses being deployed either on new chapels or on proper accommodation for preachers on circuit. As with English monarchs in the seventeenth century, Methodist preachers wanted adequate supply, but they did not wish to be placed under the authority of, or to be circumscribed by the expectations of, the suppliers.

Whatever one makes of the evangelistic strategy of building impressive urban chapels as a focal point of Methodist ministry in towns, cities, and regions, there is no denying the sheer scale of the financial achievement. Foreign missions, however, were a different story. With no property to act as collateral and no pew rents to offer a regular income, the financing of missions posed particular problems. By the time the issue was seriously addressed in the second decade of the nineteenth century there were already allegations circulating within Methodism that money raised for foreign missions had been surreptitiously and disgracefully diverted into the domestic coffers.[13] Moreover, there was widespread agreement that the "missionary intelligence" published by the connection was so late, inadequate, and depressing that it was virtually useless as a primer for missionary giving. Yet interest in foreign missions was rising as fast as the Methodist membership.

At the end of the Napoleonic Wars, therefore, an intriguing combination of financial pessimism and missionary optimism left the connection in dire need of fresh initiatives. While Methodist chapels were leaking money to collectors from the London Missionary Society (primarily a dissenting organization), Methodism's own fund-raising for missions was largely dependent on the personal networks established by the mercurial Dr. Coke. Clearly, revenue for the support of Methodist overseas missions, as with all other Methodist endeavors, needed to be placed on a more secure footing, but how was this to be done? In the midst of a cheerless rant about the deficiencies of metropolitan Methodist organization and the baleful consequences of chapel debts, Joseph Entwistle told Bunting, "We have already so many irons in the fire, that we shall do little in the 1d. a week way."[14] Bunting, as ever, was ready with his remedy.

I do not believe that missionary exertions will lessen our home-resources. Zeal, once kindled, will burn in every direction at once. The pains taken in Missionary Meetings to evince the value & necessity of a Christian Ministry & of Christian Ordinances will shew our people *their own privileges,* as well as the wants of others. They will estimate the Gospel more highly, & of consequence be more ready to support it. Besides on the new plan, a large proportion of the Mission Fund will be raised among persons not in Society, & even among persons who are not so much as stated Hearers. This will set us more at liberty in our applications to our own members for our own particular collections.[15]

In other words, Bunting was prepared to raise capital from outside the company to expand the business, without adding to the burdens of the existing shareholders. The business metaphor is not entirely fanciful, for the great public meetings on behalf of foreign missions were addressed by the best available talent and were advertised through press notices and "posting bills." Great public meetings backed by the formation of auxiliary missionary societies throughout the country delivered unimaginable financial rewards, but both in principle and in practice Methodist finances were now no longer the private business of a pious sect.[16]

Whatever was lost in terms of connectional intimacy in this transition from the political economy of a religious sect to that of a national church was, according to Bunting, more than made up by the sheer financial success of the new strategy.

The Halifax report is this day come to hand. . . . From that report it appears that the annual public collections for missions in that district in 1813 amounted to £154. 19. 5., and the extraordinary Missionary collection to £145. 8.7. whereas the moneys raised in 1814 by the new system of public meetings & Auxiliary Societies were £1292. 14. 8. This *fact* is worth more than a score of theories. There is nothing like public meetings! We have had one at Albion St., and another at the old chapel for the purpose of shewing the necessity of the proposed Chapel in Meadow Lane. . . . More is offered daily; so that we expect to raise, in this easy & delightful way, £1600 or £1800; . . . The mission business is no hindrance, but a great help. The poorer classes have now learned by experience the privilege of giving. They know the consequence & efficiency conferred on them by their number, & they seem resolved to maintain by actively assisting every good work, the dignity to which they have been raised.[17]

Bunting's sanguine assessment of the "privilege of giving," however, is not borne out by the generality of correspondence arriving on his desk in the first quarter of the nineteenth century. Itinerant preaching and the connectional system, which historians have justifiably lauded as instrumental in the remarkable expansion of Methodism throughout the world in the early nineteenth century, was an accountant's nightmare. As preachers were paid for out of voluntary subscriptions to societies, and as they were paid allowances rather than a salary, the whole enterprise depended on frugality, goodwill, and bonds of affection. The system was at its most cost efficient when it was supporting single preachers with no dependents, but by 1820 the ratio of married to single preachers was in excess of three to one.[18] Moreover, many of the older preachers were in no doubt that those in the younger brigade were less frugal and less willing to accept hardship than their predecessors. One of Bunting's correspondents stated that the finances of the connection lay "at the mercy of inexperienced, if not vain & extravagant young housekeepers." He also estimated that by 1819 married preachers cost the connection just over one hundred pounds per annum: "The young officer in the Army or Navy — The Young Surgeon & Attorney — The Young Curate in the Church — the junior Clerk in the Bank or Counting House, never dream of being in these circumstances which they have reason to hope for after 20 or 30 years' hard labour."

Even if all preachers had been infused with moral excellence and material restraint, the connectional system was not an easy one for which to make a budget. There were sharp differences in wealth within and between circuits. Membership did not expand and decline in direct proportion to the expenses of the preachers. Although guidelines were laid down for voluntary subscriptions, there were well-understood limits to the amount of moral coercion that could be employed on volunteers. In addition, trade cycles, economic depressions, war demobilization, and price and wage deflation could wreck even the most careful of plans. Not only was the administration of the system as dependent on the voluntary principle as on the contributions to be administered, but also the demands on it were everywhere increasing at an exponential rate both at home and abroad. Conference tried to regulate the system, but there were as many opinions about what to do as there were demands on the connectional purse.[19]

There was also evidence of both moral and structural decay within the Methodist organization itself, as some unscrupulous districts and circuits carelessly passed on their burden of debt to the annual Methodist Conference. At its best, connectionalism was an ecclesiastical system of mutual care and support, and at its worst it was a ramshackle model of financial evasion and irresponsibility.[20] Connectionalism had the capacity of converting failures at the periphery into crises at the center, and vice versa. The nub of the matter, however, was that Methodism had embarked upon a roller coaster ride of national and international expansion, which simply outgrew the old method of one-penny-a-week class subscriptions. As expensive new chapels were built in the great new industrial cities, and as the Methodist message was taken to Africa, India, Europe, and the Caribbean, the balance of financial power in the connection moved steadily away from class members toward men of substance, wealthy suburban chapels, and the general public.

Methodism in England grew as a business not only by expanding its markets and recruiting new consumers but also by expanding its support base beyond its dedicated core of members. The increase in Methodist membership was thus accompanied by a formidable mobilization of fresh resources. Between pietism and filthy lucre, it seemed there was tension, but no ultimate incompatibility. By 1820, to judge from the correspondence of the preachers, Methodist finances, as with real wages in the nation as a whole, were in a better position than they had been a decade earlier. Membership had increased rapidly, dozens of new chapels had been built, and foreign missions had been given a major injection of cash. The ordinary members of Methodist societies in town and country had played their part in all this, but the wealthier suburban chapels in the growing towns and cities made the decisive difference.[21] Where wealth was located, power was also, for the alliance between well-connected preachers and propertied laymen, for better and for worse, was set to lead the connection into the Victorian era.

## Methodism in New England

The system of raising money for the support of the Methodist cause in America was broadly similar to that in Britain, but there were also some significant differences. On both sides of the Atlantic the main engines of financial support were the class and quarterly meetings, which had the added advantage of devolving financial responsibility to committed members and not just hearers. In the early stages of Methodist expansion, wherever it took root, the chief expense was the itinerant ministry, which was vital to the whole connectional enterprise. Local preachers may have

Francis Asbury (1745–1816), oil on wood, by John Paradise, New York, ca. 1812
(Reproduced with permission from the Methodist Collections of Drew University)

borne the responsibility for the day-to-day ministry of Methodism in its manifold peripheries, but it was the itinerancy that more than anything else forged a national movement.[22]

The early Methodist itinerancy in America has been described as "a brotherhood of poverty," with all, regardless of social status, length of service, productivity, or talent, expected to share both the same salary level and the same privations of ministry in service of the gospel and the people.[23] The episodic references to money in Asbury's *Journal* make it clear that he regarded the itinerant ministry as a sacrifice undertaken for the sake of the gospel. He had the same deep-seated fear of the corrupting power of money as Wesley himself, and he repeatedly refused the gifts that his status in the connection attracted. In his vision of the brotherhood of preachers, fraternity and purity were dependent upon, and guaranteed by, equality and poverty. In a joint episcopal message with Dr. Coke in 1798 he stated: "Those who read this section attentively will see the impossibility of our ministers becoming rich by the gospel, except in grace. And here there is no difference between bishops, elders, deacons, or preachers, except in their travelling expenses, and consequently in the greater labours of one than the other. . . . And we may add the impossibility of our enriching ourselves by our ministry, is another great preservation of its purity. The lovers of this world will not long continue travelling preachers."[24]

With equality as the principle and frugality as the practice, the 1796 Annual Conference fixed upon an annual salary for an itinerant preacher of no more than sixty-four dollars per annum, a figure that was raised to eighty dollars in 1800 and then to one hundred in 1816. Such increases were regarded not as rewards for the increased social status of itinerant preachers, but as the bare minimum required for bringing an already inadequate salary into line with inflation. It has been pointed out that the salaries of Methodist preachers were about a fifth of those paid to Congregational ministers and were probably less than those earned by many unskilled laborers, but the salaries themselves do not tell the whole story. Not only were the salaries rarely paid in full, but they were also supplemented by a complicated set of allowances to take account of expenses, dependents, and enterprise. While on the road, preachers were theoretically entitled to expenses for traveling, food, and fuel (after 1816), though preachers' journals and autobiographies testify to the fact that this was a haphazard process and obviously depended to some extent on the wealth of the circuits to which they were assigned. Moreover, some preachers were more prepared for privation than others. A similar problem arose over allowances for dependents. As in Britain, most of the early itinerants were unmarried, a practice approved by Asbury and blessed with cheapness, but without a formal declaration of celibacy as a necessary precondition of acceptance for the Methodist itinerancy, it was inevitable that pressures to marry and have children were bound to increase. Surveys from different parts of the country suggest that the great majority of Methodist itinerants in the period 1780–1830 eventually married and settled their ministry in a particular location. Of the bumper crop of thirty-seven men who were received into the New England Conference in 1822, for example, only fifteen either died in the ministry or became superannuated preachers; the rest located, discontinued their ministry, or were expelled for undisclosed offenses.[25]

Although some Methodist itinerants remained celibate and others delayed marriage, some provision had to be made for married preachers and their families lest all the prime talent drifted out of the itinerancy altogether. Accordingly, the General Conferences of 1796 and 1800 established a chartered fund to make provision for married, superannuated, and worn-out preachers and their wives, widows, and children. The fund was to be supplied by preachers' subscriptions, circuit surpluses, quarterly, annual, and conference collections, and the profits from book sales. Under the conditions of the fund a sum not exceeding sixteen dollars was allowed for the children of preachers and, quite remarkably, the allowance of a married preacher was deemed to be double that of a single preacher. In addition preachers were allowed to keep their fees for conducting marriages and were paid a commission of between 15 and 25 percent for selling books.[26] The phenomenal success of Methodist book sales, regarded by many as the jewel in the crown of the early Methodist mission, was owed at least partly to the entrepreneurship of an impoverished itinerant ministry.

Salesmanship and enterprise alone could not save the Methodist system from duress. In fact the propensity of itinerant preachers to marry and have children imposed the same kinds of stresses and strains on American Methodism as those bedeviling the English connection. The system had worked tolerably, if erratically, under Asbury's egalitarian and ascetic regime. After his death, however, growing concerns about the extent of itinerant locations, partial locations (which created even more difficult pastoral problems for circuit superintendents), and the low quality of new recruits forced the General Conference of 1816 to address the matter with some urgency. Resolutions were duly passed to increase preachers' allowances, to provide houses for them, to pay for their food and fuel, and to improve their education.[27] Ironically, therefore, the consequences of the underfunding of the itinerancy—location and low-quality recruitment—led to the implementation of policies that, over time, would lead to the demise of the itinerancy itself. It seemed that the Methodist system of itinerant ministry, devised by Wesley for his societies in England, and further adapted by Asbury for use in America, could continue to serve the poor only as long as it was characterized by celibacy and dependency mostly on hospitality rather than cash allowances. The only available alternatives were to demand more money from Methodist societies, thereby risking expressions of anticlericalism and demoralizing allegations of corruption, or to devise structures that would have the effect of contributing inexorably to the decline of itinerancy itself.

The resolutions of the General Conference of 1816, whatever their long-term effects on the Methodist system, did not immediately solve the problems for which they were designed. The impeccably presented accounts of the New England circuits during a remarkable period of membership growth in the 1820s illustrate the extent of the problem. Preachers were paid expenses for travel, table, board, rent, and fuel; they were then due their quarterage, or annual allowance, which was fixed at $100 for single preachers, $200 for married preachers, $24 for children between seven and fourteen, and $16 dollars for children under seven. For the year ending June 1820, the sum required to meet the total quarterage was $16,487, while the deficiency was calculated to be $11,062. In short, less than half the quarterage of the itinerant preachers was actually met by the circuits they served, and the sums received from central funds, including money from the book concern, the chartered fund, and special collections, amounted to less than 10 percent of the deficiency. The reason for such a huge deficit was the fact that by the 1820s married preachers in New England outnumbered the unmarried by a ratio of two to one, and the average number of children per family was around two. Successive reports in the 1820s and 1830s showed no signs of a decline in the annual deficit, despite the growth of membership and despite impassioned pastoral addresses from circuit superintendents.[28]

Two striking facts emerge from this data. The first is the remarkably generous allowances, in principle at least, for wives and children. Married preachers were entitled to twice the quarterage of their single co-itinerants, and allowances for children were not subject to a sliding scale. Second, Methodist expansion seemed to thrive on deficit finance and the relative poverty of its preachers. Despite the propensity of married preachers to leave the itinerancy and settle down, the Methodists appeared not to experience unsustainable problems recruiting for the itinerancy, though there were periodic expressions of concern about the quality of some of the recruits.

Within the Methodist community itinerant preaching was regarded as a high-status, low-pay enterprise, sustained more by the prayers and hospitality of its constituents than by financial or material rewards. The relative poverty of the itinerants must have made life physically uncomfortable, but it did their spiritual reputation no harm whatsoever. The evidence from the diaries and reminiscences of the preachers themselves suggests that their lofty conception of the itinerant ministry far outweighed the financial hardships they undoubtedly experienced. Some complained to circuit stewards about low provision, others set their wives to work or tried to supplement their income by teaching school or exploiting the black economy, but most had their expenses, if not their quarterage, met by the local Methodist community. One old itinerant warhorse who labored in New England for fifty-six years declared at the end of his ministry that there was only one year "in which my expenses exceeded my receipts." Conversely, most itinerants frankly admitted that they were rarely paid their full "disciplinary estimate" and were never far from the poverty line.[29] Those who stayed in the ministry long enough to review their lives from the standpoint of a ripe old age looked upon the privations of their early ministry as part of the great adventure of "gospel ministry"; but poverty, as with other forms of suffering, is a far nobler thing in retrospect than in prospect.

Although there are suggestive comments both in the conference minutes and in the preachers' journals that some were more adept at securing expenses and gifts than others, in general terms the financing of the itinerancy in America occasioned much less controversy than in England. What chiefly explains the difference is that the American itinerants had more confidence in the egalitarianism of the system of appointments and rewards than their counterparts in England, for which Asbury, albeit operating in a more democratic and populist culture, must take much of the credit. Second, the American Methodist laity accepted more easily than their British counterparts that the life of a Methodist preacher was one of such affliction and poverty that none would choose it out of mere financial self-interest or personal ambition. Among the other factors to be taken into account are the general absence of established churches in the United States, which led to the establishment of the voluntary principle as the only viable model of church support and the relative absence of bitter class conflict, compared with early industrial England. There is also evidence to suggest that there were subtle differences in attitudes to money and religion between the two cultures. On the whole, Americans were more transparent in their acknowledgment of money as a suitable subject of public religious discourse than their British counterparts and

were, at least within Methodism, less inclined to believe in the malpractice of private clerical castes. Indeed, Methodist expansion in the United
States was itself facilitated by the chorus of anticlerical and anti-Calvinist
sentiment, often expressed in verse, which lambasted the careerist financial aspirations of educated clergy.[30] Nevertheless, among Methodists
there seems to be no American equivalent of the sheer volume of suspicion, criticism, and unwillingness to contribute that infected a sizable
proportion of the Methodist community in England between 1780 and
1830.

In the longer term, however, the Methodist itinerancy in the United
States, as in Britain, could not escape the consequences of its own evangelistic success, nor fail to benefit from the upward social mobility of its
support base. A few snapshots from anniversary conventions in New England indicate clearly enough the changes that took place in the culture
and financing of Methodist preaching over the course of the nineteenth
century. The first is taken from the Methodist Centenary Convention
held in Boston in the somber aftermath of the Civil War. The convention
was essentially a celebration of Methodist expansion in the New England
states from a membership of 5,829 in 1800 (1 in 211 of the population)
to 103,961 (1 in 31) on the eve of the Civil War. It was also a celebration
of increased financial muscle and enhanced social status. Pride and pleasure blended with nostalgia and millennial optimism in speeches high-
lighting the beneficial symbiosis of Methodism and American values.
Although there were ritual appeals to primitive simplicity and renewed
zeal, the overwhelming endorsement of the convention was for a more
educated, more cultivated, and more influential ministry. "The wealth of
the Church, like water," suggested one delegate, "ought to be poured
out, so that the intellectual culture shall be found even in the humblest
ones in the service of God." In the wealth of statistical information presented to the convention on the state of Methodism in antebellum New
England, three features are worthy of comment. First, Methodism's circuit system had all but collapsed; second, Methodist ministers in wealthy
states were being paid almost twice as much as those in poorer states; and
third, the capacity of the church to generate wealth from its members
had grown dramatically in the middle decades of the nineteenth century.[31] Despite greater material affluence, or more likely because of it,
Methodism in the eastern states on the eve of the Civil War had virtually
abandoned the old ideal of an itinerant and egalitarian ministry supported by local hospitality.

In yet another statistical survey of New England Methodism, this time
carried out on the eve of the First World War, it was reported to the

convention that the salaries of Methodist preachers were still too low for the role required of them. "The minister of today," the convention was told, "must be a community leader, broad minded, progressive, and aggressive. The age insists that he be a good preacher, an efficient pastor, a true leader of men. For these lofty requirements the minister must be well equipped. He must dress acceptably, for he is a leader; he must attend many assemblies, for service and the deepening of his spiritual life; he must travel for vision and culture; he must read extensively for intellectual impetus and resourcefulness. The high requirements on the part of the public make necessary heavy expenditures for adequate equipment."[32]

Traveling for vision and culture is not exactly how Asbury's preachers conceived of their itinerant ministry a century before. A conception of ministry based more on the cultivated expectations of settled congregations than on missionary expansion had triumphed within American Methodism. It was not that the history of the early itinerancy was repudiated by later generations; it was simply confined to the realm of nostalgic reminiscences and wrapped in condescension.[33] Early itinerants were regarded as those not endowed with much learning who nevertheless made good their deficiency by speaking with "tongues of fire." In this way the early privations of Methodist itinerants were confined to a different dispensation and then sacralized by memory.

Their own memories tell a different story, however. Beginning in the 1880s the New England Methodist Historical Society supplied a forum for aging Methodist preachers to recount their experiences of the "heroic age" of Methodism. What emerges from these revealing, often moving, sometimes bizarre, and always romanticized accounts is an entirely different conception of ministry from that of the later nineteenth century. Even allowing for the notorious capacity of aging Methodist "croakers" to privilege their own pioneering efforts over those of their more "worldly" successors, the contrast between the qualities admired by successive generations of nineteenth-century Methodist preachers remains striking.[34] The attributes admired most by the older preachers included: a robust constitution; a capacity for endurance; a commanding personal appearance; a voice sufficiently powerful for preaching at camp meetings; an ability to "affect" an audience; a capacity for weeping; an ability to produce religious revivals and spiritual fruit; an earnest and candid disposition; plain speaking; a good-hearted, generous, and sociable personality; evangelical unction; a passion for reforming causes (temperance, teetotalism, and antislavery); practical and scriptural preaching; frugality and exactness; demonstrated experience of special providential guidance; a fixed gaze on doing good in the here and now with the hope of eternal rewards in the hereafter; a meek, gentle, and childlike spirit; a melodious voice for singing; a keen wit; a capacity for explosive shouts of praise and enthusiasm; a desire for learning and education; a carelessness about material comforts; an ability to confound the rich, the learned, and the powerful; a willingness to celebrate the contribution of "mothers in Israel"; and above all the experience of a good death (peaceful, thankful, faithful, and anticipatory). In contrast, the qualities most admired by the end of the century were: learning and self-improvement; the ability to hold a large and intelligent congregation; a preaching ministry informed by careful preparation; facility of expression; clarity of thought and freshness of style; a status that could not be disparaged by other denominations; a capacity to keep pace with the best thought of the age; a reputation for philanthropy; and evidence of educational and intellectual attainment. Over time, a change in job specification, and the personal attributes required to fulfill it, led also to a change in status and rewards.

Although the funding of the itinerant system of ministry was the chief cause of financial disquiet within transatlantic Methodism in the period 1780–1830, there were of course other demands on the connectional purse. During the same period, for example, even larger sums of money were raised to build chapels. The financing of chapel building was not free from controversy, as the heated conference debates on pew renting made clear, but the problems were less severe and more confinable. Although the connectional system facilitated some transfer of funds for chapel building from wealthier to poorer areas, in general the sums raised to build chapels were given by the laity in a particular locality for the benefit of the laity in that locality.[35] Although the raising of such large sums of money inevitably delivered more power into the hands of those who volunteered the largest subscriptions, those who raised the money benefited directly from their investment. By contrast, raising money for the itinerancy, and also for the international missionary movement, forced into the open big questions about the nature of ministry, the relationship between committed members and the general public, and the conflict between God and mammon in the expansion of the Methodist movement. Buildings were tangible assets; preachers and missionaries were speculative investments.

Tangible assets nevertheless became ever more tangible over the course of the nineteenth century. Wherever in the world Methodism took root, a powerful combination of a sense of ecclesiastical inferiority and a surge of confessional pride resulted in the building of enormous neoclassical and gothic "cathedrals." From the cities of the north of England to those on the eastern seaboard of the United States, Methodists built big, not only to accommodate burgeoning numbers, but also to demonstrate that they sought an ecclesiastical rapprochement with the values of order, stability, and respectability. Students of second- and third-generation Canadian and Australian Methodism have detected precisely the same pattern.[36] From Leeds to Boston and from Toronto to Adelaide, huge sums of money were raised to invest in buildings declaring the social arrival of the once despised. Indeed, it was Methodism's genius that throughout the English-speaking world it was able to act for so long both as a countercultural movement of populist revivalism and as an enforcer of social stability and sobriety, though not always in the same place at the same time. It was Methodism's misfortune, at least in terms of its capacity to recruit, that it could not oscillate between these poles forever.

As every undergraduate knows, John Wesley had a particular genius for organization. The system he put in place for funding the evangelistic expansion of the Methodist movement has been regarded as stunningly successful. Its essence was that the ministry of traveling preachers was made dependent on the hospitality and regular subscriptions of a grateful laity. Whereas other churches in the eighteenth century depended for their resources either on ecclesiastical taxation or autonomous congregational giving, the Methodist pattern combined voluntarism with connectionalism. Moreover, itinerancy militated against the comfortable conformity so much dreaded by Wesley in England and Asbury in America. The regular giving of the laity in small amounts in class or quarterly meetings encouraged them to feel a stake in the movement and helped keep the controlling power of money away from the rich and the powerful. The fact that money was mostly raised and spent within the same geographical locality further aided transparency and accountability. Meticulous methods of accounting trained the laity in prudence, and careful delineation of expenses trained the preachers to expect nothing in this life but the bare necessities. If never fully egalitarian in practice, the system had an egalitarian logic to it, based on the premise that money was merely the servant of mission and not a commodity to be desired for the benefit of the individual.

For the system to work well, however, three conditions had to be established. First, supply and demand needed to be kept in some sort of rough equilibrium. Second, there was a need for trust, both among preachers and between preachers and people. Third, it was vital that money raised by voluntary donations in particular locations was spent on the agreed religious objectives of those making the contributions. In practice it proved impossible to meet these conditions either in the British Isles or North America in Methodism's great age of expansion. In both locations, the desire of preachers to marry and raise families imposed dramatic new demands on resources, as did the building of new chapels and the financing of world mission. That much was shared by the Methodist traditions on both sides of the Atlantic, but there were also important dissimilarities. In America, a combination of the self-sacrificial leadership of Asbury and the tendency of married itinerants, without too much reproach or bitterness, to locate and become local preachers, promoted greater connectional harmony than in Britain. There, allegations of financial corruption and abuse of power often accompanied the complaints of the laity against the leading preachers after Wesley's death. Class conflict was therefore generated from both outside and inside the Methodist community in Britain in the early industrial revolution.[37]

American Methodism was not entirely free from such tensions, but it was to be another form of property, human slavery, that created the real trouble for Asbury's successors. John Wesley, as his most recent biographers have made clear, was a flawed leader who left many unresolved tensions for his followers to cope with, but his strong warnings about the evils of money and slavery were both prophetic and largely ignored by many of his followers. Unsurprisingly, his economic triptych of gaining, saving, and giving all that one could proved to be incapable of mass realization. The ultimately contradictory principles of serious acquisitiveness and careless generosity were played out in Methodist minds and societies wherever the movement took root.[38] One other aspect of Methodist finances raised by this issue is the proportion that was given away as an expression of holy charity. The current state of research offers no conclusive evidence on this, but my strong suspicion is that as nineteenth-century Methodism progressed the absolute amount it gave away probably increased, but the proportion of the total income of Methodists it gave away in its manifold different sites probably decreased.

The history of Methodism in the transatlantic context reveals at least four different stages in the financing of a popular religious movement. The first, an attempt to replicate the early church's experiments with community of goods collapsed just as completely in early English Methodism as it appears to have done in early Christianity. The second, and under eighteenth-century conditions an equally radical approach, was to combine voluntarism and egalitarianism in the financing of an itinerant ministry by a grateful and supportive laity. The egalitarian component of that approach survived for longer in the United States than in Britain, but ultimately it disappeared in both places over time. A third approach, which was in nature broadly paternalistic and bureaucratic, was to exploit more structured forms of raising revenue in which richer donors came to have more power and influence than the poorer ones. A fourth stage, namely the virtual collapse of Methodist finances as a result of a declining membership and an unresponsive wider public, has been the unfortunate fate of many Methodist congregations in modern Britain and some in America. Even allowing for the reductionism implicit in such a typology, it is clear that each successive phase of fund-raising involved not only a different approach to financing Methodist operations, but also a very different social experience of religion for those giving and receiving the money. In religious organizations money is not simply a necessary and neutral commodity for getting things done; rather, money carries with it a symbolic revelation of the values for which it was collected and appropriated.

# CHAPTER SIX

# Boundaries and Margins

Here by the instrumentality of a poor coloured woman, the Lord poured forth his spirit among the people. Though, as I was told, there were lawyers, doctors and magistrates present to hear me speak, yet there was mourning and crying among sinners, for the Lord scattered fire among them of his own kindling. The Lord gave his handmaiden power to speak for his great name, for he arrested the hearts of the people, and caused a great shaking among the multitude, for God was in the midst.

— JARENA LEE, *The Life and Religious Experience of Jarena Lee* (1836)

T he marginal territory between enlightenment and enthusiasm, played out in the mind of John Wesley, had wider repercussions for the movement he pioneered. Wherever one looks at Methodism in its first century of growth, it was a movement that thrived on the boundary lines of rationality and emotional ecstasy and on the margins of traditional social hierarchies of class, gender, race, and age. Methodism and other forms of populist evangelicalism mediated a direct encounter with a vibrant supernaturalism that opened up the possibility of rapid expansion among sections of the population previously resistant to the more orthodox brands of Christianity. Although its founders and early leaders were mainly educated middle-class white males, Methodist expansion did not proceed in conventional ways. Although Methodism was not a self-consciously liberationist movement, except in the traditional Christian sense of being liberated from the bondage of sin, it did sink deep roots among people who were far from the center of cultural power in the eighteenth and nineteenth centuries, including the working classes, women, and African slaves. How was it that Methodism, which originated at the heart of the English Established Church and at an ancient seat of learning, was able to give voice to groups beyond its initial social constituency? The aim of this chapter is to follow the expansion of Methodism from the cultural peripheries of race, class, and gender to see what kind of a movement it was for those whose attraction to Methodism cannot easily be accounted for by mere social control. What was it that people on the social margins found so compelling in a movement that offered no immediate release from entrenched positions of subordination?

## Race and Culture

In the same way that Moravian Pietism helped awaken John Wesley's earnest Anglicanism, Moravian missionaries to the dense slave popula- tions of the Danish Caribbean islands blazed a trail of evangelical Protes- tant conversions that was later followed by the Methodists and the Bap- tists. It has been shown how the Moravian "pedagogy of conversion" served as a model for future Methodist success. Although the Moravians accepted slavery as a social and structural reality, they forged Christian communities in which African slaves were treated with unaccustomed respect and even introduced to the rudiments of literacy. "The mes- sage of universal fellowship" duly communicated by a range of Mora- vian gestures "had a compelling power to undermine established notions of racial inferiority."[1] Although the Moravians tried to reproduce their conversionist magic in the British Caribbean islands of Jamaica, Barba- dos, and Antigua, only in Antigua did they meet with conspicuous suc- cess, largely because they abandoned the egalitarian methods that char- acterized their earlier ventures. Although the Moravians made no great impression on the British Caribbean islands and the American colo- nies, they served as inspirational models for the Methodists who came after them.

African Americans in the American colonies, who for almost a cen- tury successfully withstood Anglican and Presbyterian forms of Chris- tianity with their emphasis on catechetical instruction and formal wor- ship, began to convert in substantial numbers to Methodist and Baptist forms of evangelical Protestantism from the 1770s. The numbers should not be overestimated, however. Recent work has emphasized both the slowness and the incompleteness of African-American conversion to evangelical Christianity.[2] By the outbreak of the American Civil War, for example, probably less than a quarter of African Americans had con- verted to Christianity. Nevertheless, no other form of social organization could compete with the various sects of evangelical Christianity for the hearts and minds of African slaves. How can this be explained?

Several of the main lines of interpretation were opened up in the first chapter. The direct supernaturalism and modes of expression of evan- gelical spirituality resonated with the content, form, and practice of West African tribal religions, the legacy of which survived for longer in the American South than was once thought. Moreover, evangelical Chris- tianity not only supplied an early rhetoric against bondage and slavery but also helped forge communal and ethical solidarity against the rapacious demands of slave culture. In short, evangelicalism offered tangible personal, social, and communal benefits to those who had been violently uprooted but who still bore trace elements of West African religion in their cultural DNA. Quite how this worked out in practice could vary from region to region, according to place of origin and longevity of African customs, but by the 1830s a noisy form of evangelicalism had become the most powerful cultural expression of African-American identity in the United States and helped facilitate the transition from ethnicity to race.[3] How did this come to pass?

Although there is evidence of some pious masters bringing their slaves with them into evangelical Christianity, the conversion of large numbers of African Americans happened in spite of, not because of, the complicity of the planters. Hence, the evangelical surge in African-American culture cannot be explained as an instrument of social control imposed from above and from without. It is nevertheless a mistake to think of the growth of African-American evangelicalism as an entirely black creation, for revivalism was borne on the wings of the southern migrations of Scots-Irish and European pietists. Methodists, who were prepared to itinerate the southern backcountry and who were accustomed to the raw edges of religious enthusiasm, and Baptists, whose public "dippings" attracted thousands of participants and onlookers, were the two religious traditions poised to make the greatest gains. It was not all plain sailing, however. White southerners, including those sympathetic to evangelical Christianity, were disturbed by some of the exotic manifestations of African-American spirituality. Ecstatic religion was not easily controlled, and for obvious reasons black ecstatic religion, though not necessarily different in form and expression from white ecstatic religion, was more to be feared by southern whites. For those southern white males who hated the emotional excesses of populist evangelicalism and who feared its impact on their domestic and social patriarchy, black manifestations of paranormal religious behavior were particularly unsettling.[4]

Southern white Methodists were less unsettled by the expression of African-American religious experiences than their white anti-evangelical opponents, but they too had cause for unease. Their unease can be measured and parsed in the softening of Methodist critiques of slavery, the exclusion of African Americans from leadership roles in the church, the close monitoring (where possible) of black religious gatherings, the denominational prescription of more acceptable forms of religious expression, the reduction of interracial intimacy in religious gatherings, and the gradual separation of blacks and whites, first within interracial churches and then into separate congregations. These changes did not entirely end contact and mutual influence between white and black Methodists in the antebellum period, but they gradually did firm up the boundaries between them. As white evangelicals repudiated their earlier opposition to slavery, they increasingly preached a theology of submission, while black evangelicals, both Methodist and Baptist, responded with an even stronger emphasis on racial separation. Long before the split between North and South in the Methodist Episcopal Church in the 1840s, therefore, came an earlier de facto racial separation between black and white in the South. Although that separation was never complete, it steadily reduced the power of the electrical charge between white and black forms of populist evangelicalism. As Methodists slowly readapted to the honor codes of the South, African Americans continued to build their own empire of the spirit on something like their own terms using their own exhorters and preachers.[5]

Although there is now widespread agreement among historians of African-American Christianity that the nineteenth-century surge of evangelicalism was not engineered from above by southern whites as an instrument of social control, there is less agreement about what created and sustained it. Some emphasize the spiritual and cosmological syntheses of evangelical enthusiasm and West African religions; some pay more attention to the social utility of a faith offering personal assurance and communal identity to those in sore need of both; others draw attention to the liturgical and linguistic rhythms of black evangelicalism as an authentic expression of African-American culture; still others have tried to grapple with the "religious" or "theological" (however those difficult terms are to be defined) content of African-American spirituality.[6] These do not have to be mutually exclusive, for they all take seriously the fact that African Americans were agents, not victims, in the formation of their own religious cultures. Those cultures were especially strong, not because they were built on a singular foundation of whatever material, but precisely because they integrated different materials into a powerful synthesis not easily undermined by any singular process of historical change.

A particularly creative way into the heart and center of the African-American encounter with evangelical Christianity is through sacred songs, rhythm, and dance. The lyrics of the spirituals, with their appropriation of Old Testament themes of bondage, exodus, and God's direct action in the rescue of his people, have been exhaustively analyzed.[7] Although there are disagreements about the strength of the liberationist, as distinct from the survivalist, message of the spirituals, there is no denying the fact that African Americans came to identify their plight in an immediate way with the biblical narratives about the journeys of the

Israelites to the promised land. The land of promise could be variously interpreted as an imagined place, a real geographical region (up north or Canada), a spiritual state, or a heavenly dream, for circles of freedom were capable of infinite expansion in the same way that Jacob's ladder had no visible terminus. More complex even than song lyrics, but perhaps just as important, is how Africans were able to carry with them a profound engagement with dance and rhythm throughout their diaspora. "To the African," writes Jon Michael Spencer, "the drum was a sacred instrument possessing supernatural power that enabled it to summon the gods into communion with the people. However, to outside observers it was the drum alone that symbolized the 'heathenism' of the 'danced religion' practiced by those so called 'cursed sons of Ham.' "[8] The drum was largely banned from circulation among Africans in North America, but rhythm survived in the bodily expressions of "hand-clapping, foot stomping, body slapping, and ring-shouting." The latter intrigued southern white Methodists, whose ethnocentric descriptions of African-American religion often betray a curious mixture of admiration and anxiety. One white observer wrote: "A practice prevails among them that is called the 'holy dance.' It generally begins just after the conclusion of the sermon, and a prayer has been made. Several persons, both male and female rise to their feet, singing some of their favorite songs; they now join hands forming a circle or ring, and keep time with their feet swaying their bodies, to and fro. This sort of exercise often continues for hours, or until weariness breaks it up."[9]

One interpretation of rhythm is that it operated as a cathartic release from stress and anxiety, a physical and emotional expression of freedom from crushing constraints of one kind or another. That Methodism could function this way in a variety of social contexts, not just among African Americans, has been articulated, both positively and negatively, by a number of Marxist and feminist historians.[10] The point is that Methodism was from the start a form of religion associated with song, music, rhythm, and emotional release from anxiety and from traditional social expressions of bodily comportment and restraint. In its encounter with the brutally uprooted Africans in North America, therefore, Methodism bridged a gap between European traditions of what Ronald Knox has generically called "enthusiasm" to ancient African traditions of folk religion. The gap between the two was superficially wide when analyzed in terms of enlightenment notions of cultural progress, but was in reality quite narrow when analyzed in terms of structural affinities.

A similar pattern can be discerned in a later period, when Methodism made spectacular gains in Korea in the late nineteenth and early

twentieth centuries. Methodism was first introduced into Korea by American missionaries in the mid-1880s. Although the religion was initially
restricted to educational and medical work, the traditional Methodist
pattern of itinerant preaching, class meetings, hymn singing, literature
distribution, disciplined spirituality, and liturgical innovation soon produced striking growth rates, which were given an additional boost by the
"great revival" of 1903–7.[11] As with the outbreak of Methodist revivals in
other parts of the world, explanations of revival need to take into account
both external and internal circumstances. The years following the Sino-
Japanese War (1894–95) and the Russo-Japanese War (1903–4) were
ones of considerable anxiety and internal strife in Korean society, made
worse by a partial Japanese occupation that occasioned popular protests.
But revival also arose out of a sense of expectancy generated by prayer
meetings, Bible studies, and testimonies to direct and paranormal experiences of the Holy Spirit. One contemporary description, allowing for the
distinctive Korean context, is remarkably similar to accounts of Methodist
revivals in the British Isles and North America in an earlier period. "The
range of the influence of the Revival was one of the marvels of it. Old
conservative Koreans, who had drunk deep of Confucius and had wor-
shiped every conceivable god, whose pride of spirit made them unap-
proachable, were among the broken-hearted and contrite. Women who
had been victims of every vile circumstance of life were given heavenly
vision and purity. Little children prayed the night through and saw won-
ders that Joel said some children would see. Western missionaries, trained
in other lands and formed of other human flesh, were likewise brought
low down."[12]

Although much of this is familiar to students of Anglo-American revivalism, the Korean version of the species took on some distinctive features. In Korean society religious revivals (Buheunghoe) came to be promoted during the first three months of the year between the Korean New
Year and Easter. They were accompanied by special weeks of prayer and
dawn prayer meetings in which prayer was often offered up in rhythmical
unison.[13] It is hard to resist the conclusion that one important factor accounting for the spread of Korean Methodism is the parallelism between
Methodist emphases on entire sanctification, disciplined self-control,
hymn singing, and corporate prayer, and the Confucian emphasis on self-
ordering and personal and communal discipline. In that respect, Methodism could be regarded as a profoundly Christianized Confucianism
made capable of mass realization by suitably amended Methodist liturgical devices. As with Methodist success among African Americans, structural affinities of belief and practice between Methodism and ancient

religions allowed for surprisingly successful Methodist cultures far removed from the original epicenters of the movement.

## Gender

One aspect of the rise of Methodism among African Americans and
among Koreans is the importance of women, often meeting separately for
social and cultural reasons, in the rise of a vibrant Methodist community.
The same is true of any geographical region in the rise of Methodism in
the eighteenth and nineteenth centuries. Indeed there is much to be said
for Ronald Knox's assertion that the "the history of enthusiasm is largely
a history of female emancipation."[14] As with many other religious traditions, the history of Methodism is really a history of female preponderance. Surveys of class membership on both sides of the Atlantic consistently show that women comprised a majority of the membership. Clive
Field's extensive survey of Methodist membership lists before 1830 (some
80,361 members) has shown a female mean of 57.7 percent. Although
this percentage varied considerably from one circuit to another, it was
remarkably consistent over time and from region to region. With women
making up 52.3 percent of adults (fifteen and older) in the general
population, as measured by the census of 1821, Field's conclusion is that
"Methodism was rather more female in its composition than the adult
population as a whole." Comparisons of marital status show that the
proportion of Methodist members who were single (24.6 percent) was
significantly smaller than in the adult population as a whole (29.3 percent
in 1851); among Methodists only, the proportion of single and widowed
women was conspicuously higher than the proportion of single and widowed men. Comparable figures, though based on significantly smaller
samples, are available for early Methodism in the United States. In the
eastern seaboard cities of New York, Philadelphia, and Baltimore from
1786 to 1801, Dee Andrews has found a preponderance of women, ranging from 59 percent to 66 percent depending on location and year. In
Boston the proportion of women members in the 1790s varied from 61
percent to 71 percent. Single or widowed women consistently accounted
for over a third of the total membership.[15]

As has been pointed out, a sober recognition of the preponderance of
women in American religious history would make a dramatic difference
to the conceptual frameworks within which that history has been reconstructed. What is true of American religious history in general is
even more important for an understanding of Methodism. Quite simply,

as purveyors of hospitality, deaconesses, visitors, evangelists, prayers, exhorters, testifiers, class members and leaders, and preachers, women
helped define the character of the Methodist movement. There were of
course constraining factors to the emergence of women as full participants in the Methodist project, in both Britain and America, including
contemporary notions of social propriety and female modesty, strained
relations with the Church of England or with the established colonial
denominations, the sometimes vigorous opposition of male itinerant
preachers, conventionally understood biblical injunctions against women
leaders, fear of unflattering parallels being drawn between the Methodists
and the Quakers, and the damaging impact of anti-Methodist publications
that delighted in emphasizing the alleged appeal of Methodism to "emotional" women. But in the context of undeniable female successes, Wesley
adopted an increasingly pragmatic view of women's public role, culminating in his characteristic invention of the device of "the extraordinary call,"
which was a way of allowing him to hold on to a conventional Pauline
hermeneutic while acknowledging that women's abilities could be successfully harnessed to the mission of the church. By the 1770s there was a
critical mass of women preachers within Methodism that could not easily
be ignored. The law enunciated by Joan Thirsk that women could make
their most substantial gains in the early stages of movements before male
controls were reimposed had come into operation. Indeed it was almost
inevitable in a movement that emphasized experience, empiricism, spiritual egalitarianism, enthusiasm, and direct empowerment from God.[16]

A similar pattern emerged in American Methodism. Thousands of
women shared testimonies and exhortations during church services,
camp meetings, love feasts, and class meetings—Methodism's distinctive social occasions. As the movement grew, women were encouraged
to "speak" in ever widening spheres, so that the rise of public female
discourse within Methodism preceded its acceptability in other social
spheres by almost half a century. Methodist emphases on liberty, orality,
and communalism facilitated women. There was also a degree of gender
blurring in early Methodist discourse. Methodism was a "women's church
because it spoke a woman's language," according to Diane Lobody; "over
and over again, with almost ritual intonation, we hear the language of
tender and uncontrollable emotionalism" as Methodists felt, wept, trem-
bled, groaned, melted, softened, and sank into God.[17]

As women's voices became more ubiquitous and significant in the
popular evangelical sects that grew prolifically in early republican America, so too did their broader contribution to the religious movements of
Methodists, Free Will Baptists, and Disciples of Christ. Catherine Brekus

has shown how women benefited from the political, economic, and social instability of the early republic to carve out important positions in Methodism as prayers, exhorters, and preachers. Although women thrived in a religious environment characterized by the lack of ordained clergy and the new emphasis on female piety and virtue, they also encountered limits. Their public voice was greater in the North than in the South; they were not ordained or permitted to administer the sacraments; and they were kept out of positions in ecclesiastical governance. It would be a mistake, however, to underplay the significance of what was being achieved by female agency: "Given the failure of the American Revolution to extend true equality to either women or blacks, the decision to allow them into the sacred space of the pulpit was radical indeed."[18] By dressing and speaking plainly, by sustaining "islands of holiness" in an otherwise raucous environment, and by building a grander Christian family out of their manifold and diverse families, women not only reshaped the American denominational order but also made a remarkable contribution to the shaping of the American republic.

There is one further twist to the story of women, Methodism, and nation building. Gregory Schneider has persuasively shown how Methodism was instrumental in ushering in a distinctive kind of evangelical domesticity in which the "idea of the family as belonging to a private sphere of affection and moral discipline that was to be set over against a public sphere of competition and self-interest." In this interpretation Methodism not only helped undermine an eighteenth-century American cultural ethos based on patriarchal sovereignty and honor codes, but also helped establish a new domestic ethic in which mutual affection and self-denial were inculcated, first in class meetings and love feasts, and then in homes. "The way of the cross," so assiduously cultivated by the Methodists in building a new religious family of fathers and mothers, brothers and sisters, came to be applied to actual families. In these secluded spaces women, men, and children sought to replicate "relationships within the family of God." In this way the Victorian cult of domesticity was at least in part a Methodist creation. The consequences both for women and for the church were mixed. Over time actual family units undermined and then subverted the familial mechanisms of the church, most notably its class meetings and love feasts. Families came to monopolize domestic piety while voluntary reform movements and political parties helped organize Methodism's public face. What was left for the church, in Schneider's words, was to become "a nascent bureaucracy made up of specialized agencies and programs designed for denominational self-propagation."[19] The balance sheet for women was similarly ambiguous. While they gained as instruments of the middle-class domestic piety that shaped great tracts of American culture in the nineteenth century, they also lost as public agents of the religious movement that helped domesticate them. As in Britain, the prescribed religious behavior of American women subtly began to change. Before 1810 female domesticity on the whole was not paraded as a model in Methodist publications; women were admired rather for their religious experience, progress in holiness, and contribution to the religious and social mission of the church. Asbury's ubiquitous "Mary and Martha" sermon privileged Mary over Martha. Yet by 1850, women came to be admired more for their pious domesticity than for their public contribution to the work of mission.

If the language of Methodism supplied a vocabulary and a grammatical structure that allowed women to articulate their religious experience without alienating men, the same was true of their pursuit of sanctification, which brought with it the possibility of a dramatic subversion of traditional hierarchies at least within the Methodist spiritual economy. For sanctification was no respecter of conventional boundaries. If women, even African-American slave women, could aspire to entire sanctification (and most of the credible claims were made by women), then here was an aspect of life, and for Methodists the most important aspect of human life, in which gender was not a disadvantage. Indeed, the most influential popularizer of a modified version of John Wesley's perfectionism was the Methodist lay revivalist Phoebe Palmer, whose "altar theology" helped reduce the old Wesleyan pursuit of sanctification to three simple steps: consecration of one's life fully to God; belief in God's promise to sanctify; and bearing witness to what God has done. Palmer's theology and revivalist energy made an important contribution not only to the rise of the Holiness traditions, such as the Church of the Nazarene in the United States and the Keswick Movement in Britain, but also to the later emergence of Pentecostal and charismatic movements.[20]

## Female Piety

There is widespread agreement that within Methodism there were no *concerted* attempts to challenge established gender boundaries, either within the denomination or in the wider society. On both sides of the Atlantic there were few demands for ordination, few members were involved in women's rights movements, few refused to submit to male authority, and most female preachers were single or widowed, thereby avoiding opprobrium as deserters of domestic responsibility. Moreover, as time went on women's sphere of activity and influence first expanded and then was reined in and diminished, as Methodism settled into denominational mode.[21] So much is relatively well known, but there is a need to probe even deeper. In what sense was Methodism really a woman's movement, and not just a movement in which a few especially talented women could attain important roles in the public ministry of the church? How did all this work out in practice, not among the female preachers who were exceptional, but among the many thousands of women who were not? Did gender matter to Methodist women, not in the obvious sense of understanding their place within the overwhelming maleness of institutional power in Methodism, but more importantly in any distinctively "religious" sense, however that is to be defined?

The more than twenty women who are allowed to tell their own stories in Paul Chilcote's helpful edition of their diaries, memoirs, journals, and letters are to some extent a pious elite writing for a prescriptive purpose, and therefore not a representative sample of the rank and file of Methodist women. Moreover, there is no way of knowing for sure how heavily edited were the surviving texts to meet the requirements of pious consumption, but they are nevertheless revealing of the nature of female piety within early Methodism.[22] Most of the women had at least one pious parent, but many also had to encounter family opposition before acting as a conduit into Methodism for their fathers, brothers, husbands, and children. All experienced a decisive religious conversion before engaging in an eager if sometimes unpredictable quest for entire sanctification. Many experienced help along the way from men, but the striking feature of their quest for holiness is how much they relied on other women as class and band leaders, prayer partners, exhorters, mentors, friends, confidantes, and correspondents. Men could sometimes be nuisances or opponents, but on the whole they were regarded either as facilitators or partners in the expansion of the Methodist movement.

Although there is some suggestion that women deliberately muted their voices out of deference to men, or that they were sometimes forced to accept unwelcome limitations on their spheres of action, the evidence mostly suggests that gender conflicts among the faithful were regarded as much less significant than the great divide between the saved and the lost, or even that between pious and troublesome believers. Mary Barritt Taft, for example, a gifted preacher and wife of a preacher, suffered at the hands of a male Methodist in Dover, England, who could not accept her right to preach, but her account of the episode focuses more on his troublesome spirit than his gender, and she was defended by other more pious and supportive men.[23]

The language employed by women to describe or evoke religious experience is particularly enlightening. Although introspective melancholia is far from absent in these accounts, as is profound suffering and grief (especially after the loss of children), the overwhelming tone, appropriate to their prescriptive purpose, is one of celebration and happiness. The triad of "holiness, happiness, and heaven" enunciated by Ann Ray in a letter to Elizabeth Hurrell is a common feature of female Methodist discourse, as is the sense of loving and being loved by a crucified savior. Although the quality of the relationship with Jesus, described by Elizabeth Mortimer as "Saviour, Husband, Brother, Friend," was vital to these Methodist women, their conversion experiences propelled them into a life of service as well as a life of devotion. Sarah Crosby, widely regarded as Methodism's first woman preacher, wrote in her diary: "I was much quickened in prayer. My soul was deeply sensible of the presence of God. I saw great perfection in him and many imperfections in myself, which I desire to be saved from. I felt my soul humbled before him, and had also power given me to rejoice with joy unspeakable, and great liberty to pray for friends and all mankind." Sensible experience, power, and liberty unlocked gender reticence. In the following months her scruples about public speaking were removed, and she preached to hundreds of people in a variety of public settings.[24]

Phyllis Mack has drawn attention to another distinctive feature of female as distinct from male Methodist discourse, namely its greater preoccupation with physical pain, suffering, and the sheer fragility of life. Acquainted with suffering and death through their visitations of the sick (more directly a female role), and schooled in the endurance of pain by childbirth and brutal medical treatments, women's spirituality was shaped by the hard edge of endurance and affliction. Some were crushed by pain and grief, while others proclaimed a state of spiritual exultation through identification with the crucified Christ, but there is no denying that women were more frequently and protractedly brought face to face with life's sufferings than men. Since suffering could not be avoided, it had to be dealt with, sometimes with the support of other women, caring families, or religious societies, but sometimes alone in afflicted solitude. With high rates of infant mortality, an almost complete absence of effective anesthesia, and the social and religious expectations on women as caregivers unto death, the discourse of Methodist women is unmistakably full of pain.[25]

One question often asked of early Methodist spirituality is in what respect does it differ from either traditional expressions of Christian devotion recorded over the centuries or from the spirituality of other contemporary evangelical movements in the eighteenth century. There are of course shared similarities with wider Christian traditions, including devotion to a suffering savior, serious reading of the scriptures, diligence in prayer, concern for the poor, and patient forbearance in the face of suffering and death. But there are also distinctive Methodist emphases. Sarah Colston, a member of the Methodist society in Bristol, took comfort from the fact that "the lord was no respecter of persons, but willing that all should believe and be saved." Ann Gilbert, a Cornish Methodist preacher, "went one evening to the class, and while we were singing the first hymn, I found an uncommon hardness of heart, such as I had never found before. This induced me to cry mightily to the Lord, that he would soften and melt it into tenderness, by his dying love." Isabella Wilson became attracted to the Methodists because "if any knew their duty to God, they did, and that they were his people. And I was always ashamed before them for fear they should speak to me concerning my soul; yet I loved to hear them talk of the things of God."[26] The recorded *Experience of Frances Pawson* is a classic tale of Methodist spirituality. She read William Law's *Serious Call,* Thomas à Kempis's *Imitation,* and Wesley's *Life of De Renty.* She met Wesley, who inspired her "with a veneration for him I cannot express." She attended love feasts and class and band meetings that were often led by women whose spiritual mentoring became very important to her. Then came the moment of conversion.

> Jan 7, 1775. This evening my spirits were uncommonly low and much depressed. I went to the chapel at seven o'clock, and on my return, "the love of God was shed abroad in my heart" [cf. Rom. 5:5], and in such a degree that my soul was humbled into the dust. The sentiment of my past ingratitude was so strong that I saw, if the Lord had sent me to hell for it, he would have done me no wrong. I had, indeed, read many Calvinistic books on justification, but I never saw the fullness and freedom of God's pardoning grace in such a light as I do now.[27]

Conversion was followed, as with most early Methodists, by a devoted pursuit of entire sanctification through the public ministrations of the Methodist system and the private cultivation of the life of devotion. As the wife of John Pawson, who was a senior preacher in the connection, Frances Pawson was close to the furious battles that took place within the Methodist polity in the decade after Wesley's death, as contests for power and control threatened the unity of the movement. "I have likewise wrestled much with God for the whole connexion," she wrote in July 1795, "lest it should be torn to pieces about points of discipline — points which

will subside of themselves, if the parties will have a little forbearance."
The following year, at the peak of the Kilhamite disturbances that produced Methodism's first secession, she wrote:

> The Conference is just at hand, and the preachers are beginning to
> come. My heart is enlarged for the prosperity of Zion. It is a day of
> trouble to the connexion. Alexander Kilham has agitated the minds
> of the Methodists by the circulation of many anonymous printed
> letters, &c. His whole attack seems levelled at the old preachers. He
> seems to wish the Methodists to adopt, as far as possible, the laws of
> the French National Assembly. But to insinuate that my husband and
> other venerable men have defrauded the connexion, after devoting
> our lives and fortune to the cause, is cruel in the extreme. Well, the
> church has often had to endure the contradiction and the sneers of
> restless men. The preachers have all been united in his expulsion,
> and if he do not retract his slanders, God will inflict upon him a
> heavier punishment. Had he wept over our defects I would have
> joined him in spirit.[28]

Ironically, John Pawson's private correspondence indicates that Kilham's allegations of financial malpractice had some justification, but the
important point about Frances Pawson's recorded experience is what it
reveals about the differences between men and women in their approach
to the conflicts of the 1790s.[29] Although women were a clear majority
within the connection, the decisions about the future of the movement
were worked out in Conferences, district meetings, connectional courts,
and public pamphleteering, all organized and presided over exclusively
by men. Frances Pawson's pleas for forbearance and weeping over "our
defects" fell largely on deaf ears during the turbulent debates within
Methodism at the end of the eighteenth century.

A few years later a similar fate befell Dorothy Ripley on the other side of
the Atlantic. Born in Whitby, Yorkshire, in 1769, Ripley left England for
America in 1801 to plead the cause of African slaves in the New World, and
quickly secured a private interview with the president, Thomas Jefferson.
She wanted Jefferson's personal approbation, as a slaveholder, for her to
continue her work on behalf of "distressed Africans." Jefferson was polite
and courteous, but he repeated his opinions in *Notes on the State of Virginia*
that the mental powers of Africans were not equal to the Indians. Ripley
replied that

> God had made all nations of one blood and that ancient Britons
> were degraded very much once in their powers of reason and this
> people being neglected many centuries, their power of reason was

dimmed from long abuse of the same. I was inclined to think, if the present generation of children were separated from their parents and educated by virtuous persons, who would teach them habits of industry and economy, they might then prove a blessing to the country. To train them up with the view that they were not the same race would prove only a curse to the land, especially the females, whom I felt myself concerned for the most on account of their exposed situations to the vile passions of men.[30]

Although the recorded experiences of Frances Pawson, Dorothy Ripley, and others show clearly the limits of the power and influence of Methodist women, they also show their extent, for Methodism was without question preponderantly a women's movement. Allowing that statement to sink in has enormous consequences for writing the history of Methodism as a popular religious movement. If Ann Braude's polemical statement that "women's history *is* American religious history" were applied with equal rigor to the history of Methodism, what difference would it make? In Methodist historiography the sad truth is that women have been ignored not only by the male writers of institutional history, but also by historians whose stated goals were to bring humble people back into the narrative mainstream of social and cultural history. The impact of feminism on the writing of religious history has dramatically expanded the amount of literature on women in Methodism, but most of the writing, excellent though it has been, has been devoted to either the exceptional women who became preachers and leaders, or to the role of women as a generic category within Methodism, which is often confined to a separate chapter in a much bigger book. Taken together, whatever their weaknesses, these studies have made a major contribution toward the reorientation of Methodist history away from institutions and theology and toward praxis and experience.[31] What then remains to be done?

Olwen Hufton has shown how women's history came on the radar screens of social historians writing under the influence of the Annales School in the 1950s and '60s before evolving into a largely separate enterprise.[32] Women's history then evolved into gender history and was soon influenced by postmodernist theories about texts and how they were to be read. According to Hufton, what is most needed now is for women to be reintegrated into the past (without a past there is no dignity or memory), not as mere appendages or as small groups of elites, but as full participants in the movements they built. Given the state of the surviving evidence such a task is almost impossible, but it is at least important to start asking more intelligent questions. For example, why were women in the preponderance almost everywhere Methodism took root, and how

can one properly reconstruct the history of Methodism taking that preponderance into account?

It is at this point that the relative undersupply of primary sources
operates as a barrier, for even a temporary immersion in the memoirs,
diaries, and letters of women begins to reformulate one's settled impressions of a movement allegedly built by male itinerant and local preachers.
Indeed, until recently the two most common historiographical traditions of Methodism, focusing on those cultural insiders who emphasized
the building of the institutional apparatus of the church and on those
"croakers" who urged a return to the primitive simplicity of the old
itinerant preachers, each had a vested interest in playing up the contributions of men in the public sphere. The preachers, the structures, and
the theology of Methodism are far from absent in female discourse, nor
were they resented as unnecessary restrictions to female spirituality, but
they occupy an entirely different place. It is not just that women wrote
more about the domestic location of Methodist spirituality or about sis-
terhoods of faith outside the home, but their whole approach to the
mission of the church is conceived in different terms. They spent more
time thinking and writing about the domestic ramifications of professing
faith, including what it meant for parents, husbands, and children. Their
view of mission built out from domestic spheres into extended families of
faith (classes and bands) and then into wider communities linked by
expressions of charity or visitation. Mary Barritt (Taft), the most famous
woman preacher in early-nineteenth-century England, recounts a domestic visitation where she heard the cries of a starving child. She asked
the mother to bring it to her house every day for food, and the episode eventually resulted in the entire family's conversion to Methodism.
"What a vast variety of circumstances," Barritt wrote, "does God overrule
and make subservient to the salvation of souls."[33]

Just how vast a variety of circumstances is clear from the following
incident in the early history of Methodism in the United States, which is
worth reproducing in some detail for what it reveals both about the way
relatively humble women contributed to the movement's expansion and
about how Methodism's high-octane "spirituality" processed that contribution in a particular social setting. The incident took place in a newly
established New England preaching station called Shirkshire in Buck-
land, western Massachusetts.[34] In the 1830s a popular struggle for religious power and control took place in what was virgin territory for the
Methodists. The story is recounted in some detail by an unpretentious
Methodist itinerant preacher named William Gordon, whose record of
his ministry, given the standards of the genre, is unusually blunt, honest,

and self-deprecating. He writes that Shirkshire was the home of a religious group called the Truarites, and their preacher, a man named
Stearns, was still in the area. According to Gordon, he "had preached
until his congregation had dwindled to nothing." After apparently reaching some kind of consensus regarding their future direction, the small
congregational remnant requested the service of Methodist itinerants,
and "filled the house" with eager hearers when they came to town. Although this new initiative bore some fruit, the people wanted more; "they
wished a 'four day's meeting' to be held with them." Stearns showed up
at the meeting, according to Gordon, "to recover lost influence and
ground." Though earnestly conducted, the meetings were unfruitful in
the unwelcome presence of Stearns and a few of his supporters. The
scene was set for a showdown.

> The prayer meeting Friday morning was remarkably impressive
> and searching. Some of the people trembled on the occasion. A
> preacher named Stearns came to our meetings, and appeared en-
> vious on account of the interest manifested in our service. There
> was in the place a very good woman by the name of Flagg, an elderly
> lady, tall and portly, of unusually impressive appearance and re-
> spected by all who knew her. She had not been able to attend these
> meetings until that Friday morning prayer meeting. She had had a
> dream shortly before this, that had made an impression on her. She
> thought she was standing by the bed of a stream in which water had
> formerly flowed, but at the time of her dream there was but little
> water in it. In this water, however, there were snakes and poisonous
> reptiles that presented a very repulsive appearance. She did not
> understand the significance of the dream at the time, but at this
> remarkable prayer meeting the interpretation came to her.
>
> During the progress of the meeting she arose from her seat,
> went to this Stearns, stood boldly before him, and charged him with
> being the hindrance to the success of the meeting. Referring to her
> dream, she said that his spirit and conduct were represented by the
> poisonous reptiles that she saw in the stagnant water. At the conclu-
> sion of that terrible, scathing personal address, he took his hat and
> left the house. As soon as he had gone, the house seemed to be
> filled with the glorious Spirit and power of God. When this extraor-
> dinary manifestation of the presence of God subsided, Reverend
> Oaks, our local preacher, and a sister Hawks who was present, each
> testified that if Sister Flagg had not delivered this unusual message,
> they must have done it. Thus Sister Flagg was corroborated in the
> service she performed. After this, the work went on and conver-
> sions took place.

Aside from the sheer entertainment value of this passage, how should it be read? Since we know nothing else from other sources about the lives of Stearns or Flagg, it is obviously dangerous to infer too much from one recorded encounter written from a pro-Methodist viewpoint. In modern parlance the encounter could be read as an exercise in "charismatic authority" on the part of a female mystic openly flaunting male opposition to a popular religious cause. Empowered, emboldened, and enabled by her roots in the community, Sister Flagg expressed the pent-up feelings of communal frustration against an unpopular male leader and opened the way for a cathartic release of religious enthusiasm. Once the offending male had been ejected, the community reinforced its latent solidarity amid scenes of standard religious revivalism. In other words, the incident in Shirkshire could be portrayed as essentially a social conflict with gender dimensions played out in the rituals, language, and theater of a religious revival. To leave the event with such a tidy explanation in place satisfies the rules of engagement of the social historian, but it still leaves unexplored the mental and religious worldviews of the main participants, who interpreted the event as a "spiritual conflict" in which they were instruments of good against the forces of evil. The structure of Gordon's account, as well as the recorded event, operate within a framework of interpretation that accepts as normal the operation of special providences and that human beings, regardless of gender, age, and social status, could be chosen instruments of divine empowerment. But Gordon is also interested in establishing the credibility of Sister Flagg as a reliable witness. Here is another example of that distinctively Methodist fusion of enlightenment and enthusiasm. Brian Clark, who has worked intensively on Gordon's writings, comments:

> Gordon is clearly interested in the factors that made Sister Flagg credible as a deliverer of the divine brush-off. She is described as "an elderly lady, tall and portly, of unusually impressive appearance and respected by all who knew her." No shrinking violet, no flighty young thing, no extra from the teenage cast of *The Crucible* is Sister Flagg, but a respected matron of great substance, both metaphorically and literally. Above the equivalent line in Gordon's more extensive personal reminiscences is a note to the effect that she was affectionately called Mother, not Sister Flagg, which speaks to her moral and social authority as a spokesperson for the group, which is our chief concern, and her credibility as a divine dreamer, which is his interest. The account from the autobiography clearly takes Mother Flagg at her word regarding the substance and circumstances of the dream, and endorses her inspiration in interpreting

and acting on its implications. It places her action in the context of a spiritual struggle and corroborates her by reference to "the extraordinary manifestation of the presence of God," which followed her speech and the testimony of two mature witnesses who discerned the same message from the Spirit. Most decisively, Mother Flagg's authority was testified to by its fruit, as "the work went on and conversions took place." So this newly rechristened church, now free from stain, was graced with the divine immanence as the covenant is sealed and God moves into the purified sanctuary.[35]

This peculiar little tale, though not peculiar in the sense of being unusual in the records of early Methodism, where dreams, visions, and special providences are ubiquitous, reveals a world of meaning that insists on the primacy of the spiritual dimension of conflict. Here is a way of seeing the world that explicitly describes the human dimensions of conflict, but refuses to grant that the political, social, or gender element is the most fundamental. If we are to obey Edward Thompson's injunction to make the effort to penetrate to the heart of the Methodist experience as a way of understanding its power, then trying to understand it in something like its own terms (however that is to be judged) is an essential first step, if certainly not the only step that needs to be taken. Unfortunately, we social historians inhabit the intellectual space of the Enlightenment, which as we have seen in Chapter 2, has condemned as fanciful the very enthusiasm that we are now called upon to interpret.

The statistics showing a female preponderance within Methodism together with the above accounts of the religious experience of some of Methodism's "silent majority" indicate that Methodism was not only a religious movement in which women had an important role, but that Methodism was comprehensively shaped by women in ways that we still do not fully understand. This Copernican revolution not only has significant implications for how the history of Methodism needs to be written, but also poses intriguing questions about how the movement developed in the nineteenth century. By prescribing pious domesticity as the most appropriate role for women, male Methodists were able to consolidate their control over all the instruments of power within the connection, including control over theological education, church property, preaching, publishing, ecclesiastical committees, and the construction and implementation of church policy. They also wrote the history of Methodism in ways that privileged their own contribution and thereby became guardians of the church's collective memory. By steadily closing down the ways in which the majority of Methodists could influence the function and

shape of the movement, men, who in the late eighteenth and early nineteenth centuries had made room for a surging female membership
(whether consciously or not, and willingly or not), steadily implemented
policies that fenced in its social space. In that respect, part of the explanation for the decline of Methodism in the Anglo-American world in the
twentieth century may be due to its inability to accept the radical implications of its own history of gender relations. Throughout its history Methodism has had a predominantly male leadership and a predominantly
female membership. The ways in which that fundamental asymmetry has
been negotiated and reformulated over time and place are as deeply
revealing of Methodism's character as a religious movement as any other
analytical category.

# CHAPTER SEVEN

# Mapping and Mission

Providence has clearly designed this country as a land of Protestants; and
God has prepared us to receive the nations of the world by the vigour and
purity of our civil and religious institutions and by the successive and vast
extensions of our territory.

   — BISHOP MATTHEW SIMPSON, *Annual Report of the Methodist
   Episcopal Church Missionary Society* (1854)

T
he first foreign missionaries commissioned by the Protestantism
of the New World, Freeborn Garrettson and James Cromwell,
were sent to Nova Scotia by the founding conference of the Methodist Episcopal Church in Baltimore in 1784. As was almost universally
the case in early Methodist missions, the missionaries were sent not to
export Methodism but to service and expand an existing constituency of
migrants. The Methodists they found in Nova Scotia were a mixture of
flotsam and jetsam from earlier missionary activity by Episcopalians, Baptists, and Presbyterians, some awakened New England Congregationalists, a committed group of Methodist migrants from Yorkshire in England, and a number of black refugees who had sought freedom and
protection from British forces during the American Revolutionary War,
and who fetched up in Nova Scotia as unlikely Empire loyalists.[1] After
the incorporation of the Sierra Leone Company by the British parliament
in 1791 most of these black Methodists sailed from Halifax to Sierra
Leone, where they and their descendants greeted the first English Wesleyan Methodist missionary to West Africa, George Warren, in 1811. This
serendipitous story of population migrations, missionary support, and
restless mobility is emblematic of Methodism's rise to globalism in the
late eighteenth and the nineteenth centuries. By the 1880s, only a hundred and fifty years after Wesley's heartwarming experience in London,
Methodism, either of the English or the American variety, had established a foothold in most countries of the world. The aim of this chapter is partly to map that growth within the context of two expanding
world empires, but more specifically to pose the question why Methodism had such an expansionist dynamic and to identify some of its main

characteristics. What is particularly striking about Methodism's mission-ary expansion is how often the same issues that caused debate within its domestic sphere occasioned similar controversies as the movement ex-panded into new spaces overseas. In that respect, seeking to penetrate to the heart of Methodism as a missionary movement is as good a way as any to understand the essence of the movement in its entirety.

Writing from Liberia in 1859, Bishop Francis Burns stated: "This stay-ing within hearing of the ocean's waves will be the death of us! Chris-tianity, in order to preserve its vitality among any people, requires expan-sion, and we must spread or die." Similar sentiments were penned by Stephen Baldwin, a veteran of Methodism's China mission, who claimed that Methodism's most distinguishing feature was "its constitutional habit of pushing on." More recently, Dana Robert has suggested that Method-ism thrived in a messy tension between expansion and consolidation, individual creativity and corporate regulation, "or between calls to honor the Spirit and references to the Book of Discipline." She goes on to say that "optimism, faith in human nature, life-risking evangelical zeal, and opportunistic pragmatism characterized missionary expansion." Indeed, these had been the characteristics of the entire Methodist project right from the beginning as it expanded throughout the British Isles and then to North America in the eighteenth century.[2]

## Mapping

The mapping of Methodist expansion is relatively straightforward. From the British side Methodism followed the trade routes and military deploy-ment of early imperialism, which carried it to the West Indian islands (some thirty-five hundred members in 1790, mostly in Antigua), Upper and Lower Canada, the Canadian Maritimes, South and West Africa, Cey-lon and South India, and Australasia, all before the accession of Queen Victoria in 1837.[3] From the American side the push westward to the Pacific Ocean was equally relentless and inexorable. The decision of the American missionary society to supply missionary preachers with a spe-cific missionary objective to frontier communities rather than saddling the inhabitants with the expense of sustaining an itinerant preacher en-abled Methodism to capitalize on the remarkable demographic growth of western states and territories. At its peak in the mid-1870s the Missionary Society of the Methodist Episcopal Church was supporting more than three thousand "domestic" missionaries. By then Methodism had made sweeping gains in Ohio and Indiana, had been established in Illinois,

Wisconsin, Minnesota, and Iowa, and had footholds in Kansas, Nebraska, and Colorado. Expansion begat expansion; as missions in one territory barely stabilized, plans were made to push yet farther. In the decades just before and after the Civil War, Methodism spread rapidly through the northwestern and southwestern states and territories.

The Methodists generally followed, but sometimes anticipated, population migrations, constantly aware that the religious spoils went to those who were in first. Soon after the Mormons arrived in Utah, soon after the beginnings of the Californian gold rush, soon after settlers arrived in Washington territory west of the Cascade Mountains, Methodism appeared with its characteristic fusion of zeal and organization. There was a Methodist society in Dakota months before the Territory of Dakota was even created, and by the end of the century Methodism had extended its tentacles into Wyoming, Montana, and Nevada. The same story could be told of the southwestern states as Methodism penetrated Arizona and New Mexico. This remarkable surge westward was facilitated by a fast-moving population, by the flexibility of the Methodist system with its conferences, districts, circuits, stations, and classes, and by the availability of resources (people and money) in sufficient quantities to keep up the momentum. Above all Methodism grew because it wanted to and because those who carried out the missions regarded themselves as sacred emissaries in the spread of scriptural holiness across the land. In this task Methodists encountered little structural opposition. In the American west there were no established churches, a seemingly endless supply of new people and new land, and a relative undersupply of cultural institutions of all kinds. Not all was plain sailing. Methodism's western expansion was a rumbustious affair with any number of squabbles over slavery, jurisdiction, tactics, relations with other expanding denominations, and money. Moreover, Methodist expansion was sometimes more rapid than it was deep. In the founding of new Methodist congregations, there are any number of accounts of false starts, premature ends, and bitter recriminations in between.[4]

The Methodist advance to the Pacific Ocean in the nineteenth century needs to be mapped ethnographically as well as spatially. Methodists encountered migrants from different parts of the world and established missions to the French, Germans, Scandinavians, Chinese, Japanese, and many others. Sometimes reinforced by personnel from European evangelical or pietist movements, and sometimes by exporting ethnic Methodists to native homelands, Methodism was able to service and exploit one of the most dramatic population movements in human history. In this story of mobile and expanding populations, however, Methodism

The Wyandot Indian Mission at Upper Sandusky, Ohio, ca. 1825, from a photograph of an oil painting by Frank H. Halbedel (Reproduced with permission from the Methodist Collections of Drew University)

encountered a population group that was neither growing numerically nor expanding geographically — the Native Americans. Despite sporadic efforts by Thomas Coke, Francis Asbury, and Nathan Bangs at the turn of the century, Methodism made almost no impact on Native Americans until the conversion of John Stewart, a free-born mulatto, part Native American, who ministered among the Wyandot Indians in the period 1814–23. Stewart, like Peter Jones who worked for the Methodists among the Mississauga Indians (and probably some others not yet identified), made use of his biracial identity to reach across cultural barriers.[5] This period also coincided with more serious efforts by the United States government to assess the state of the Indian tribes and, through the Civilization Act of 1819, to supply small sums of money at executive discretion to organizations prepared to "civilize" the native nations. This early example of a "faith-based initiative" did not yield huge sums of money, but it did supply an impetus for Methodists to expand their missions among the Indian tribes east of the Mississippi. In the ensuing years Methodist societies were established among the Wyandots, the Cherokee, the Chickasaw, the Choctaw, the Creeks, and among the various tribes of Algonquin, Iroquois, and Sioux. The Methodist tactics of preaching, building schools, and forming societies had to cope with the results of brutal government policies, forced relocations, and the rapaciousness of white traders.

Although the Methodists systematically organized missions among the migrating Native Americans west of the Mississippi, progress was slow and uneven. Wade Crawford Barclay records that in the twenty-five years between the authorization of the first missionary to the Wyandots in 1819 and the division of the Methodist Church in 1844, the Methodists established missions among some thirty-five tribes, sent more than two hundred preachers to Native American mission appointments, and organized almost four thousand Native Americans into membership of Methodist societies. This was far from negligible progress, but it did not rival the speed of Methodist growth among the expanding African-American population of the southern states. The context was not propitious. Broken treaties, commercial exploitation, white violence, land confiscations, rampant white-borne disease, and immense cultural chauvinism all made it difficult for Methodism to establish a strong presence among Native Americans. But the explanation goes deeper than that. Right from the start the Methodist mission was defined in terms of bringing the blessings of "civil and domestic economy" to the native population. Peddling the superiority of a settled farming economy over a nomadic hunting tradition, the Methodists found it difficult to make connections with the radically different Native American culture. With little appreciation of the customs, ceremonials, and symbols of their evangelistic targets, the Methodists relied on their traditional methods but could not convert a sufficiently critical mass to enable the mission to proceed dynamically with indigenous leaders, language, and methods. The language problem was particularly formidable, for the Methodists so much relied on preaching, teaching, and reading that the lack of linguistically qualified personnel and materials in native languages was a serious barrier to progress. Perhaps even more profoundly, the Methodists, no doubt sharing the general chauvinism of the age, were unwilling to commit sufficient time and resources to a mission that seemed to be declining in worth and importance throughout the nineteenth century. With a few notable exceptions, most Methodist missionaries to the Native Americans were itinerant preachers who served for relatively short periods of time, never mastered the native language, and placed a low value on the culture to which they were assigned. The Methodist mission to Native Americans in the nineteenth century was by no means a total failure, but neither could it be described as a conspicuous success. It limped along with enough accomplishments to fuel the annual reports of the missionary society, but with insufficient éclat or dynamism to attract energetic enthusiasts from without or a vital leadership from within.[6]

However one evaluates the success of Methodist missions to the Native Americans, there is no doubt that they supplied early testing grounds for the potential effectiveness of the Methodist message among non-English-speaking populations outside the matrix of Anglo-American civilization. Methodists believed that the power of the Gospel would "convert the savage hearts" and then "the light of civilization" would change their habits: "Thus, while Christianity shall reform the heart, science shall enlarge and refine the understanding, and the arts of civilized life, meliorate and adorn their conduct in domestic and civil society." This tidy vision of Native Americans converting to Christianity, forsaking nomadic customs, opting for a settled and domesticated lifestyle, and becoming "a generation of good citizens, pious Christians, and industrious farmers" proved to be incapable of mass realization. The geographical mobility from which Methodist expansion profited among Anglo-American whites did not work the same way among Native Americans, despite some heartening tales of Wyandot transmission from the upper Midwest to Upper Canada. One difference was that Native Americans did not choose to move in search of self-improvement but were victims of draconian removals perpetrated by the very civilization the Methodists represented.[7]

The Methodist missionary society at first saw Indian removal as an opportunity for an accelerated westward expansion of missions, but soon the annual reports were littered with complaints about the devastating effects of disease and migration on the fragile Methodist societies among Native Americans. So devastating were the baleful effects of white cruelty that the Methodists attempted to evangelize the Flathead Indians of Oregon by establishing a whole colony of missionaries, teachers, doctors, tradesmen, and families.[8] In order to protect the Flatheads from the "contaminating influences" of unprincipled white Americans, the Methodists proposed to set up a virtual prototype of a mission station such as those later established in parts of Africa.

American Methodism's surge westward in the nineteenth century was also accompanied by a growing commitment to overseas missions. The story begins with the Liberian mission in the 1820s, when Methodism established a toehold in West Africa through the migrations of African-American Methodists organized by the American Colonization Society. A decade later the Missionary Society of the Methodist Episcopal Church added its support to the Methodist cause in the Liberian colony by sending missionaries and providing resources for the establishment of schools. The Liberian mission established patterns that were to be repeated again and again in Methodist missions to Africa: most white missionaries died within a few years of arriving in Africa, the burden of the preaching was carried by Africans, and the thrust of the mission was the education of the native population. By 1840 the Methodists had established the Liberia Conference Seminary, the Millsburg Female Academy, the White Plains Manual Labor School, and a little network of Sunday schools. Although the scale of these enterprises was small, the pattern of using education as the chief device of christianizing native populations became the Methodist hallmark. Schools supplied new generations of native preachers and teachers to continue work that white missionaries with their health frailties and cultural chauvinisms could not begin to accomplish on their own.[9]

The 1830s also saw the small and uncertain beginnings of Methodism in Latin America. Lay migrants in Buenos Aires formed a Methodist society in 1832, provoking the missionary society to commission a scouting mission to visit Brazil and Uruguay in 1835. In the following decades the speed of Methodist overseas expansion quickened: the church set up operations in China, Argentina, and Germany in the late 1840s, India in 1856, Japan and Mexico in 1873, Korea, Angola, and Singapore in 1885, Zimbabwe and the Philippines in the late 1890s, and the Congo in 1911. Barclay's sweeping narrative shows that American Methodism also established a presence in other European lands, notably Switzerland, Bulgaria, Italy, and Scandinavia, before the end of the nineteenth century; after growing slowly at first, Methodism became established in the 1880s and '90s in Mexico, Brazil, Uruguay, Venezuela, Bolivia, and Chile.[10]

Methodism mapped the world on the back of two expanding civilizations. The first, the British, was to begin with an informal then a formal empire within which Methodism made its way through soldiers, sailors, migrants, traders, civilizers, and colonial governors. The second, the American, was an expansionist commercial empire, which sucked in migrants from all over the world and exported traders, educators, and doctors. A mobile laity, whose pioneering efforts were then supported by the great Methodist missionary societies, which were respectively the largest missionary societies in Europe and North America, did most of the mapping. One does not have to capitulate to the hagiographical traditions of missionary biography to appreciate the many remarkable tales of sacrifice and heroism by the first generation of Methodist missionaries. Many were quirky and unusual figures often on the underprivileged side of boundaries based on color, gender, and social class. Most paid a heavy price for their missionary zeal. Few survived for very long. But Methodist expansion was not dependent on individual initiative alone, for it was fueled by a characteristic combination of personal zeal and corporate organization. It is to the latter that we must now turn.

## Organizing

It is difficult to give a precise date for the origin of the Methodist missionary society in Britain. The standard histories opt not for the dates of the sending out of conference-supported "missionaries" to Ireland, Scotland, and the Shetland Islands, nor for the appointment of "missionaries" to the North American colonies in 1769, nor for the appearance of Antigua on the list of stations for 1785. The preferred dates are either 1786, which saw the publication of Thomas Coke's *Address to the Pious and Benevolent, proposing an Annual Subscription for the support of Missionaries in the Highlands and adjacent Islands of Scotland, the Isles of Jersey, Guernsey and Newfoundland, the West Indies, and the provinces of Quebec* (a proposal that received Wesley's blessing), or 1813, when the first Methodist missionary meeting was held in the Old Chapel at Leeds. In the United States Methodist missionary societies were organized in eastern seaboard cities in 1819, partly in response to the success of John Stewart's work among the Wyandot Indians, and the General Conference of 1820 formally adopted the constitution of the Missionary Society of the Methodist Episcopal Church. The reasons for the formation of Methodism's two great missionary societies are surprisingly similar. Nathan Bangs stated that the American society was organized to impose formal ecclesiastical control over missions, to improve fund-raising, to carve out a separate denominational niche by stopping money given by Methodists from going to their rivals, to seize new opportunities, and to spread the ideals of scriptural holiness to the entire world. These are almost identical to the reasons given by Jabez Bunting for the formation of the Wesleyan Methodist Missionary Society in Britain. Bunting was particularly concerned about the leakage of Methodist resources to the London Missionary Society and the Church Missionary Society, and was optimistic that a new Methodist missionary society would be able to raise funds from sources beyond the denomination itself. Methodism thus set out on foreign missions, not only to convert the heathen, but also to compete for resources and influence with other Christian denominations hoping to do the same thing. As with the empires that sheltered them, the Methodist missionary enterprise was a complex mixture of idealism, competition, self-interest, and control.[11]

Frailties of organization, inadequate resources, and lack of experience of the world they were determined to convert limited the impact of the missionary societies. Among the more promising developments was the formation of large numbers of auxiliary societies, including some organized by women and some organized for children. The first female auxiliary of the Methodist missionary society was founded in New York City in 1819, and others followed in piecemeal fashion until 1869, when the Woman's Foreign Missionary Society of the Methodist Episcopal Church was founded, largely as the result of the efforts of Clementina Butler, an Irish Wesleyan who emigrated to the United States and then served as a missionary in India. The feminization of missions in the last third of the nineteenth century was partly a product of the social changes occasioned by the American Civil War, not least the death and disability of large numbers of men, and partly a response to the new opportunities of mission that allowed women to support other women in ways that were impossible in their male-dominated home churches. In this way married women supported educated single women to go abroad to christianize and civilize foreign populations in ways that would raise the lowly status of women, which was regarded as the hallmark of non-Christian civilizations. As teachers, doctors, social reformers, and evangelists, women flowed out of American colleges and training institutes to raise the standard of Methodist piety and civilization in surprisingly large parts of the globe.[12]

The mobilization of women, both as fund-raisers and as missionaries,

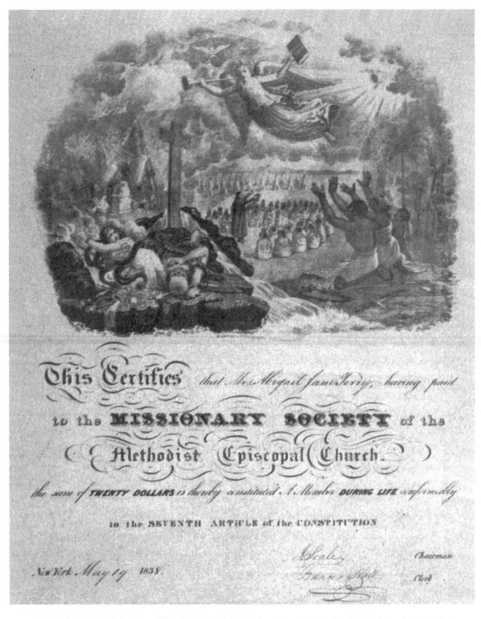

A certificate conferring life membership in the Missionary Society of the Methodist Episcopal Church on receipt of a donation, engraved by N. Currier in New York, ca. 1838 (Reproduced with permission from the Methodist Collections of Drew University)

helped solve two of the most pressing problems of early Methodist missions: the inadequacy of revenue, especially during periods of economic
depression, and the undersupply of willing and capable male candidates,
especially in light of the immense toll taken by diseases in foreign lands.
It also had incalculable effects on the nature of the Methodist mission
and its message. If Methodism was largely a woman's movement in the
North Atlantic region in the eighteenth and nineteenth centuries, it
was no less a woman's movement as it spread across the world in the
second half of the nineteenth century. It has been shown that within
Methodism the early dominance of the three-self mission theory propagated by Rufus Anderson (secretary of the American board from 1822 to
1866), namely the founding of self-supporting, self-governing, and self-
propagating churches, gave way in the later nineteenth century to a more
pragmatic and holistic view of mission that emphasized evangelization
and civilization as parallel objectives in "raising" foreigners to become
Christians and appropriate the blessings of Western culture in the process. "The late nineteenth century woman's missionary movement con-
flated culture with religion, attributing the strengths of western culture
to its Christianity, and the weaknesses of non-western culture to other
religions," in Robert's words, but by so doing it also made Christian
missions more vulnerable to the charge that they were both witting and
unwitting bearers of imperialism. The Methodist empire of the spirit,
largely through its female majority, had by the end of the nineteenth
century taken on some of the characteristics of an informal religious
empire. As Robert has shown concerning the pivotal founding of the
Fuzhou Anglo-Chinese College, Methodism's empire was increasingly
built on its remarkable propensity to establish universities and colleges of
higher education all over the world, not as deflections from evangelism as
is sometimes portrayed, but as ways of disseminating educated Christianity among native populations, many of whom welcomed it. The benefits of Western education, especially for women, mostly outweighed the
risk of tasting the bitter fruits of imperial chauvinism.[13]

## Reporting

The annual reports of the Missionary Society of the Methodist Episcopal
Church are not only mines of information about the spread of Methodism in the United States and overseas, but are also deeply revealing of
the attitudes, characteristics, and assumptions underpinning American
Methodist expansion. The most obvious point to note is how confident

American Methodists were in the message they were propagating and in the civilization they were exporting. Although the reports are not without self-criticism over lack of missionary zeal, poor fund-raising, and a sense of missed opportunities, there is an unwavering conviction not only in the righteousness of the cause but also in the belief that the time was ripe for evangelical Protestantism to liberate the world from its various bondages. After twenty years in existence the missionary society, despite claiming only fifty thousand conversions in its domestic and foreign missions, stated that the missionary enterprise was the "crowning glory" of the nineteenth century.[14]

More colorfully, the Methodists declared their goal to be the evangelization and salvation of the world: "to place the emancipated tribes of this world's population under the immediate outbeamings of the Sun of Righteousness. In a word it is to roll back the thunder of the divine malediction from six hundred millions of undying spirits, and bid them rejoice in the smile of an approving Father, and to triumph in the hope of a blissful eternity." Although the Methodists based their optimism partly on the Bible's millennial prophecies about the "future dominion of Christ over the entire globe" and partly on their own demonstrable success in christianizing the American west, they believed that the goal of world evangelization depended upon means, energy, and self-reliance to seize the opportunities opened up by divine providence. They were neither passive millenarians nor robotic instruments of providence, but rather energetic collaborators with God in the greatest adventure of world history. "Our success depends not upon miraculous power, but upon the ordinary operations of the Holy Spirit, through the instrumentality of a Gospel ministry, supported by the liberality of a generous people."[15] If the world was to be saved, Methodists and other evangelical Protestants would have to work for it, give to it, and if necessary die for it.

Nevertheless as American, English-speaking, and "civilized" Methodists, they perceived God to be on their side in a very particular way. The growth and progress of America, of science and enlightenment, of trade and industry, of freedom and democracy, and of evangelical Protestantism and the English language were all thought to be linked in a great divine plan in which the Methodists were destined to play a central role. The enemies of the plan, but also complicatingly and compellingly the objects of Methodist mission, were Roman Catholics, Muslims, pagans, savages, despots, and the ignorant. By midcentury a combination of American manifest destiny as exemplified in the Treaty of Guadalupe Hidalgo (1848), English imperial expansion, and European revolutions persuaded the Methodists that "the hand of God" was opening up the whole world to "the churches of England and America to the work of its evangelization." Everywhere things were being shaken: "the walls of China, the infallibility of Rome, the changeless mould of caste, the iron girdles of Mohammedism, are all shivered." The world was in a state of upheaval as people clamored for freedom and progress. Only in America and England was there rest: "Our moral ascendancy will much grow amid the paroxysms of other nations and the repose of our own."[16] In this way Anglo-American Methodism basked in the perceived superiority and divine sanction of Anglo-American civilization in the mid-nineteenth-century world order.

This sense of world mission and divine empowerment somehow survived the bitter internecine struggles in both British and American Methodism in the 1840s and '50s and the very obvious lack of repose in the political histories of the two nations. In 1853 Bishop Ames's address to the missionary society suggested that American Christians had a special obligation for missions due to the distinctive history of the nation, especially its roots in the pursuit of religious liberty and the fact that the voluntary principle in religion conveyed great freedom and power to its inhabitants. Moreover, the fact that immigrants from China and the Pacific islands were landing on the Pacific Coast of North America to meet up with predominantly European migrants moving westward across the states ("blending into one mild and gentle people, under the influence of the Protestant religion") was regarded as a symbolic encircling of the globe for Protestant Christianity.[17]

This idea that America had a particular talent for Christian missions owing to its demonstrated capacity to receive the nations of the world and christianize them was a favorite theme of missionary society addresses and reports. This sense of providential favor survived even the vicissitudes of the American Civil War, which allegedly "proved the heroism and durability" of the American republic. At the fiftieth anniversary meeting of the missionary society in Washington in 1869, it seemed that American Methodist missions had achieved their place in the sun. Chief Justice Salmon P. Chase presided at an evening meeting, Bishop Ames reported that the society collected more revenue than any other religious organization in the United States, and Cyrus Foss stated that God would make Christian America "that mighty instrument which shall cut through all oppression, and which in the end shall be the avenging sword of the Almighty on all the tyranny of the nations of the earth, before which they must melt away or come to justice and the love of man." Interestingly, Foss employed the use of the metaphor of a mill to describe American greatness, as people from every nation were poured in and ground between the lower stone of the common school system and the upper stone of the Bible until "at last there comes out an enlightened and Christianized Protestantism." To American pride was added a belief in the purifying force of civilization. One lecturer talked of the spread of telescopes, steam engines, telegraphs, and microscopes as destroyers of paganism and superstition. Commerce, science, technology, and global trade would combine to usher in a new civilization in which American Protestantism would be the guiding light.[18]

Not all was sweetness and light in Methodist missions, however. The missionary society constantly struggled with inadequate resources and disappointing results. The original plan of asking Methodist members to contribute one cent a week to missions, which was hardly a stellar ambition, was never properly realized.[19] As with the financing of British Methodist missions, it was not until the democratic principle of the penny a week for all was largely abandoned in favor of mobilizing the wealthier bourgeoisie through auxiliary societies, annual appeals, and better publicity that the society was able to bring its finances more into line with its ambitions. A more serious problem facing the society was that, notwithstanding its rhetoric of global transformation, the stubborn reality captured by the ubiquitous membership tables in the annual reports was the relatively slow progress of Methodist missions. The Native American missions disappointed, the Liberian toehold in Africa remained a toehold, the early adventures in South America yielded remarkably little, the reconversion of Europe foundered on the rocks of the old state churches, the surge east into India, Russia, and China produced modest results, and the Methodist advance through the Pacific islands and Southeast Asia was spotty and uneven. It was not that Methodist foreign missions were unsuccessful when judged against reasonable standards of what could realistically be accomplished in the first half-century of a new enterprise, but that their achievements paled in comparison with the spectacular success of Methodism's westward expansion in the United States, and in the light of the movement's self-declared overseas expectations. Naturally the gap between aspiration and accomplishment had to be interpreted, and it was done so in ways that are deeply revealing of Methodism as a religious movement.

In the same way as British Methodism's early missionary endeavors brought it face to face with a strong Roman Catholic presence in Ireland, American Methodism's missionary aspirations soon ran up against the Catholicism of the Spanish, French, and Portuguese empires. The early results were no more propitious for the Americans than they were for the British. Early attempts to make headway among the Spanish and French populations of Florida, Louisiana, and Canada came to little and soon disappeared from the annual reports. By the 1840s further Methodist expansion was starting to run into Catholic competition in Oregon, Texas, California, and South America. Indeed, by the middle of the nineteenth century American Methodist missions were encountering Roman Catholic hostility and competition in a bewildering range of sites from the banks of the Rio Grande to the mouth of the River Plate, and from the migrations of European Catholics to countless American cities to the religious scramble for Africa. Everywhere competition bred hostility. Nothing is more ubiquitous in the pages of Methodist missionary reports than anti-Catholicism. Portrayed as despotic, priest-ridden, superstitious, illiberal, and ignorant, Roman Catholicism was the creed of the Old World enslaving superstitious victims in the New World.[20] As is always the case in the rhetorical conflict between evangelical Protestants and Roman Catholics, there are any number of colorful incidents and stories upon which to draw. The Methodist missionary reports include plans to subvert Catholic influence among Amerindians, encourage democratic movements in South America, continue the work of the Reformation among German Catholic migrants, seize Corsica for the evangelical cause, and use British colonial influence to keep Catholicism in check in Bulgaria.

One of the most colorful stories was reported from New Mexico, where a converted Roman Catholic priest, Benigno Cardenas, preached the Methodist cause in Santa Fe in the early 1850s despite the use of every trick in the trade by the Catholic bishop of New Mexico. The bishop allegedly protracted his services, rang chapel bells, threatened his flock, and tore up Methodist publicity. Although this incident was portrayed as a Methodist success story, the sober reality of the missionary reports is that Methodism did not do well in Catholic and non-English-speaking regions. Although colored by the usual anti-Catholic prejudice, one missionary's account of the lack of success of Methodist missions among French Catholics in the United States was not far off the mark. He drew attention to their ignorance of English, their poverty, their religious schooling by Jesuits, their lack of biblical knowledge, and their unwillingness to accept a form of religion so much predicated on a conversion experience as opposed to one based on rituals and festivals.[21] Even among the French who abandoned Catholicism, Methodist missionaries more frequently encountered skepticism and rationalism than any interest in evangelical Protestantism.

Although American Methodists were supremely confident that Roman Catholicism would eventually wither with the old despotic European empires that exported it to the New World, there was little supporting data for such a belief in their own reports. Sometimes the lack of progress caused internal friction. William Butler, who organized Methodism's first annual conference in India, later found himself as a missionary in Mexico, but without the resources to carry the fight to native Catholics. After a promising start he was forced by increasing debts and decreasing appropriations to cut missionary support to new Mexican congregations: "One of these congregations was in the City of Leon, with a population of 110,000 souls, this congregation was the only ray of evangelical light that these people ever saw. I had to extinguish it, and surrender to Romanism ground we had won after hard conflict and much danger! So of the other two places closed. This is work which I am not used to—I cannot understand *sounding a retreat* on the field of history, and being subject to the exultation of Romanism that the Meth. E. Church has been obliged to surrender the City of Leon to them."[22] Not only were Methodists surrendering foreign cities to their great enemy—they were also losing ground in the United States as immigration from Catholic parts of Europe swelled eastern seaboard cities faster than Methodist missions could evangelize.

If encountering Roman Catholicism was the perceived bane of Methodist missions in the New World or in areas new to Protestant Christianity, running up against the influence of state churches was Catholicism's corollary in the Old World. Once again the encounters between Methodism and Europe's old state churches are instructive about the kind of movement Methodism perceived itself to be. The reports of missionary encounters with state churches in Germany, Switzerland, and Scandinavia are almost direct parallels to eighteenth-century English Methodist accounts of dealing with the Church of England, or indeed New England accounts of dealings with established churches in America.[23]

State churches, according to Methodists, produced "dead formalism" with low pastoral standards and bred a deep intolerance of religious competition. As protected monopolies they were more interested in social control than in "vital religion." Thus the Methodists reported slow progress in Denmark because of the population's timid reluctance to "contract out" of the state religion; slow progress in Sweden because the authorities employed fines and the license of the mob to deter religious enthusiasts; and slow progress in Germany because of the bigoted intolerance of both Lutherans and Roman Catholics. But Methodists also reported how their injection of voluntary religious zeal into cities like Zurich and Bremen encouraged state churches to be more pastorally engaged with their host populations.[24] The point is that Methodists believed, as with Adam Smith, that religious monopolies were good for established churches, but bad for the cause of enthusiastic religion, espe-cially among the poor. American Methodists firmly believed that Eu-rope's old established churches were mere midwives of infidelity and secularization, while the competitive structure of American religion, from which they as a voluntary religious association had benefited, of-fered a demonstrably more successful model for the dissemination of religion. In this way American Methodism's European missions, though not particularly successful, confirmed Methodists' belief in the religious and cultural superiority of American Protestantism over the dead and formal religions of old Europe.

Whether confronting the Catholic remnants of old European empires, the state churches of nineteenth-century Europe, the lack of "civilization" among Native Americans or African tribes, or the apparent subjection of women in India and China, American Methodists' encounters with the wider world persuaded them that both their faith and their country would be at the center of a new global culture of peace, prosperity, and Protes-tantism. According to the leaders of the Methodist missionary enterprise, all they needed from their followers was energy, money, sacrificial service, and perseverance. Results would surely follow, as they had done during Methodism's remarkable westward march across the United States. What the Methodists were slow to diagnose was that new space was easier to conquer than old space, that preexisting civilizations were more deeply entrenched than they imagined, that non-English-speaking peoples were harder to reach than they expected, and that their confidence in the joint march of faith and civilization was exaggerated.

The painfully slow progress of their missions to Native Americans and their apparent inability to expand their support base from English-speaking colonists to the indigenous peoples of Africa forced new ques-tions into the open. Did saving faith precede civilization or the reverse? The Methodists had traditionally believed and practiced the former, but their experience among Native Americans made them think harder about the latter. To what extent should Methodist missions build out from colonies of English speakers, school and college foundations, and posi-tions of economic and political influence, or alternatively, how fast should Methodists aim for indigenization with all the messy cultural baggage (from their point of view) that came with it? To what extent should Meth-odists aim to convert societies through their educated elites, or should they pin their faith on the spread of raw religious populism from below? How should domestic and foreign missions be controlled? Should new conquests be regularized into traditional Methodist conferences with episcopal oversight as quickly as possible, or should the metropolitan mission board retain responsibility for policy and funding? What were the respective roles of independent initiative and centrally dictated strategy? These and other questions came to the forefront as Methodism increased its stake in the world but was unable to evangelize it with the speed its early optimism demanded.

## Strategizing

The pattern of Methodist overseas expansion was not all that dissimilar to its pattern of domestic expansion. The mobility of the laity, the importance of itinerant preachers-missionaries, the organization of locals into classes and conferences from which local preaching talent could flow, the use of education at all levels from Sunday schools to more advanced learning, the outbreak of periodic bursts of revivalism, the communication links between the center and the peripheries, the slow development of indigenous liturgies and styles, and the formidable enterprises of fund-raising and institution building are all as common in the spread of Methodist overseas missions in the nineteenth century as they had been in the expansion of Methodism in the Anglo-American world. Methodist missions were entrepreneurial and pragmatic, opportunistic and optimistic, flexible and adaptable. Missioners believed in the power of the Holy Spirit, the perfectibility of humanity — any humanity — and in the utility of using "providential means," whether the growth of empire or the spread of the English language, to further their objectives. On the whole they believed in forming partnerships with local people and not lording over them. This was the characteristic Methodist style, especially its remorseless pragmatism and sheer optimism about what could be accomplished by a zealous minority.[25]

Many of these characteristics, along with the inevitable squabbles surrounding policy formation, can be followed through the remarkable career of William Taylor, American Methodism's most traveled overseas missionary in the second half of the nineteenth century. Converted at a camp meeting on the American frontier in 1841, Taylor established his reputation as someone who could make things happen during his first missionary appointment to the California gold fields in the late 1840s and '50s, before successive overseas appointments brought him to England and Australasia (1862–66), South Africa (1866), the West Indies (1868–69), India (1870–75), South America (1877–84), and the Congo and Liberia (as missionary bishop to Africa, 1884–96).[26] In addition to his work in the establishment of American Methodist missions on

"The Struggle at Shaw's Camp Meeting," depicting the conversion of William Taylor as drawn by the distinguished American illustrator Frank Beard

An illustration by Frank Beard from William Taylor's *The Story of My Life* (1896) shows Taylor as an itinerant preacher

six continents, he also worked cooperatively with English Methodist missions in Australia, South Africa, and the Caribbean islands.

In a unique way Taylor personified how American and English Methodism embraced the world in a kind of pincer movement of expanding empires. A prolific author and self-publicist, Taylor not only traveled but also found himself at the raw edge of missionary innovation and strategy in many different parts of the world. In the best traditions of Methodist individualism, Taylor was a rough diamond who raised hackles among the members of missionary boards back in the United States. For good or for ill, he was rarely out of the limelight, and probably did "more than any other individual to expand the geographical frontiers of Methodism during the last half of the nineteenth century."[27]

Taylor first experienced a mission to indigenous populations in his visits to Australia, Tasmania, and New Zealand, where he simultaneously exploited the opportunities of empire and sympathized with its aboriginal victims, but it was his remarkably successful trip to South Africa in 1866 that established his international reputation as a revivalist. As was often the case with Methodist revivals in other parts of the world, the preceding years in Cape Colony had been characterized by economic dislocation, social deprivation, some forms of preexisting Christian penetration, and in this case military defeat. The key to Taylor's remarkable success as a revivalist preacher in Natal and Cape Colony appears to have been his partnership with an African interpreter called Charles Pamla. Taylor, on his own admission, could make little progress with black audiences without Pamla, whereas Pamla could achieve significant results without Taylor. The reverse was of course true with English-speaking audiences, which were Taylor's specialty wherever he went in the world. According to Taylor the secret of Pamla's success as an interpreter was the fact that his own spiritual experience, including his characteristic Wesleyan experience of entire sanctification, was so in tune with Taylor's that his sensibility and intonation were in almost perfect harmony. Taylor was able to work with some other interpreters, though some were disastrous, but none achieved results comparable with Pamla's. Taylor cheerfully admitted that Pamla was so talented as a preacher "that it became a work of supererogation for me to preach through him, for he could do it as well, or better, without me."[28]

Taylor's experiences in southern Africa, both positive and negative, left an indelible impression on the way he thought Methodist missions ought to be conducted. The mission station model, in which missionaries became civil magistrates, preachers, school superintendents, and cultural regulators, had some value as models of Christian practice and sanctuaries of refuge for persecuted converts, but they were expensive to maintain and encouraged a settler mentality that militated against rapid evangelization of the African interior. Taylor's preferred method was to select the most gifted native African preachers, supply them only with a rudimentary training, send them to the main centers of population, encourage them to establish self-supporting churches, and then move on as quickly as possible. He did not want native Africans theologized into ineffectual preachers, and he did not want mission stations to become isolated cultural stockades. His vision was for an aggressive, heroic kind of Christianity that would fight heathen superstitions, Mohammedanism, and the "worldly spirit that creeps into Christian countries." Taylor had a particular contempt for the first fruits of European theological liberalism as it entered Africa through a preaching tour by the Anglican bishop of Natal, John Colenso. Taylor noted that during Colenso's much-hyped episcopal tour of his diocese he managed to baptize only two children, while in the same five weeks Taylor along with his "Zulu and his black legion" had seen more than a thousand converts. Taylor also records a conversation between Pamla and someone warning him to avoid Colenso for fear that he would shake his faith in the truth of the Bible and the divinity of Christ, to which Pamla replied, "He proved the truth of the Bible and the Divinity of Jesus Christ in my heart thirteen years ago." In this case Methodist experience trumped theological erudition. Taylor left Africa in 1866, claiming to have seen some eight thousand converts in seven months. Although many were white colonists, the great majority was African. Taylor came to believe that the principles he had seen work in Africa, which were after all uncannily similar to those he thought had won the American frontier for the Methodist cause, would work anywhere. In particular his enthusiasm for fast native transmission has found an echo in modern mission historiography as it moves inexorably away from a narrow focus on white missionaries to a more inclusive emphasis on indigenous efforts. It has become clear that whatever the contribution of people like Taylor as catalysts, long-term success depended on the swift development of partnerships with local people who alone could act as bridges between traditional society and the outposts of imperialism.[29]

Taylor's arrival in India in 1870 ushered in a more controversial phase of his career as a Methodist missionary. Taylor's expansive style soon breached the comity arrangements between national religious traditions within which Christian missions had operated in India, and he soon imitated the early history of Methodism by evangelizing Anglicans and then organizing converts into Methodist bands for spiritual nourishment. He was also critical of a dependency culture in Indian missions, which kept missionaries dependent on home-based support and converts dependent on missionaries. According to Taylor this pattern led to a decline in evangelism and a lack of indigenization. His solution as described in his book entitled *Ten Years of Self-Supporting Missions in India* (1882) was to set out the "Pauline Method" in which independent and self-supporting churches could commit to evangelism and discipleship with a minimum of outside control and interference. He thought that that was how Methodism had always worked. "Most of the pioneer work of Methodism in America has been done on principle number one," he wrote, "by laymen, and women, and local preachers. In the cities, east and west, and throughout the length and breadth of the land, the old plan was for a few earnest laymen to enter every open door, by establishing a weekly prayer-meeting, or a little Sunday-school; then, after some preparation, to build a small chapel, develop the work, hold a series of special services, and have a hundred outsiders converted to God; then build up a strong self-supporting church."[30]

The alternative method of missionaries being sustained by great institutions with reputations to protect, in Taylor's view, led inexorably to missionaries becoming masters rather than servants, with baleful consequences for the future of the mission. Taylor buttressed his arguments with illustrations from livestock farming (overcosseted animals develop no independent survival muscles) and from his own experiences. Behind the theological, missiological, and ecclesiological disputes between Taylor and the executive board of the Methodist missionary society lay deep class cleavages between Taylor's simple rural upbringing and the "*nouveau riche* urban constituency" of the board. As Taylor moved on from India to South America and then on to Africa he remained a thorn in the flesh of the missionary society's board, whose members simultaneously admired his energy and enterprise and distrusted his cavalier sense of independence from official constraints. Taylor's example and his missionary theory had a profound impact both on the Keswick tradition of holiness missions and on the worldwide spread of Pentecostalism. The rise of Pentecostalism out of the Methodist mission to Chile is a particularly revealing example.[31]

Taylor was not an easy man to manage, and his methods, despite his own publicity, were not always as successful as he had hoped. It was partly to elbow him out of the chaotic and largely unsuccessful South American missions that the General Conference of 1884 elected Taylor missionary bishop to Africa. Taylor established self-supporting missions in Angola, Congo, and Mozambique before being retired from the work by the Annual Conference in 1896, some fifty-five years after the old warhorse

## Dedication.

I humbly dedicate to my Divine Sovereign, and to my fellow Subjects, the Story of my Life. It is not a book of fiction, but of facts, not remote reminiscences, but facts, written mainly in the present tense, fresh from memory, occupying thus the leisure of about a hundred voyages at sea, covering a period of nearly forty years; illustrative facts in vast variety. A picture all shine, or all shade, would not truthfully represent real life. Some may not like the shade, but the shine abounds, and is open to free selection. My special work for edifying and energizing the hosts of God's elect in climes remote, and for the birth and development of churches in purely mission fields, is the work of God, and it abides, and spreads out like an Asiatic Banyan, or like the Eucalyptus forests of California. There were no such trees on that coast when I went there in 1849. I sent the seed from Australia to my wife in California in 1863. Her seed sowing made such a marvelous growth that a horticulturist neighbour of ours wrote me, and send him a pound of seed — the smallest of all seeds, and the nurseries, thus seeded, dotted the whole country with great forests of evergreen, the most prominent land marks of The Pacific Coast.

"But you did not cultivate them with your own hands."

No, I can't do the work of a million of men, but such seed sown in good soil makes such a showing as will arrest attention, excite interest, enlist co-operative agency and furnish work for millions of workers through the roll of the ages till our Lord shall come.

"And you furnished the seed and started the movement?"

Yes, in the variety of fields, methods of work, and skilful rendering of the word of God, as illustrated in this life story.

"Well, if you had not put in the seed which set all this work into vital activity, other persons of greater renown might have done it." All I have to say is, that they didn't & I did.

150 Fifth Ave, N.Y.
August 13th 1895.   Respectfully submitted.

Wm Taylor, Bp. of Africa.

Handwritten frontispiece to William Taylor's *The Story of My Life* first gave his life to the Methodist cause. John Wesley, his evangelistic inspiration, was actively engaged in itinerant evangelism and church organization for almost exactly the same length of time between his Aldersgate experience in 1738 and his death in 1791.

Taylor's career, though he was not always officially endorsed by the denomination he served, is instructive of a distinctively Methodist approach to world missions. He was a rugged individualist who believed in heroic enterprise. He was suspicious of bureaucratic paternalism because he thought it sapped energy, gobbled up resources, and produced a dependency culture. He thought that the once promising Methodist missions to Africans in Antigua and the Wyandots in Ohio had been ruined by the English and American missionary societies. He feared the growth of what he called religion by proxy, whereby increasingly the Methodist laity were giving over their religious responsibilities to professionalized preachers, choirs, teachers, and missionaries. He eschewed the millennialist vision of the world's transformation by divine fiat in favor of the gradual advancement of the kingdom by earnest endeavor and faithful witness. He believed that Christianity preceded civilization and that to reverse the order was to court disaster. He unashamedly believed that "the English Colonization System, including America, is a part of a grand providential programme for the extension and establishment of a universal Christian empire throughout the world." He regarded the dispersion of English-speaking people, the growth of global trade and communications, and the growing ascendancy of Anglo-American culture as divine gifts to the nineteenth-century church in the same way as the dispersion of Jews and the spread of Greek opened up the Roman empire for Pauline Christianity in the first century.[32]

In spite of having firsthand experience of the slowness of Protestant missionary expansion, especially in South America, Taylor retained a fierce optimism that, if the Protestant churches exploited their advantages and avoided the evils of paternalism, the whole world could be converted to Christianity within fifty years. As an old-fashioned Wesleyan believer in entire sanctification, he believed that such experience was the foundation of world mission. Sanctification existed not for personal benefit alone, but to send people out to win souls: "Pentecostal experiences have sent a Pentecostal Church into the streets, bazaars, fields, and villages with irresistible soul-saving power," he wrote. In short, he was an American Methodist converted on the frontier who believed that what he had experienced had transformed the United States and would ultimately transform the world. To accomplish that task he believed in means and pragmatism. As America's first missionary bishop to Africa he used

his connections to gain interviews with the king of Portugal and King
Leopold II of Belgium to get their blessing for Methodist missions in
Portuguese Angola and the Congo Free State.[33] In his own review of his
life and ministry, Taylor, whose ego was not inconsiderable, stated that he
"received my appointments from God by indirect internal light and leading, and by external providential indications," and claimed never to have
been misled. Whatever his foibles, which the board of the missionary
society came to know better than it wished, Taylor was a remarkable
product of the Wesleyan school of revivalism, missionary optimism, and
sturdy self-reliance. As he strove to expand the reach of the Methodist
message, few parts of the globe escaped Taylor's energetic attention,
whether they liked it or not.

What is striking about the globalization of Methodism in the nineteenth century is how it spread through the arteries of two expanding
civilizations, the British and the American. Moreover, as Methodism
spread, many of the same patterns and conflicts that occasioned its rise in
Britain and America were played out in many different parts of the world.
Methodism's old tensions between its authoritarian ecclesiology and its
egalitarian message and between expansion and consolidation played
out in new and exotic locations throughout the world. By 1900 Methodism had not conquered the world for evangelical Protestantism as it had
hoped to do, but it had established a toehold on all six continents and in
most countries of the world. Moreover, through its Holiness offspring,
Pentecostalism, its empire of the spirit was poised for even more extensive triumphs in the twentieth century.

Behind the mapping, organizing, reporting, and strategizing of Methodist missions, and behind the printed ranks of annual reports, balance
sheets, and missionary stations, the private correspondence of Methodist
missionaries shows the human cost of the great missionary adventure.
Missionaries set out with fierce optimism, crusading faith, and even a
kind of martyr complex. Many died within weeks of reaching their desti-
nation; still others were ravaged by diseases that weakened them for the
rest of their lives. But despite unimaginable suffering and personal trag-
edy, few seemed disappointed with the choices they made or with the
message they carried. Whether reading the account of a young widower
movingly reporting the death of his twenty-two-year-old bride to her
American parents (the first death of a Methodist missionary in South
America), or reading about the privations of living through the Indian
Mutiny, a common theme is the resilience of faith in the Methodist mes-

sage of personal conversion, the witness of the spirit, the cultivation of perfect love, and the anticipation of heavenly rewards for faithful service. The Methodist message may not have conquered the world with quite the speed of its most optimistic advocates, but it seemed to satisfy those who suffered most in the cause of its dissemination.[34]

# CHAPTER EIGHT

# Consolidation and Decline

If there is anything in religious inheritance, or in the influence of a religious environment, I should be, if not an actual Pastor of a flock, at least one of the most devout of the faithful, a snooping Brother concerned only with good works. But instead of carrying on the work of my forefathers I find myself full of contempt for the Church, and disgust for the forms of religion. To me such things are silly; I cannot understand how grown people can believe in them, or how they can repress their giggles as they listen to the ministerial platitudes and perform such mummeries as are the rule in all churches.

— HERBERT ASBURY, *Up from Methodism* (1926)

In the summer of 1878 in the Massachusetts town of Newton, local civic and religious leaders and their families turned out to honor the life of a local worthy called Marshall Spring Rice. Rice was born in Framingham in 1800, the son of Unitarian parents. Orphaned at eighteen, he worked the family farm in the summer and went to school in winter. He prized his education more than farming and soon became a schoolteacher. Rice, along with his brothers, was converted to Methodism through the ministry of Methodist circuit riders, and he soon raised the money for a meetinghouse to establish Methodism in the nearby town of Newton Upper Falls. Over the course of his life he founded Sunday schools, became a temperance activist, opposed slavery, and was elected to the state legislature. He became a railroad pioneer, planned cemeteries, and worked as town clerk. He vigorously supported the Northern cause in the Civil War, in which his son was tragically killed in the battle of Fredericksburg. He had six children; two died, one other became a substantial Boston merchant, and a daughter married the president of the Baptist Theological Institution. The secrets of his success, according to his biographer, were work discipline and a "truly Catholic piety . . . he was the busiest of men; he never blustered but *worked*. Tho' always cordial and courteous to his many guests, he suffered himself to be diverted but little from his home or outdoor business. Persistent work with him was both a born and constantly cultivated faculty."[1]

So it was that the town of Newton turned out to celebrate the life of one of its favorite sons. A marquee was duly assembled, music was played, afternoon tea was eaten, all religious traditions were represented, and the town's lawyers, teachers, and ministers delivered suitable eulogies. Rice was presented with an "elegant and comfortable armchair" by a Boston University professor. Small-town America celebrated not only the life of Marshall Spring Rice but also its own core values of godliness and good learning, hard work, civic pride, sturdy self-reliance, and moral reform. Here was an example of that fusion of Methodist and American values that drew attention from many commentators on American life just before and after the Civil War.[2]

Similar tales to this one could be told of Methodism throughout the English-speaking world in the third quarter of the nineteenth century.[3] Methodism, it seemed, had arrived at somewhere near the center of middle-class culture. Gone were the old hostilities and prejudices against religious enthusiasts and firebrand itinerant preachers. The Methodists had apparently earned their place in the sun, and only diehard establishment bigots and cultural snobs like Matthew Arnold in England questioned their credentials. As great classical and gothic chapels with their balconies and mahogany pews sprang up in dozens of western cities, and as Methodist philanthropy endowed new schools and universities all over the world, it seemed that all was well with a once primitive religious tradition. Yet the tables and graphs of Methodist growth and decline since its beginnings in the eighteenth century tell a somewhat different story.

Methodism had been founded as a religious society within the Church of England. It was organized initially as a voluntary association divided into cells served by itinerant and local preachers. In the early stages of its growth in any particular region it thrived on flexibility and low administrative costs. Meetings took place in cottages, local halls shared with other groups, or, as time moved on, in relatively modest Methodist chapels. Since early growth was volatile and unpredictable it seemed expedient not to invest heavily in buildings, for some societies could literally be here today and gone tomorrow. There was a revolving door in and out of the movement as increased demands outstripped levels of commitment in a significant section of the membership. Careful plotting of the early societies shows that not all centers of strength in one period survived to become bastions of Methodism in a later period.[4]

Some early societies evaporated or were absorbed into other populist brands of religious enthusiasm. As the movement grew, however, its areas of strength became more clearly demarcated, and it was common for a

# WESLEY'S GHOST.

## BY VETUS.

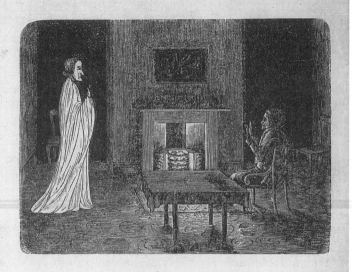

" Then a spirit passed before my face, the hair of my flesh stood up, and
I heard a voice saying."—Job iv. 15, 16.

SECOND EDITION.

MANCHESTER:
J. GADSBY, NEWALL'S-BUILDINGS, MARKET-STREET.
LONDON:
R GROOMBRIDGE AND SONS, 5, PATERNOSTER ROW;
AND J. GADSBY, BOUVERIE-STREET.
1846.
PRICE TWOPENCE.

The title page from "Vetus," *Wesley's Ghost* (1846). In the book, Wesley's ghost returns to castigate his current followers for their "present backslidings." (Courtesy of the John Rylands Library) significant town or city to emerge as the focal point of connectional organization and distribution of resources within a given region.[5] As the movement settled it had to face the consequences of settlement. All the predictable questions had to be answered. When and how was independence from Anglicanism to be declared? When could Methodists expect to receive the sacraments from their own preachers? How were those preachers to be stationed, paid, and educated? What kinds of buildings were required and how were they to be funded? Who was to exercise pastoral care over the incoming multitudes? Vigorous debate accompanied each issue. Romantics and "croakers" held out for primitive simplicity and the "old plan," while self-conscious modernizers went about building churches, founding colleges, establishing periodicals, constructing disciplines, and forming committees. Each side, or more accurately, those at different points on a long continuum, shamelessly invented tradition and claimed it as authentically theirs. Wesley's famed and much-praised eclecticism then had its drawbacks, for almost every position could be defended by an appeal to a Wesleyan precedent. Wesley's ghostly presence was everywhere in the debates. But in resolving the questions outlined above, appeals to ecclesiastical authority and tradition were often less important in defining positions than were the emerging social identities of preachers and laity as they inched slowly from being cultural outsiders to insiders. Underlying disputes about polity and religious style often were superimposed on deeper issues of social aspiration and achievement.

## Interpreting the Graphs

Graphs of Methodist growth on both sides of the North Atlantic, expressed as a percentage change from the previous year, show some striking similarities and some important differences (see Appendix). In all locations the early history of the movement (the first thirty years or so in each place where it took root) included the most rapid but also the most volatile growth. Huge spikes of growth are often followed by deep troughs, resulting in a chart of membership increase that reads like an abnormal cardiograph, though the upward gradient is still remarkable. Methodist numbers in the American colonies, for example, increased fivefold between 1773 and 1776, fell in 1777–78, and then doubled from 1778 to 1782. Although some of this variation can be explained by institutional frailties in the collecting and reporting of the data, most of it cannot. Once established, the trajectory of growth settles down to a more regular rhythm of annual increase with occasional spikes. In the United States these came between 1787 and 1790 and between 1801 and 1803. Most striking, however, are the differences between the average annual rates of increase from country to country. In 1776, for example, there were almost identical numbers of Methodists in Ireland and America. Half a century later there were ten times as many Methodists in the United States as there were in Ireland, a stunningly different trajectory, even allowing for the fact that the total American population was increasing about three times faster than the Irish population. As with compound interest in a savings plan, different rates of growth produced over time a vastly different aggregate total. In Ireland growth rates of Methodists per year for the last quarter of the eighteenth century averaged 6.6 percent, compared with 14.2 percent in the United States, which consequently had more than three times as many Methodists by 1800 as there were in Ireland.

No country across the North Atlantic could match the growth rates in America, but those rates, in common with those from other countries, began to decline in the middle decades of the nineteenth century. Once again, the American decline in growth rates (but not in absolute numbers) was not as steep as in other places, but the trajectory was nevertheless downward. The question is how to explain this decline in average growth rates. To put it crudely, was this pattern the inevitable trajectory of the growth of a popular religious movement as it moved from sect to church to formal denomination? Is this the stereotypical pattern, deviance from which, not conformity with, would require explanation? Or is it the case that Methodism, by deliberately choosing a more settled structure of church and ministry, collaborated in its own demise by taking decisions that seemed appropriate at the time but ultimately proved to be flawed?

The first of these possibilities, the consequences arising from Methodism's transformation from a revivalist sect to an established denomination, has obvious attractions as an explanatory model, especially since all Methodist traditions throughout the North Atlantic region appeared to follow a roughly similar trajectory of growth and decline. The model would look something like this. The first and second generations mount a serious challenge to an existing religious establishment by emphasizing voluntary commitment, the priesthood of all believers, and a popular egalitarian message. The third and fourth generations mobilize their resources and build an infrastructure capable of sustaining expansion. Growth comes from a combination of successful recruitment from outside and an ability to socialize the children of Methodist believers into the movement as active participants. Widespread intermarriage and high fertility rates based on a more optimistic worldview and a strong sense of the "blessings" of fruitfulness further contribute to high growth rates. The fifth and sixth generations orchestrate a working rapprochement with the established values their forebears reacted against. They begin to occupy a position much closer to the center of the opinion-making middle classes and steadily lose their distinctiveness, but they also manage to influence the culture around them. Both recruitment from outside and socialization of the young slow down dramatically, but the institution cranks on with no immediate sense of crisis partly because greater respectability improves recruitment from the middle classes, which in turn produces more resources for ministry. In fact in the case of Canadian Methodism, the union of small Methodist churches in 1884 and a greater investment both in urban churches and in a greater national coverage led to very respectable growth rates from the mid-1880s to the mid-1920s. In these forty years the total Canadian Methodist membership doubled to more than four hundred thousand. This fact alone should be a reminder not to exaggerate the speed of Methodist decline in many parts of North America. In the United States Methodism ceased to make rapid gains as a percentage of total population around 1860 (though there were modest spikes in the 1870s and 1910s), but it was not until the 1950s that Methodism began its long march of decline as a proportion of all Americans, and not until the 1970s did absolute numbers of Methodists begin to fall.[6]

Even facts like these, however, can be accounted for within the broad analytical framework of consolidation and decline by suggesting that the chronological incidence of decline is different from country to country. Moreover, advocates of this interpretation of Methodist decline argue that religious denominations, as with ocean liners, can take a long time to slow down even after the engines are turned off, but they are also harder to get moving again. Once the consolidation phase is over, subsequent generations then have to manage a slow, steady, but inexorable decline punctuated sometimes by bouts of nostalgic romanticism about the good old days or by vigorous debates about the essence of the tradition, which then gets invented as well as debated. In this phase institutional management can become an end in itself, partly because managed decline is both expensive and time consuming. This phase is often accompanied by the reunification of Methodist traditions that were fractured in the nineteenth century. But greater size and unity do not halt the decline. The precise dating of all these changes, and their manifold causes, may vary from place to place, but the overall pattern has a kind of ruthless inevitability. In Britain, for example, Methodist church membership barely held its own in the first third of the twentieth century, but it has declined more than 50 percent, from a total membership greater than nine hundred thousand in 1930 to around four hundred thousand by the end of the century. Similarly, in the United States during the period 1991–96 the United Methodist Church closed 1,025 churches and opened only 210, a ratio of five to one.[7] Neither trend offers much hope for the future prospects of Methodism in the North Atlantic region.

A second explanation for the shape of the Methodist graph stems from the "croaking" tradition of Methodist historiography, which has been surprisingly influential not only among "insiders" but also among professional historians who are often critical of ecclesiastical bureaucracy. By emphasizing the superiority of the heroic generation of founders over the tame accommodationism of successors, it is possible to construct a view of Methodist history not too dissimilar from the sociological model presented above, but for its advocates the causes of decline are regarded very differently. Far from succumbing to the inexorable consequences of irresistible forces, Methodists, according to this view, contributed to their own decline by moral and spiritual failures that resulted in mistaken policies and poor choices: itinerancy was watered down; class meetings lost their dynamism; parents failed to instruct the young in their own tradition; the raw edge of enthusiasm as represented in camp meetings was blunted by a desire for social acceptance; theological education introduced liberal ghosts into the machine; the building of large urban chapels sucked in resources, built up debts, and materialized Methodism's spiritual culture; the desire to spread scriptural holiness collapsed into civil religion; entire sanctification became a forgotten illusion; a crusading social activism inspired by holy faith disintegrated into a depersonalized social gospel; vibrant liturgical and ritualistic innovations were first routinized and then etherized; the attempt to reform the wider culture ended more often with accommodation, not transformation; the transcendental became incidental; voice became mere sound; and the pursuit of holiness became a quest for respectability. In this scheme Methodism was not eroded by inexorable forces acting from without, but by a thousand shoddy concessions to worldliness emanating from within. Such an interpretation had obvious attractions for pious insiders and aging itinerant preachers who either looked back nostalgically to an epic age of evangelistic energy, or looked overseas to a new generation of heroic missionaries. Within this general framework of interpretation some have sought to emphasize particularly salient elements such as the decline of class meetings, the dilution of itinerant preaching, or the liberalization of theology.[8] The implication is that the decline in Methodist fortunes could be reversed only by paying attention to a particularly important feature of the early primitive tradition without which historic Methodism could not thrive.

This is the version of Methodist history that was often served up in the biographies and autobiographies of early Methodist itinerant preachers and in the anniversary lectures and sermons of nineteenth-century Methodism. One example of this ubiquitous tradition is Howard Cary Dunham's lecture titled "Methodists of the Olden Times," delivered to the New England Methodist Historical Society in 1888. Dunham was obsessed with Methodist relics (Wesley's bed, Whitefield's skull, itinerants' saddlebags), and with the ancient heroes of the faith: "These were venerable men, intelligent, devout, thoroughly Methodistic, in their convictions and lives, to this hour, their memory comes to me like a grateful benediction. . . . They have gone hunting and fishing for souls all the way from Scusset to Poverty Lane, they have leveled forests, tunneled mountains, bridged chasms, set rivers on fire, they stand before you scarred from battles fought for the Lord, and now, what do you propose to do with them?"[9]

In a similar vein George Steele's centennial address to the New England Conference posed the question of why Methodism grew so quickly, and answered it by appealing to the heroic quality of the itinerant preachers: "These preachers had quick perception of the adaptation of the means to ends, both as preachers and as administrators of great ability in organization. . . . One secret of their success was in their ability to speak to the intuitions of men. . . . They attacked the old orthodox dogmas with resolution and energy."[10] Through ubiquitous obituaries, biographies, anniversary lectures, and early histories, Methodists were given a version of their history that magnified the heroism of the pioneers, and unfavorably compared the piety of the late nineteenth and early twentieth centuries with that of a century before. This paradigm also helped shape the content of Methodist archives throughout the North Atlantic region and not surprisingly found its way into the history books, often as the dominant interpretive framework. The secret of its power lies in its brilliant celebration / invention of tradition, its capacity to evoke guilt and admiration in almost equal amounts from contemporary Methodists, and in the uncomfortable fact that amid the undeniably nostalgic language, there was at least a glimmer of truth in the message. The contrast is indeed stark between this emphasis on primitive Methodism serviced by heroic itinerants and more modern concepts of church and ministry. Consider, for example, this account of Methodist ministry penned by Frank Pomeroy in the 1930s.

My religious instruction was begun early, founded on the Bible and the Catechism. Later I was interested in some of the "protracted meetings" of the Methodist Church, where sinners were warned of "the wrath to come," exhorted to repent, and urged to come to the "Mourner's bench" and be "saved." I responded to these appeals but had little of the emotional excitement and psychological reaction to which others bore testimony. These were very highly valued as proofs of "conversion." If these were essential, then I still am outside the fold. I was admitted to church membership at an early age. When I face my life work I had no dramatic "call to preach" and struggle against it, as has been the experience of many others, but accepted the ministry, cheerfully, in accordance with early and continued influences, and my own intelligent choice.[11]

Pomeroy's light-hearted account of his ministry is full of irony, self-mockery, urbane wittiness, and playful illustrations, all of which would have been unthinkable for a Methodist preacher writing in the eighteenth or nineteenth centuries. At stake here is more than a change in style, but rather a sea change in concepts of church, ministry, and society from Methodism's early self-understanding.

One stage on from Pomeroy's avuncular liberalism was the bitter rejection of the whole tradition by men like Herbert Asbury, Francis Asbury's great-great-nephew, whose *Up from Methodism* published in 1926 is a kind of fierce American parallel to Edmund Gosse's *Father and Son*. But Asbury's tone is even more savage than Gosse's. His book is a wickedly irreverent look at what it was like growing up in a small Missouri town at the turn of the century (Asbury was born in 1891 and grew up in Farmington). Far from carrying on the American Asbury dynasty of Methodist leaders, Herbert poked fun at the sabbatarian narrowness and bigotry of the fin de siècle Methodism in which he grew up, supplying one of the most compelling accounts in literature of what it was like to be a young person at the receiving end of a psychologically manipulative revival service. Asbury was indeed "converted" under duress, but vowed never again to darken the door of a church except on a journalistic reconnaissance mission. He was nevertheless sufficiently haunted by his great-great-uncle's elevated stature to subject his ancestor's journals to intense analysis. The picture of Francis Asbury he takes away from his immersion in the journals is of a melancholic hypochondriac, driven by a fierce yearning for constant religious thrills, and mourning because his yearnings were never satisfied. Asbury's infamous energy and zeal are interpreted by Herbert as the sad results of an unhappy temperament worked over by a vicious religion. Indeed, Asbury's portrayal of early American Methodism as a dialectical disease of the human spirit is not too dissimilar in language and tone from that other great repudiator of a Methodist dynasty, Edward Palmer Thompson. Herbert Asbury ends his book with a grim promise to break the chain of Methodist DNA in his family. "If I ever have a son," he writes, "he shall be permitted to choose his own religion if he decides that a religion is necessary to his happiness and peace of mind. But if he ever shows any signs of becoming a preacher, priest or rabbi, or even a Brother, I shall whale hell out of him. I am that intolerant."[12] The bitter rejection of the tradition by liberal or Marxist intellectuals in the twentieth century is as much a feature of Methodism as its global expansion.

A third way of interpreting the shape of the Methodist graphs of growth and decline throughout the North Atlantic region is to view Methodism as either the beneficiary or the victim of much larger historical forces with which it was structurally connected. In such a scheme, Methodist expansion could be variously interpreted as a religious form of popular enlightenment (a theology emphasizing human agency) coming of age in an age of enlightenment, a voluntary association growing in an age of crisis for religious establishments, a free market species of religion benefiting from the rise of market economies, and as a democratization of religious culture in the age of the democratic revolutions. But what came in with the tide of larger historical forces could also go out with them. It is commonly alleged, for example, that processes of industrialization, urbanization, and modernization led inexorably to secularization. In the second half of the nineteenth century, therefore, Methodism ceased to grow as a percentage of the total population before declining in absolute numbers in the twentieth century. In short, Methodism was a kind of religion well adapted to a particular moment in the history of Western culture, but was incapable of sustaining momentum when the culture moved on. Its religious offspring, in the shape of Holiness and Pentecostal movements, were able to reproduce equally dazzling growth rates in places other than Europe and North America as they too rose with changes in non-Western cultures. The fact that Methodism's trajectory of stabilization and decline from the mid-nineteenth century broadly paralleled those of other mainline Protestant traditions throughout the British Isles and North America would seem to suggest that Methodism was subject to roughly the same influences with some of the same results as were Baptists or Congregationalists or Presbyterians. In Britain, for example, the graph of Methodist decline almost exactly parallels those of the other Free Churches.

The three analytical frameworks presented so far are neither exhaustive nor mutually exclusive, and each set of hypotheses needs proper testing to separate more useful from less useful interpretations. But the rise and decline of Methodism throughout the North Atlantic region also supplies enough national sites to invite a comparative analysis. What seems most obvious from such an analysis is that Methodism in the United States grew faster for longer than in any other country. Methodism's early and complete separation from religious establishments, including its own parent movement, and its vigorously populist style enabled it to make sweeping gains in its first century. In comparison with other places of Methodist expansion, America offered the fastest-growing and most mobile population, the most unsettled geographical space, the most egalitarian political structures, the culture least effectively controlled by social elites, and the most unregulated religious market. In response the Methodism that took off in the United States was the most radically pietist in its language and the most populist in style of any of the North Atlantic Methodist species. Paradoxically Methodism in the United States was able also to position itself closer to the center of national culture by the later nineteenth century than anywhere else, with the possible exception of Wales, where Methodists participated with other evangelical Nonconformists in a vigorous and largely successful overthrow of Anglican paternalism. In England, Methodism tore itself from within and slowly adapted to an Anglican religious establishment that simply absorbed and outlasted its bombastic challenger. In Ireland, Methodism leaked its prime talent across the Atlantic and was slowly squeezed between the forces of a resurgent Catholic nationalism and a largely Presbyterian Ulster Protestantism. Methodism thus became a predominantly northern sect, occupying a narrow ground with no realistic prospect of further expansion.

By 1860, therefore, Methodism in the North Atlantic region had become an established part of the denominational landscape — no mean achievement in such a short period of time — but its future prospects were less certain. In England and the United States, the two countries in which it made its greatest impact, Methodism had suffered major internal divisions. These were not the kind of divisions that led to a more pluralistic surge of growth, as was largely the case in the period 1790–1830, but were rather of the bitterly fought variety that absorbed institutional energy and produced collective disillusionment.[13] Moreover, the annual growth rates of the movement across the North Atlantic had slowed to a fraction of what they had been half a century earlier. Methodism was no longer growing substantially faster than the population in any of its old heartlands. Although absolute numbers continued to rise throughout the second half of the nineteenth century, there was no mistaking the fact that the era of surging growth was over. Ironically, through the newly founded foreign missions, and the remarkable rise of Pentecostalism, Methodism, or churches with roots in the Methodist holiness tradition, was on the brink of becoming a world faith just at the point that its North Atlantic revolution was beginning to run out of steam. Methodism's empire of the spirit was still expanding into new parts of the world, but its old imperial capitals were slowly crumbling from within.

So much for the broad outlines and interpretations of Methodist growth and decline across the North Atlantic region; what the rest of this chapter will seek to do is to look more closely at the interpretive frameworks outlined above in the light of creative new work on the history of secularization before attempting to offer a more nuanced explanation for the shape of the Methodist graph.

## Methodism and the Old Secularization Paradigms

As a powerful master narrative embracing such complex social processes as industrialization, urbanization, and modernization, the idea of secularization has been remarkably successful as an organizing concept of religious change, but almost useless as an explanatory device. While missiologists, who have to take real cultural encounters seriously, have a dazzling array of conceptual frameworks to choose from, sociologists and social historians of modern Western Christianity have really only one. Despite the near universal collapse of confidence in the explanatory power of secularization theory, no convincing alternative has been offered, and even those who attack it most skillfully seem wedded to the idea of religious decline.[14] The argument rages not so much over the reality of decline as over its timing and mechanisms. It is perhaps prudent briefly to recall the range of multidisciplinary building blocks, by no means mutually exclusive, that have gone into the construction of the old secularization edifice.

The first could best be described as the steady expansion of the enlightenment project and has its most coherent formulation in the work of the Australian historian Alan Gilbert.[15] Since the assumption was that religion was predicated on a need for consolation in the midst of powerlessness and poverty, it thrived in preindustrial societies where life was nasty, brutish, and short. With the coming of improved standards of living, the rise of a material culture, the development of greater institutional security (primarily through state welfare), and the slow growth of enlightenment ideas of progress and popular scientism, religion began to lose its explanatory power. In short, the religious tide was on the way out owing to major and irreversible social trends subsumed within the broad concept of meliorism. The more economic and social conditions improved in the West, the less recourse its population had to the consolations of religion. Within this scheme Methodist decline in advanced Western countries was inevitable, because its predominantly religious view of the world could not survive improvements in material culture, scientific progress, and the growth of state power.

A second building block was put in place by sociologists of religion eager to apply the insights of the classical nineteenth-century sociologists to the thorny problem of the perceived decline in the social salience of Christianity, especially in Europe. The most intellectually coherent explanation was supplied by Peter Berger in his brilliant and influential book *The Sacred Canopy*. His stated aim was "to apply a general theoretical perspective derived from the sociology of knowledge to the phenomenon of religion." He ingeniously suggested that the Western religious tradition carried the seeds of secularization within itself. Although the roots go back deep within the Judeo-Christian tradition and the Hebrew Scriptures, the Protestant Reformation, by divesting itself of the three most ancient and powerful concomitants of the sacred — mystery, miracle, and magic — sped up the process. Moreover, the accompanying growth of religious pluralism led to a corresponding decline in the plausibility of religion. The operational processes were the rise of a modern industrialized society (the secular eye of the storm), the separation of Church and State, the establishment of highly rational bureaucracies, and the rise of privatization, choice, and pluralism. The de-monopolization of religious institutions is ipso facto a secularizing phenomenon. Once allegiance to religion becomes voluntary, it becomes less certain. Religion becomes part of the market economy, a consumer product vulnerable to changes in taste and fashion. It makes religion vulnerable to the secularized lives of its consumers. It also entails bureaucratization and ecumenism as a way to organize competition and reduce its collateral damage. Thus, "the two global processes of pluralization and secularization are closely linked."[16] Pluralism forces churches either to compete in attracting increasingly secular consumers or else to shelter behind old traditions and risk becoming marginal. Neither strategy, according to Berger, has much chance of long-term success. Within this framework, it could be argued that Methodism ultimately became a victim of its own success. By challenging established religious traditions and expanding religious pluralism in the British Isles and North America it was making religion increasingly a matter of consumer choice, within which it had little chance

of maintaining its market share over the long term. As an agent of pluralism, Methodism ultimately paid the price of pluralism.

A third framework stems from the work of social historians of religion
on British industrial cities and European cities in the nineteenth century.
Based largely on statistics of declining religious practice and the pessimistic observations of contemporaries, it seemed clear to most social
historians writing before 1980 that industrialization and urbanization
posed serious, even insurmountable, problems for the churches.[17] Unprecedented demographic growth simply made it difficult for churches to
get the right people and the right buildings in the right place at the right
time. Here was a European-wide problem resulting from growing needs
and declining resources as the old state churches appealed unsuccessfully
to their respective governments and traditional social constituencies for
more support. Whether the state churches were Protestant (Lutheran,
Presbyterian, and Episcopalian), Catholic, or Orthodox, the same pattern
of huge ratios of laity to clergy and insufficient religious accommodation
shows up in the literature. So too does an unmistakable pessimism about
the state of religion among the fast-growing working-class suburbs of
most European cities with populations greater than a hundred thousand.
In the face of such evidence from cities as denominationally disparate
as Glasgow, Manchester, London, Barcelona, Paris, Berlin, Vienna, and
St. Petersburg, it is not surprising that most social historians of religion
thought they saw a clear connection between industrialization, urbanization, class consciousness, and secularization in nineteenth-century cities.
Hence religious denominations of all kinds simply could not thrive in new
urban landscapes.

This explanation has some force when applied to Methodism, for
there is widespread agreement among social historians of religion in the
different countries where it took root that Methodism was never able to
sweep large cities in the way that it once did in rural communities and
smaller towns. This pattern was clearly detectable by the middle of the
nineteenth century. A recent local study of Methodism in the city of
Birmingham and its surrounding Black Country towns and villages shows
a dramatic difference between Methodist fortunes in the city and its
hinterlands, where Methodism thrived among the artisan populations of
early industrial England. As the century progressed, the Methodist tactic
of building imposing new urban "cathedrals" in cities as far apart as
Toronto, Baltimore, Boston, London, Leeds, Manchester, and Sydney
established a serious presence among the urban middle classes in all
these places, but it did not lead to the mass conversion of the urban

proletariat. Nothing is more indicative of the decline of Methodism in twentieth-century Britain, for example, than its disconcertingly poor performance in inner cities and council estates.[18]

A fourth building block of the old secularization edifice was supplied by theologians, who felt that their task was to reflect on the data of religious decline, accept its irreversibility, and come up with some creative theological accommodation to new realities. The most articulate proponent of this view was Harvey Cox, the Harvard theologian who wrote his modern tract for the times, *The Secular City*, in 1965. Cox's first sentence stated that "the rise of urban civilization and the collapse of traditional religion are the two main hallmarks of our era and are closely related movements." According to Cox, cities "achieved" a number of things: they translated technological and scientific advances into everyday life; they "exposed the relativity of the myths men thought were once unquestionable"; they operate as powerful symbols of the reality that humankind has become the center of its own universe ("We experience the universe as the city of man"). Cox's metaphorical constructions are the most interesting and, as is the way with metaphors, the most revealing: secularization is a "force," "a swift flowing current," "it rolls on." Secularization is itself an actor on the human condition. Secularization has children called pluralism and tolerance. It calls for our immersion. It is, of course, "irreversible." Above all, secularization, and the liberty of urban anonymity it brings with it, is to be embraced and welcomed.[19] Hence Methodists should be neither surprised nor upset by the relative weakness of denominational religion in Western cities.

All four of these frameworks have come under serious pressure in the past twenty years. Enlightenment assumptions about the decline of religion in tandem with the decline of the "God of the gaps" looks less convincing now than it did in the 1960s and '70s. Second, the rise of pluralism as an explanation of religious decline has had to take into account the inconvenient fact that American pluralism seems to have delivered stronger religious adherence than the established churches of Europe that sought to retain the sacred canopy. Perhaps pluralism operated differently in Europe and America. In America the dynamics of pluralism developed stronger voluntary muscles and compelling new forms of populist religiosity, while in Europe pluralism did not so much throw up new forms of religious devotion as set up debilitating tensions within and between the power structures of states and their churches over who had control, and who supplied the resources. Third, most social historians of religion no longer think there is an *automatic* link between urbanization and secularization, even though there is a great deal of evidence from European cities suggesting that the rapid growth of working-class suburbs created conditions more likely to benefit new socialist movements than traditional forms of religious piety. But in American cities, churches reaped the benefits of acting as agents of assimilation for millions of European migrants. In a powerful analysis of different patterns of religiosity in three late-nineteenth-century mega-cities (London, Berlin, and New York), Hugh McLeod has shown how patterns of religious adherence held up much better in New York than in big European cities.[20] Finally, theologians, sociologists, and historians who take time to set aside their presuppositions and look at the real world outside their cloisters are less confident of the merits of secularization theory than they once were. Compare, for example, Harvey Cox's earlier vision of religion in the modern world from the vantage point of Harvard Square with his later writing after visiting some African-American, Asian, and Hispanic Pentecostal churches in Boston.

> The signs and wonders that appeared at Azusa Street and in the global movement it loosed included far more than speaking in tongues. People danced, leaped and laughed in the Spirit, received healings, fell into trances, and felt themselves caught up into a transcendent sphere. In retrospect we can also describe the revival as the principal point in western history at which the pulsating energy of African American spirituality, wedded by years of suffering to the Christian promise of the Kingdom of God, leaped across the racial barrier and became fused with similar motifs in the spirituality of poor white people. It marked the breaking of the barrier that western civilization had so carefully erected between the cognitive and the emotional sides of life, between rationality and symbol, between the conscious and unconscious strata of the mind. In this context, the mixing of the races was not just an early equal opportunity program. It had powerful archetypal significance as well. It presaged a new world in which both the outer and inner divisions of humankind would be abolished, and it was the harbinger of one of the great surprises of the twentieth century, the massive and unanticipated resurgence of religion in a century many had thought would witness its withering away.[21]

There is therefore increasing unease about the explanatory value of each of the four traditions outlined above, as much from those within these interpretive frameworks as from those who have attacked them. All four operated largely from unexamined assumptions or an overdependence on the pessimistic literature of nineteenth-century commentators, who often exaggerated decline because of bourgeois neurosis about the rise of a godless proletariat, or because of hopelessly unrealistic expectations about what the churches could achieve. Many English social commentators, for example, were alarmed by the apparently low turnout of churchgoers on Census Sunday in 1851, when around 58 percent of the population who could go to church did go to church, whereas estimates of church attendance in the year 2000 were around 8 percent for England and Wales and 13 percent for Scotland. By comparison with what came after (and maybe even what came before), therefore, Britain's great age of industrialization and urbanization from roughly 1780 to 1914 witnessed extraordinarily high levels of measurable religiosity.

There are, of course, more nuanced versions of traditional secularization theory available, including that offered by Steve Bruce and Roy Wallis, whose argument that the social significance of religion in Europe has indeed declined owing to the operation of social differentiation, societalization, and rationalization is moderated by real historical examples (including Ireland, Poland, and the southern United States) where these processes have been slow to operate.[22] Religion can still survive strongly when it acts as cultural defense or cultural mediation, but even in such places the arrow of secularization is sooner or later inexorable. Bruce and Wallis also met head-on some of the most common arguments against secularization theory: the survival of common and implicit religion; the rise of functional substitutes for religion (such as sport); the recognition that there never was a medieval golden age of religious belief and practice; and the fact that religion performs all kinds of generic psychological functions that are difficult to replace. Indeed, the more nuanced the approach, the more convincing is their central hypothesis, that secularization theory survives because it offers the best explanation for the self-evident decline of the social significance of religion in the West, especially western Europe.

The relevance of this debate for the study of Methodism is obvious. The idea that Methodist growth slowed down and went into decline because of inexorable historical processes relied heavily on the assumptions of the old secularization theories. Of course some of these ideas still merit some attention, but their limitations also need to be acknowledged. There is no question, for example, that the old Methodist tradition of community-based revivalism that swept parts of England, Wales, Ireland, and North America in the eighteenth and nineteenth centuries was simply inappropriate for twentieth-century urban populations.[23] Similarly, the whole superstructure of Methodist providentialism, which did so much to persuade Methodists of the direct intervention of God on their behalf, took a beating from the rise of more rationalist interpretations of events. No mainline religious denomination, especially those within the Protestant tradition that invested heavily in education, could remain untouched by wider changes in culture and society. Moreover, simply regretting the decline of itinerant ministry, camp meetings, and class meetings without understanding the cultural conditions that eroded them inevitably leads to invidious comparisons between old enthusiastic Methodism and its modern lukewarm successor.

## New Secularization Paradigms

Fresh work on secularization, based either on innovative local studies or on a more general conceptual challenge to older work, has opened up intriguing new interpretations of how churches of all stripes began to run out of steam during the twentieth century. Three ideas are particularly germane to the study of Methodism. The first comes from the work of Simon Green, whose study of religion in industrial Yorkshire from 1870 to 1920 concluded with the suggestion that during this period institutional religion "became more responsive; it became more inclusive; and finally it became more complex. Characteristic religious experience changed too: it became more ordered; also more devotional; and lastly more learned." His basic argument is that the voluntary religious associations of late Victorian and Edwardian Britain tried so hard to be more inclusive institutions that they saddled themselves with unrealistic expectations, heavy debts, an unsustainably large portfolio of activities, and a more mundane, ordered, and procedural form of religion. In the process they undermined the very associational ideal that had generated so much energy in the eighteenth and nineteenth centuries. "As associational membership declined, attendances dropped and finances wilted," the churches became increasingly vulnerable to a host of urban counterattractions from the world of entertainment to the world of politics.[24] Put crudely, late Victorian churches tried so hard to reclaim the wider secular culture that they overreached themselves and failed both to nurture their inner core of associational members and to concentrate on congregational recruitment. They were so keen to influence their cultural penumbra that they neglected the umbra at the heart of their mission. The problem was compounded when the state, with incomparably greater resources, took over many erstwhile religious functions, including education and welfare, leaving the churches almost high and dry. Institutional amalgamations and ecumenical platitudes, the characteristic response of Methodists to these problems, if anything hastened the speed of their decline, for increases of denominational scale and organizational rationality proved to be no solutions to the actual problems facing them.

Green's insightful analysis ends with the provocative suggestion that people stopped going to church in twentieth-century Britain not because they had ceased to believe in the Christian message, but rather the reverse: "they stopped believing because they stopped going."[25] Put that way, one interpretation of Methodist decline in twentieth-century Britain is not that the church was victim of an increasingly secularist culture, but rather that the church helped create a more secularist culture by the institutional choices it made almost at the height of its powers in Victorian and Edwardian Britain. These choices were not the result of a lack of missionary ambition, as is often suggested, but rather were determined by an inappropriate diagnosis of how voluntary associations actually worked both in the past and in the present. Green's conclusions, though from a different conceptual starting point, broadly parallel those of another influential local study of late-nineteenth-century religion by Jeffrey Cox, who suggested that churches in London were remarkably successful in projecting a diffusive Christianity in the wider society at the same time as their power to recruit active participants in voluntary associations went into a marked decline.

A second new formulation of religious decline with obvious relevance to Methodism is Callum Brown's work on the decline of religion in modern Britain. Brown, who wrote a number of influential articles arguing that secularization was not the product of industrialization and urbanization, has suggested in a more recent book that it was not until the 1960s that Christianity lost irrecoverable ground in British society. The important mechanisms were not those usually cited by secularization theorists, who Brown believes were largely seduced by enlightenment empiricism and an evangelical obsession with numbers into adopting a pseudo social scientific approach to religion that failed to see the wood for the trees. By contrast, Brown has concentrated more on the ways the British people constructed their Christian identities in the period 1800 to 1960. By listening to their own voices and narrative structures, he suggests that Britons regarded themselves as decidedly Christian up until the 1960s, "when new media, new gender roles and the moral revolution dramatically ended people's conception that they lived Christian lives." So, far from seeing secularization as a long product of enlightenment modernity beginning in the eighteenth century, Brown suggests that the churches were astonishingly successful in shaping the identities of Britons until the 1960s, when a rapid decline of female religiosity, the virtual collapse of the old evangelical construction of the self, and a host of cultural changes emanating from a new youth culture changed everything.[26] The implications of this stimulating analysis for the history of Methodism are profound. Of all the religious movements of the last quarter of a millennium, Methodism was the most addicted to statistical measurements of religious progress and to empirical methods. Moreover, probably no religious movement was more successful in using the media of sermons, hymns, magazines, tracts, and obituaries to help shape the construction of evangelical religious identities. Finally Methodism, which always had a female preponderance and which relied heavily on women to socialize new generations into church membership, was particularly susceptible to a decline in the religious commitment of women. Methodism stood to suffer from any cultural revolution that threatened the erosion of traditional conceptions of the religious self and any diminution of the religious influence of women. According to Brown that is exactly what happened in Britain in the 1960s, and it either has happened or will happen to other Western cultures in due course.

A third fresh approach to the issue of religious decline is based on the cumulative work of a generation of European social historians on religion and urbanization and can perhaps be best introduced as a historical metaphor. The metaphor stems from an idea derived from an exhibition at the Museum of Fine Arts in Boston on the ancient Egyptian city of Amarna. At the center of the exhibition was an ingenious set of computer programs that reconstructed Amarna, brick by brick, from ancient ruins into a living urban society. Each new program added a fresh layer of sophistication to the urban reconstruction without obliterating the work of the previous programs. Something similar could be done for European religion in the age of great cities. "Programs" could be developed for the complex variables that affect the vitality of religious belief and practice. These would include: the religious characteristics of regional hinterlands from which urban migrants arrived (often these reveal distinctive patterns of religiosity established over centuries); the relationship between churches and emerging political movements such as liberalism, socialism, and nationalism (churches survive better in tandem with new national projects than against them); the progress of enlightenment ideas among the opinion-forming classes (the earlier and more complete the impregnation, the greater the extent of cultural secularity); the speed of urban growth and the supply of fresh resources to the churches (the faster the speed of urban growth and the greater the degree of class or social conflict the more difficult it was for churches to operate successfully); the differential rates of religious observance revealed by gender, class, age, and denomination (young, mobile, working-class male

Protestants are the most secular); the strength of the survival of populist forms of eclectic religiosity based upon seamless syntheses of church and folk religion (showing that religiosity is not amenable to mere statistical tabulations alone); the rise of more pluralistic religious cultures, sometimes augmenting, sometimes replacing older patterns (for example, the shift from denominational allegiance to more informal structures of belief and practice); changes in the use of language over time about the nature of religion and irreligion (the distinction between the public and private spheres of religion, for example, is of comparatively recent origin); the revival of popular religious enthusiasm (popular evangelicalism in some Protestant countries and processions, cults, and shrines in some Catholic countries); periods of continuity and periods of rapid change caused by warfare or pronounced value shifts such as occurred in the 1960s; asymmetries in the decline of different kinds of religious belief and practice (for example, rites of passage ceremonies hold up best almost everywhere, while regular church attendance rates are comparatively low); the relationship between churches and new emancipation movements based on "Liberty, Equality, and Fraternity," including the precise point at which churches made some accommodation (too little, too late, hurt ecclesiastical institutions of all sorts); the relationship between religion and the mapping of social space and the measurement of time (ground lost here is hard to recover); the power of symbols and who or what fills the popular imagination; the effectiveness of generational transmission of religious beliefs and practices (collective memories once interrupted are almost impossible to reconnect); and the influence of individuals and ideas from place to place (creative individual initiatives could make a difference to the fate of churches in particular localities).[27]

The aim of all this would be to construct a map of European, and indeed American, conglomerate belief systems, rather like a set of detailed aerial pictures of landscape and its change in use over time. The final picture may resemble a theoretical model to some extent, but it will be more richly textured and will indicate life, vitality, variety, complexity, and the dignity of human instrumentality. The virtual city package need not necessarily show up inexorable forces of urbanization, industrialization, modernization, and pluralization, but rather might show an emphasis on function, contingency, choice, and change. Moreover, change does not have to be interpreted as decline; transformation and adaptation may be more important concepts than rise and fall.

Proponents of secularization theories would no doubt argue that the only thing at stake here is that a historian uncomfortable with theoretical models, and sensitive to problems of historical inevitability, is simply constructing a more complicated but equally inexorable metaphor of religious decline. Mere *description* of a process, they might argue, can be as complex and variegated as scholarly scruples determine, but the end result is roughly the same. In other words, a descriptive framework is simply being employed to replace a more theoretical one. What is at stake, therefore, is not so much a challenge to secularization as a concept, but guild wars about which academic discipline can supply the most convincing explanation of an agreed decline. My response to that would be that the approach outlined above substantially reconfigures the issues at stake in the debate. Far from seeing secularization as an inevitable component of modernization, a kind of religious asphyxiation from breathing the toxic fumes of modernity, the "virtual city" approach lays bare contingencies, mechanisms, and instrumentalities. If Christianity has declined in large parts of modern Europe (a proposition difficult to resist), it did not do so because of some irresistible social process or processes, but because of real choices made by real people in real social situations. In particular, the propensity of Europe's old state churches to align themselves with forces of conservatism and traditionalism (out of perceived self-interest) in a period of fast-moving political, economic, and social change was nothing short of disastrous. The same old arguments of lack of state support and massive popular indifference are peddled everywhere from the exploitative clerical landlords of southern Spain to the confessional Lutherans of German cities, and from Chalmers's advocacy of the godly commonwealth in Scotland to the Orthodox clergy in St. Petersburg.[28] But if one pauses to look at the differential ratios of priests to people in a host of European cities, one finds the same pattern of conspicuous underprovision in working-class neighborhoods compared with middle-class districts. The point is that secularization did not simply engulf people; rather, they collaborated with arrangements that facilitated it.

The same, it could be argued, is true of Methodism. The church's nineteenth-century investments in property, education, publishing, and ecclesiastical organization along with its inculcation of personal qualities of work discipline, sobriety, self-improvement, and civic responsibility among its members allowed Methodists to achieve a more central position in the cultures of most of the countries in the North Atlantic region. But with respectability and cultural acceptance came an inevitable decline in the otherworldly zeal of its earlier manifestations. In short, Methodism's cultural diffusion and ecclesiastical ambitions increased out of line with its power to recruit members and effectively disseminate its message both to its own children and to those outside the Methodist constituency. The result was increasing influence and decreasing recruitment, a pattern that is obviously unsustainable over the long haul.

The pattern of decline described here is not too dissimilar from that portrayed by Roger Finke and Rodney Stark, Mark Noll, and Robert Wuthnow. In different ways they have all shown how mainline denominations decline as they make fewer demands on their own members, have no very obvious recruitment mechanism, and steadily lose ground to new, more energetic movements. According to Finke and Stark's table of "market share" of American religious denominations from 1940 to 1985, United Methodism lost 48 percent of its market share, a figure directly comparable with other mainline Protestant denominations, such as Presbyterianism, Episcopalianism, and Congregationalism. By contrast, Southern Baptists, Assemblies of God, Church of the Nazarene, and the Latter Day Saints made market-share gains of similar proportions. So common has been this pattern of American religious growth and decline since the colonial era that it is tempting almost to establish it as a kind of law of religious movements.[29]

More concentrated work on patterns of Methodist growth and decline in the 1990s suggests a refinement of this law. In a sociological survey of church closures and new church openings (as stated earlier the ratio is a decline of five to one), it has been shown that Methodism, regardless of theological characteristics, was able to establish new churches in areas of substantial population movement. New Methodist churches are being founded mostly in "revolving-door communities" or, less frequently, in areas of primary population growth.[30] Conversely, Methodism is not thriving in older, more stable populations in which aging, lack of recruitment, and poor generational transmission take their inevitable toll. This conclusion parallels some of the arguments presented in Chapter 1 about Methodism thriving on mobility and change. Perhaps the most salient conclusion one can offer of Methodism's patterns of growth and decline throughout the world is that it is not a religious movement that can survive for very long on institutional consolidation alone. For Methodism to thrive it requires energy, change, mobility, and flux.

To go back to the story forming the introduction to this chapter, the life and death of Marshall Spring Rice offers some suggestions for an appropriate conclusion. Less than a year after his life was celebrated by the Methodist church and the Sunday School Union of Newton, Rice died. Further celebrations, this time of a more somber kind, drew together the Christian congregations and voluntary organizations of Newton. What was clear from the conduct of Rice's funeral is that not only had Methodism achieved respect in local civic culture but local civic culture had been to an extent Methodized. A kind of pan-evangelical moral culture rooted in the Sunday schools and the local churches had become the dominant shaper of Newton's public life. What the Methodists had achieved here and in many other social spaces across the North Atlantic region was something very close to Simon Green's portrait of chapel culture in industrial Yorkshire in the same period. As Methodism along with other evangelical churches and voluntary organizations fought for and achieved a more inclusive model of religious adherence, it steadily undermined its own associational roots. Whether this was desirable, inevitable, or even reprehensible is not the point. The point is that Methodism, which drew so much of its energy from the old Wesleyan imperative to spread scriptural holiness across the land and then the world, could not sustain the same momentum and commitment from its followers when the gap between the ideals of scriptural holiness defined internally by the movement and achieved externally in the wider society narrowed to quite respectable proportions. Methodism at its heart and center had always been a profoundly countercultural movement. It drew energy and personal commitment from the dialectics arising from its challenge to accepted norms in religion and society. It thrived on opposition, but it could not long survive equipoise.

# CHAPTER NINE

# Methodism's Rise and Fall

The story of Methodism's rise from a small coterie of religious societies in Oxford University in the 1730s to a major world communion by the beginning of the twentieth century is compellingly complex. The serried ranks of official statistics tell the story in its most reductionist form. By 1908 Methodism had almost 9 million members, at least four times as many adherents, 7 million Sunday scholars, more than 150,000 ministers and lay preachers, half a billion dollars' worth of property, and thousands of schools, colleges, universities, seminaries, and training institutes all over the world.[1] These estimates, frozen in time, take no account of generations past, or generations yet to come. They tell nothing of the lives lived and changed, cultures shaped and absorbed, private and public spaces altered and molded.

Telling Methodism's worldwide story poses special problems. As a religious movement it transcended boundaries of nationality, ethnicity, gender, race, social class, and culture. It changed over time and was shaped by its geographical contexts. Its noisy enthusiasm, sometimes extravagantly so, has provoked strong reactions, among both contemporaries and historians. Adding to the sense of complexity is the uncomfortable reality that interpretations of the movement have oscillated dramatically over time, sometimes flatly contradicting one another. In the eighteenth century, for example, Methodism was frequently criticized for disrupting patterns of work by holding too many meetings and promoting a heart religion of emotional excess at odds with the daily disciplines of productive labor and familial support. By the twentieth century predominantly Marxist historians and Weberian sociologists attacked "methodical" Methodism for creating a slavish work ethic among the emerging industrial proletariat.[2]

Similarly, in the eighteenth and early nineteenth centuries Wesley and his movement were castigated by Roman Catholics for their anti-Catholic bigotry, while in the late twentieth century Wesley's *Letter to a*

*Roman Catholic* was seized upon by ecumenists as a model for interfaith dialogue. In politics, Wesley's Methodism was lampooned by an early generation of political radicals in Britain for its narrow devotion to the status quo, while members of the British Labour Party have nostalgically searched for their radical roots in the religion of the Methodist chapels. Feminist scholars still disagree about whether Methodism advanced or hindered women's liberation. African-American Methodists are both proud of their denomination's early opposition to slavery and ashamed of its later capitulations. Twentieth-century intellectuals who grew up within Methodist traditions fiercely disagree about the effects, whether noble or baleful, of Methodism on their lives. The list goes on and on. Some of these disagreements result from Methodism's changing over time, and from place to place, but others are located in genuine disagreements about how to interpret ambiguous evidence. Early Methodism seems to have promoted both godly discipline and emotional excess, a work ethic and a devotion to ecstatic rituals, female empowerment and submissive domestication, emancipation for those at the bottom of social pyramids and an unrelenting bourgeois ethic of acquisitiveness.[3] In other words, Methodism was complex, multifaceted, and, like all great movements, brought forth both intended and unintended consequences.[4]

In past works I have tried to come at this complex movement from a number of directions — local and regional studies, biographies, politics and public debate, gender, and popular culture — but this book has attempted some different approaches.[5] First, and most important, my aim has been to treat Methodism as a transnational religious movement not easily confined to, or interpreted within, purely national boundaries. As it spread throughout England, the British Isles, North America, and the wider world, Methodism changed and adapted to new contexts, but it remained recognizably Methodist, not just evangelical, wherever it became established. In an attempt to explore what "recognizably Methodist" might mean, this study has concentrated on eight themes, many of which employ a dialectical or comparative approach to the Methodist essence.

The book began with an attempt to answer the most fundamental, and perhaps the most difficult, question of all: why did Methodism grow when and where it did in the North Atlantic region in the eighteenth and nineteenth centuries? What supplied this new empire of the spirit with its expansionist zeal and what social, economic, and political factors facilitated its expansion? Any satisfactory answer to these questions must emphasize both endogenous and exogenous factors and, more important, seek to relate them to one another. My application of an evolutionary biological metaphor, competition and symbiosis, was an attempt to emphasize that Methodism is a recognizable religious species, but that it grew, adapted, and procreated according to the suitability of its environmental conditions. Determining what were the most suitable conditions is deeply revealing of the kind of movement Methodism was. Much later, when Methodism sought to expand throughout the world in the contexts of two global empires, British and American, its growth patterns, and its growth limitations, also reveal much about the nature of the movement. Although it had deep roots in the Pietist traditions that came out of the European Reformation, Methodism, it should not be forgotten, arose directly out of Anglicanism and expanded in those parts of the world where Anglicans and English speakers migrated. In order to survive and thrive Methodism needed to break free from Anglicanism and benefit from the tide of anti-establishment sentiment that reconfigured religion and political culture in the age of the democratic revolutions. How this rupture took place from country to country, and the surviving strength of establishment religion in various regions, helped determine the speed and characteristics of Methodist growth.

Right from the start, Methodism was a religion that carried the genes of dialectical tension; it could scarcely have been otherwise, given the background of its founder. The most pervasive was the tension between enlightenment and enthusiasm, between rational calculation and the direct inspiration of the spirit. Wesley was both an Oxford-trained logician with roots in the old High Church tradition of Anglican spirituality and an incorrigible enthusiast for signs of direct divine intervention in the lives of his followers. As the enlightened pinned their faith in human progress free from the dark clouds of fanaticism and superstition, Wesley pinned his on human perfectibility free from the dark pits of willful sinning and cold, formal religion. Wesley could be fiercely logical in his many polemical arguments with opponents and deeply gullible when evaluating the religious experience of people like George Bell, the London-based millenarian perfectionist. Others have seen similar dialectical tensions: between the spiritual egalitarianism of the Methodist message and the authoritarianism of its ecclesiastical structure, between the religion of the heart and the methodical disciplines of the holy life, between the libertarianism of grace and the works-righteousness driven on by fear of backsliding or lack of progress toward perfection, between the freedom of the spirit's leading and the ubiquitous rules and disciplines governing Methodist societies, and between religious revivalism as a way of transforming the human condition for the life hereafter and a focus on political reform as a way of redeeming life here and now.

There was more at stake here than mere rival ideas, for the Methodist dialectic could operate within the hearts and minds of ordinary believers and could extend to different styles of leadership and governance. Compare and contrast, for example, the two most influential leaders of Methodism after Wesley's death, Francis Asbury in America and Jabez Bunting in England. Asbury, a metalworker's apprentice and the son of a farm laborer, struck up a remarkable rapport with American preachers who were also mostly farmers or artisans. His leadership was based on personal piety, a determination to ask nothing of others that he would not do himself, and a pragmatic devotion to the spread of scriptural holiness across the land. He first opposed slavery and then backtracked for fear of losing the South; he embraced camp meetings and fielded the inevitable criticisms against their emotional largesse; he ruled with an iron hand, but was sensitive to local circumstances. He was a populist bishop who subjected his episcopal ordination to a vote of the preachers. He saw himself as a *Wesleyan* Methodist, even outstripping his mentor in miles traveled, households visited, and privations suffered. As Donald Mathews has pointed out, Asbury came "to dominate the American Wesleyan imagination through his iron will, fierce piety, clever maneuvering, fabled ubiquity, self-discipline, and monumental life."[6]

Jabez Bunting was an entirely different kind of Wesleyan leader. The son of a Manchester radical tailor, Bunting was educated by Unitarians, read widely among theological classics, and after some unpleasant confrontations with Methodist revivalism red in tooth and claw, he became an ecclesiastical bureaucrat par excellence.[7] Fearful of popular radicalism and unrestrained revivalism, Bunting placed his faith in sound management and connectional discipline. He more or less gave up itinerating and settled mostly in London where he sat on committees, shaped policy, managed the budget, edited Methodist publications, represented the connection in the public arena, and laid down the law on almost everything from theological education to missions, and from educational policy to political campaigns. He was a consummate ecclesiastical politician whose desire for control provoked a massive counterattack in the late 1840s from which British Methodism never fully recovered. Bunting and Asbury could scarcely be more different, yet both claimed to be in the authentic Wesleyan tradition. Each thought that Wesley's ghost approved of their interpretation of the tradition. Both owed something to Wesley's style of connectional management, yet there can be little doubt that Asbury captured better the essence of the Methodist project and oversaw dramatically faster numerical gains than Bunting. Leadership style, as this book has shown, was not the only issue at stake in the differential

growth rates of British and American Methodism, but the sheer distance
between the respective visions of Bunting and Asbury shows just how far
the Wesleyan membrane could be stretched.

If the abiding tension between enlightenment and enthusiasm, the
head and the heart, is one way of penetrating to the center of the Methodist movement, another is to consider the nature of its message, how it
was transmitted, how it was heard, and how it was implemented in the
lives of the rank and file. This is the most difficult task of all, for Methodism was noisy, eclectic, and populist, and academic historians and theologians often have neither displayed imaginative empathy nor constructed
convincing analytical paradigms for coming to terms with such religious
expression. There are insightful exceptions. Leigh Eric Schmidt has engaged the culture of sound in evangelical religion with splendid creativity, and Donald Mathews and Diane Lobody have written with sensitivity
about the centrality of noise and voice in the whole Methodist project.[8]
Mathews, ever a discerning interpreter of the tradition, writes: "The
movement provided a process through which ordinary people found
their own voices. They spoke. Others listened; and then they too spoke.
Others joined them. They sang and wept and felt renewed — in the love of
Christ. The language of origins was dynamic and evocative; its testimonies
in the vernaculars of the people was the dynamic creativity of the movement."[9] Interior experience became public testimony; public testimony
became community discourse; and community discourse was written and
disseminated. From its class meetings to its great universities, Methodism
expanded from the religion of the heart to the religion of the public
square. The speed of transmission and of social elevation was uneven and
unpredictable, but many women, African Americans, and ordinary laborers expanded their access to the public sphere in tandem with the
movement they embraced. There were, of course, resistant factors, such
as male chauvinism and naked racism, some of which were sponsored by
the Methodists themselves, but the overall tendency was to promote the
voices of ordinary people in ever-expanding circles.

The Methodist message was neither uniform nor completely formulaic, but wherever it was spoken it had a number of common characteristics. It spoke of the possibility of salvation and a new start, not at the
dictates of an authoritarian divinity, but as the result of divine love inspiring a willing human response. It dared hope for a transformed life, even
to the point of perfect love, though it urged fierce vigilance to guard
against backsliding and worldliness. It emphasized discipline, fellowship,
and social responsibility. It was spoken through hymns, sermons, testimonies, confessions, extempore prayers, and ecstatic rituals. It was ab-

sorbed into the rhythms of birth, life, and death, and was tested ultimately by the believer's capacity to slide peacefully into eternity, where
the rewards of the holy life awaited those who persevered. It mattered
that the message was carried by submissive and exemplary volunteers, not
by paid officials of the state, for in a powerful way the medium was the
message. Of course, it is wise not to overromanticize the grandeur of all
this. As well as heroism there was emotional manipulation, charlatanry as
well as purity, and terror as well as loving persuasion. It is impossible to
read the melancholy diaries of teenage Methodists without concluding
that there was a frightening intensity to prescribed Methodist piety that
unsettled minds and spirits. The ubiquitous deathbed scenes of holy
dying are as emotionally indulgent as they are inspiring. Much of this is a
matter of taste; but altering taste away from casual licentiousness to moral
earnestness, and from a concentration on this life alone to a consideration of eternal life, was also part of the Methodist message.

Millions adopted the Methodist message, but it was rejected and opposed by millions more. Wherever Methodism took root, especially in
the first decade of its existence in any given place, established social,
economic, and political interests vigorously opposed it. Social superiors,
including the owners of slave plantations, who feared that religious enthusiasm would be the midwife of social dislocation, whipped up opposition against it, but ordinary people who disliked its puritanical zeal
and exclusivist claims also resisted Methodism. The nature of the opposition Methodism occasioned was as revealing about the structure of
eighteenth- and nineteenth-century society as it was about the nature of
Methodism itself. Forceful opposition generally settled down as Methodism became established, but internal conflicts did not. Methodism's authoritarian ecclesiology was a source of contention for many on both
sides of the Atlantic who thought they had joined a voluntary association
of equals, not an organization run by a clerical hierarchy. Given the
content of the ideas swirling around Methodism's artisan constituency in
the age of revolutions, it would have been surprising if Methodism had
not been agitated by Paineite notions of popular sovereignty or by populist campaigns for the rights of the laity. Methodism also suffered from its
capacity to absorb conflicts from its environment, including divergent
views about the great issues of the day such as slavery, social class, and
political reform. To that list the late twentieth century has added questions about sexuality, marriage, and lifestyle.

The greater participation of Methodists in public debate was accompanied by structural changes in the way the connection was governed,
financed, and organized. Controversial topics soon came on the agenda.

How were Methodist preachers to be trained and educated? What kind of investment in property was appropriate? How was the movement to be financed? How was the movement's expansionist mission to be accomplished? What were the respective roles of clergy and laity, blacks and whites, men and women, rich and poor? Methodism's slow drift away from its revivalist roots to somewhere closer to the cultural center of its host environments can be charted in any number of different ways. Changes in the style and content of theological education are very revealing, but my choice was to follow the money, which provides the clearest picture of how early practices of egalitarianism inevitably gave way to less associational and more stratified ways of facilitating Methodism's world mission. Increasingly, power lay with those who gave the most, or in the case of the ministry, those who earned the most. The sense of collective ownership of the movement, and the sense of a brotherhood of itinerants sharing equal privations, could not long survive the increased differentials. The same issues that disturbed the domestic peace of the movement also played out in foreign missions. Self-sufficient idealists like William Taylor could accept neither bureaucratic control nor the money it supplied.

Methodism's declining growth rates in the twentieth century are, if anything, easier to explain than its meteoric rise. What is striking in retrospect is not that the Methodist graph began to resemble more closely the decline of other mainline Protestant denominations, but that nineteenth-century Methodists dared believe the whole world order could be converted to evangelical Protestantism. What fired their optimism was not only belief in the righteousness of their cause, but also the conviction that they were marching in tandem with the unstoppable progress of a superior Western civilization. It seemed to them that English-speaking Anglo-American culture was poised to sweep the world and that they would be both its agents and its beneficiaries. This belief was not pure fantasy. The speed with which Methodism expanded across North America, from the Delmarva Peninsula to the Californian gold mines, and its capacity to absorb people from different ethnic and racial backgrounds, supplied a powerful case study of how it all could work. William Taylor, who was converted on the frontier, took the message to California, and then helped establish Methodism on five continents, was both a self-proclaimed exemplar of Methodism's heroic tradition and an emblematic figure of what the future held in store. But Taylor's mission turned out to be more unique than ubiquitous. As it turned out, it was not Methodism that was poised to sweep the world but its Holiness offspring, Pentecostalism. Here was another movement giving voice to ordinary people, thriving on mobility, depending on women, privileging personal transformation over public reform, and vigorously organizing dislocated people into noisy cells of perfectionist excitement. Above all, Pentecostalism is an enormously successful continuation of Methodism's energy and mobility, which transformed the religious landscape of the North Atlantic region and beyond in the eighteenth and nineteenth centuries. The next Christendom, already under construction in the global south, would not look the same if Methodism had never existed.[10]

# Methodist Membership and Rates of Change, United States and United Kingdom

Data for the following tables and graphs are derived from *The Methodist Experience in America: A Sourcebook,* vol. 2, ed. Russell E. Richey, Kenneth E. Rowe, and Jean Miller Schmidt (Nashville: Abingdon, 2000), C. C. Goss, *Statistical History of the First Century of American Methodism* (New York: Carlton & Porter, 1866), and Robert Currie, Alan Gilbert, and Lee Horsley, *Churches and Churchgoers: Patterns of Church Growth in the British Isles Since 1700* (Oxford: Clarendon, 1977). Unlike the tables in Currie, Gilbert, and Horsley, the figures for Ireland include both Methodists and Primitive Methodists, and are taken from the conference journals. All figures refer to membership, not adherents or attendees. To estimate the number of people under direct Methodist influence, historians conventionally multiply membership figures by a multiple ranging from three to seven, but there is no universally agreed formula for this computation. Given the propensity of Methodism to fragment into countless different groups, and the difficulty of obtaining reliable figures for African-American Methodists, the following tables cannot claim impeccable accuracy, but they do at least offer the possibility of making fruitful comparisons from place to place and from year to year.

Rates of change for each year were calculated by taking the current year's membership and subtracting the previous year's membership, then dividing the result by the previous year's membership, producing a percentage figure. Dashes indicate a gap in the statistical data. See Chapter 8 for an interpretation of these tables and graphs.

United Methodist Lay Membership and United States Population
(from U.S. Census), 1790–1990

| | United Methodist Lay Membership | | | | United States Population | | |
|---|---|---|---|---|---|---|---|
| Year | EUB* | Methodists | Total | % Change | Number | % Change | % UMC** |
| 1790 | — | 57,858 | 57,858 | — | 3,929,214 | — | 1.5 |
| 1800 | — | 65,181 | 65,181 | 12.7 | 5,308,483 | 35.1 | 1.2 |
| 1810 | 528 | 174,560 | 175,088 | 168.6 | 7,239,881 | 36.4 | 2.4 |
| 1820 | 10,992 | 257,736 | 268,728 | 53.5 | 9,638,453 | 33.1 | 2.8 |
| 1830 | 23,245 | 478,053 | 501,298 | 86.5 | 12,866,020 | 33.5 | 3.9 |
| 1840 | 38,992 | 855,761 | 894,753 | 78.5 | 17,069,453 | 32.7 | 5.2 |
| 1850 | 61,175 | 1,185,902 | 1,247,077 | 39.4 | 23,191,876 | 35.9 | 5.4 |
| 1860 | 141,841 | 1,661,086 | 1,802,927 | 44.6 | 31,443,321 | 35.6 | 5.7 |
| 1870 | 190,034 | 1,821,908 | 2,011,943 | 11.6 | 38,558,371 | 22.6 | 5.2 |
| 1880 | 270,032 | 2,693,691 | 2,963,723 | 47.3 | 50,189,209 | 30.2 | 5.9 |
| 1890 | 346,751 | 3,441,675 | 3,788,426 | 27.8 | 62,979,766 | 25.5 | 6.0 |
| 1900 | 423,699 | 4,226,327 | 4,650,026 | 22.7 | 76,212,168 | 21.0 | 6.1 |
| 1910 | 498,551 | 5,073,200 | 5,571,751 | 19.8 | 92,228,496 | 21.0 | 6.0 |
| 1920 | 609,519 | 6,140,318 | 6,748,837 | 21.1 | 106,021,537 | 15.0 | 6.5 |
| 1930 | 667,294 | 7,319,125 | 7,986,419 | 18.3 | 123,202,624 | 16.2 | 6.5 |
| 1940 | 663,817 | 7,682,187 | 8,346,004 | 4.5 | 132,164,569 | 7.3 | 6.3 |
| 1950 | 801,105 | 8,935,647 | 9,736,752 | 16.7 | 151,323,175 | 14.5 | 6.4 |
| 1960 | 763,380 | 9,884,484 | 10,647,864 | 9.4 | 179,323,175 | 18.5 | 5.9 |
| 1970 | — | — | 10,671,774 | 0.2 | 203,211,926 | 13.3 | 5.3 |
| 1980 | — | — | 9,519,407 | −10.8 | 226,505,000 | 11.5 | 4.2 |
| 1990 | — | — | 8,853,455 | −7.0 | 248,709,873 | 9.8 | 3.6 |

*Evangelical United Brethren
**United Methodist Church

United Methodist Membership Growth (percent), 1790–1990

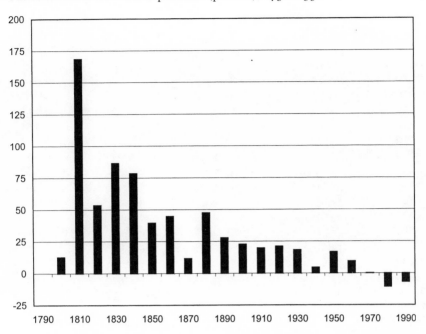

United Methodists' Share of U.S. Population (percent), 1790–1990

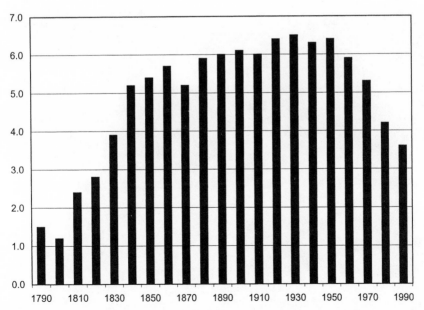

## Methodist Membership in Great Britain and Ireland, 1770–1990

| | Great Britain | | Ireland | |
| --- | --- | --- | --- | --- |
| | *Methodists* | *% Change* | *Methodists* | *% Change* |
| 1770 | 26,282 | — | 3,124 | — |
| 1780 | 37,721 | 43.5 | 6,109 | 95.6 |
| 1790 | 57,657 | 52.9 | 14,106 | 130.9 |
| 1800 | 96,078 | 66.6 | 19,292 | 36.8 |
| 1810 | 145,210 | 51.1 | 27,801 | 44.1 |
| 1820 | 208,412 | 43.5 | 36,527 | 31.4 |
| 1830 | 302,048 | 44.9 | 36,903 | 1.0 |
| 1840 | 451,433 | 49.5 | 42,133 | 14.2 |
| 1850 | 518,156 | 14.8 | 31,766 | −24.6 |
| 1860 | 525,332 | 1.4 | 38,201 | 20.3 |
| 1870 | 602,727 | 14.7 | 28,028 | −36.1 |
| 1880 | 653,403 | 8.4 | 24,463 | −12.7 |
| 1890 | 726,106 | 11.1 | 25,365 | 3.7 |
| 1900 | 770,406 | 6.1 | 27,745 | 9.4 |
| 1910 | 841,294 | 9.2 | 29,357 | 5.8 |
| 1920 | 801,721 | −5.0 | 27,247 | −7.2 |
| 1930 | 841,462 | 5.0 | 30,087 | 10.4 |
| 1940 | 792,192 | −5.9 | 31,053 | 3.2 |
| 1950 | 744,815 | −6.0 | 31,933 | 2.8 |
| 1960 | 728,589 | −2.2 | 31,909 | −0.1 |
| 1970 | 617,018 | −15.3 | — | — |
| 1980 | 487,972 | −20.9 | — | — |
| 1990 | 424,540 | −13.0 | — | — |

Methodist Membership Growth in Great Britain and Ireland (percent),
1770–1990

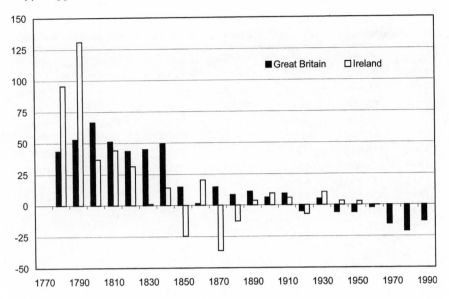

Five-Year Growth Rates of Methodism in the United States, Great Britain, and Ireland, 1775–1830

| | United States | | Great Britain | | Ireland | |
|---|---|---|---|---|---|---|
| | Methodists | % Change | Methodists | % Change | Methodists | % Change |
| 1775 | 3,148 | — | 30,760 | — | 4,237 | — |
| 1780 | 8,504 | 170.1 | 37,721 | 22.6 | 6,109 | 44.2 |
| 1785 | 18,000 | 111.7 | 44,614 | 18.3 | 7,817 | 28.0 |
| 1790 | 57,631 | 220.2 | 57,657 | 29.2 | 14,106 | 80.5 |
| 1795 | 60,291 | 4.6 | 74,931 | 30.0 | 15,266 | 8.2 |
| 1800 | 64,894 | 7.6 | 96,078 | 28.2 | 19,292 | 26.4 |
| 1805 | 119,945 | 84.8 | 106,862 | 11.2 | 23,321 | 20.1 |
| 1810 | 174,560 | 45.5 | 145,210 | 35.9 | 28,801 | 19.2 |
| 1815 | 211,165 | 21.0 | 189,579 | 30.6 | 29,357 | 5.6 |
| 1820 | 259,890 | 23.1 | 208,412 | 9.9 | 36,527 | 24.4 |
| 1825 | 347,195 | 33.6 | 272,612 | 30.8 | 34,217 | −6.3 |
| 1830 | 476,153 | 37.1 | 302,048 | 10.8 | 36,903 | 7.8 |

Five-Year Growth Rates of Methodism in the United States, Great Britain, and Ireland (percent), 1775–1830

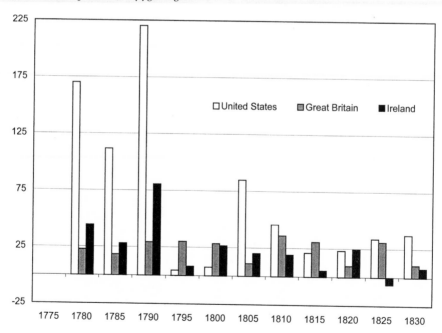

# Chronology

| | |
|---|---|
| 1692 | Society for the Reformation of Manners founded. |
| 1698 | Society for the Promotion of Christian Knowledge founded in London. |
| 1703 | John Wesley born at Epworth in Lincolnshire. |
| 1707 | Charles Wesley born at Epworth in Lincolnshire. |
| 1714 | Birth of George Whitefield in Gloucester. |
| 1720 | John Wesley matriculates at Christ Church, Oxford. |
| 1724 | John Wesley receives his baccalaureate degree. |
| 1726 | John Wesley elected Fellow of Lincoln College, Oxford. |
| 1727 | John Wesley receives his M.A. |
| 1728 | John Wesley ordained a priest in the Church of England (September 22). |
| 1729 | William Law's *Serious Call to a Devout and Holy Life* published. |
| | Oxford Methodists appear. |
| 1735 | John and Charles Wesley appointed as missionaries to Georgia by the Society for the Propagation of the Gospel in Foreign Parts. In February 1736 they arrive in Georgia, where they encounter German Pietists (Moravians and Salzburgers). |
| | Howell Harris undergoes a religious experience and becomes an itinerant evangelist in Wales. |
| 1736 | Charles Wesley returns to England. |
| 1737 | John Wesley publishes *A Collection of Psalms and Hymns* in Georgia. |
| | Publication of Jonathan Edwards's *Faithful Narrative,* an account of the Northampton revival of 1735. |
| | John Wesley leaves Georgia under controversial circumstances (December); arrives in England early in 1738. |
| 1738–39 | Whitefield's first tour of America. |

1738      Organization of the Fetter Lane Society in London under the
          leadership of Peter Böhler.

          John Wesley experiences assurance of sins forgiven at a society
          meeting in Aldersgate Street (May 24).

          Wesley visits Moravian community at Herrnhut and Pietist
          stronghold at Halle.

1739      Bristol revival; Wesley begins open-air preaching.

          Wesley acquires the Foundery in London and begins holding
          services there.

          Conversion of Selina, Countess of Huntingdon.
          Kingswood School founded to educate the sons of Methodist
          families.

1739–41   George Whitefield makes a second preaching tour of America.

1740      Wesley breaks with Moravians due to their emphasis on quietism.

          Great Awakening in North America.

1741      Dispute between Whitefield and Wesley results in the division of
          the Methodist revival between Calvinist and Arminian wings.
          John Wesley issues tickets to the band members.

1742      Wesley organizes first class meeting at Bristol and issues quarterly
          tickets to members.

1744      First Conference of Methodist preachers takes place at the
          Foundery in London.

1745      Birth of Francis Asbury.

          Methodism introduced into Scotland.

1746      Establishment of the first Methodist circuits in England.

          John Wesley publishes the first volume of *Sermons on Several
          Occasions* (volume 2 published in 1748; volume 3 in 1750; volume
          4 in 1760).

1747      Birth of Thomas Coke (d. 1814).

          John Wesley makes his first trip to Ireland.

1749      John Wesley begins publication of *A Christian Library*, completed
          in 1755.

          Anglican Bishop Lavington of Exeter attacks the Methodists in *The
          Enthusiasm of the Methodists and Papists Compar'd*.

1755      Wesley's *Explanatory Notes Upon the New Testament* published.

1756–63   Seven Years' War.

1758      John Wesley baptizes two African-American slaves.

1760        Methodist colonists arrive in America.

            Philip and Margaret Embury and Paul and Barbara Heck
            emigrate from Ireland to New York.

            John Strawbridge settles in Maryland and begins itinerating,
            organizing a class around 1763 and a society several years later.

            Nathaniel Gilbert introduces Methodism into the West Indies,
            forming a society among his slaves in Antigua.

1765        Wesley's sermon *The Scripture Way of Salvation* published.

1766        Philip Embury and Barbara Heck establish first Methodist society
            in America in New York.

            The first Methodist mission in the future Dominion of Canada
            begins with the arrival in Newfoundland of Laurence Coughlan,
            an Irishman.

1768        John Street Church built in New York City.

1769        Methodist Conference in England sends Richard Boardman and
            Joseph Pilmore as the first Methodist itinerant preachers in
            America.

1770        George Whitefield dies in Newburyport, Massachusetts.

            Mary Evans Thorne appointed class leader by Joseph Pilmore,
            becoming the first woman in the colonies to hold such a position.

1771        Francis Asbury and Richard Wright sent to America.

            John Fletcher's *Checks to Antinomianism,* written to defend
            Arminian theology during the Calvinistic controversy, appears.

1773        First Methodist Conference in America takes place in
            Philadelphia, under the presidency of Thomas Rankin, whom
            Wesley had appointed as superintendent of the work in America.

1774        Wesley attacks slavery and the slave trade in *Thoughts upon Slavery.*

            Lovely Lane Chapel built in Baltimore.

1775–83     American Revolutionary War.

1775        Wesley issues *A Calm Address to our American Colonies,* condemning
            the colonists' actions.

1777        Conversion of Richard Allen.

            Thomas Coke is forced out of his parish and joins the Methodists,
            becoming Wesley's top assistant.

1778        Wesley begins the *Arminian Magazine.*

1779        Fluvanna Conference in Virginia determines to ordain Methodist
            preachers to administer the sacraments.

            Birth of Jabez Bunting in Manchester (d. 1858).

1780        Publication of *Collection of Hymns for the Use of the People Called
            Methodists.*

1781    Methodism arrives in Nova Scotia.

1784    Wesley ordains Richard Whatcoat and Thomas Vasey to be
        preachers for America and authorizes Thomas Coke to ordain
        others, including Francis Asbury.

        Christmas Conference in Baltimore and establishment of
        Methodist Episcopal Church in America; ordains general
        superintendents (subsequently called bishops) and preachers,
        and adopts Wesley's hymnbook and prayer book.

        Wesley's Deed of Declaration establishes Annual Conference as
        governing body of British Methodism.

1785    Wesley ordains preachers as elders for Scotland.

        First *Book of Discipline* published in Philadelphia.

1786    Thomas Coke arrives in the West Indies.

1788    Death of Charles Wesley.

1789    Bishops Francis Asbury and Thomas Coke visit President
        Washington.

        Methodist Book Concern established in Philadelphia.

1791    Death of John Wesley.

        Beginnings of Methodist activity in France.

1792    First General Conference of American Methodism.

        James O'Kelly secedes over episcopacy controversy to form the
        Republican Methodist Church in the United States.

1794    African-American Methodists form first separate black Methodist
        church — Bethel Church — in Philadelphia.

        Beginnings of Camp Meeting movement in North Carolina.

1795    Plan of Pacification permits Methodist itinerant preachers in
        England to administer the sacraments under certain
        circumstances.

1797    Foundation of the Methodist New Connexion following the
        expulsion of Alexander Kilham and the refusal of the Wesleyan
        Methodist Conference to permit lay representation.

        Wesleyan Conference adopts the Form of Discipline.

1799    Jabez Bunting becomes a Wesleyan preacher.

1800    Cane Ridge Camp Meeting begins the Great Revival in the West.

        General Conference issues Pastoral Letter on Slavery.

1804    Nathan Bangs ordained.

        Methodism introduced into Sweden.

1806    Methodism introduced into South Africa.

1807    First English Camp Meeting held at Mow Cop.

1808    William McKendree ordained as a bishop, the first American-born
        bishop of the Methodist Episcopal Church.

        Methodist Episcopal Church adopts a Constitution.

1811    Sidmouth's Bill, proposing increased restrictions on preaching,
        defeated in the English Parliament, partly through the efforts of
        Methodists.

        Primitive Methodist Connexion founded by revivalists Hugh
        Bourne and William Clowes.

        First Methodist missionary arrives in Sierra Leone.

1812    Toleration Act, repealing Five Mile and Conventicle Acts and
        extending scope of religious toleration, passed with the strong
        support of English Methodists.

        Methodist services and class meeting begin in Australia.

        Methodist Episcopal Church General Conference composed, for
        the first time, of elected delegates.

1813    African Union Church formed.

        Foundation of Methodist Missionary Society in England.

        Beginning of Methodist mission to Ceylon.

        Methodism introduced into Germany.

1814    Bishop Thomas Coke dies.

1815    Bible Christians formed in Cornwall by former Wesleyan
        Methodist local preacher William O'Bryan (originally called
        William Bryant).

        First Wesleyan missionary to Australia arrives in Sydney.

        African-American layman John Stewart begins mission to Wyandot
        Indians in Ohio.

1816    Organization of the African Methodist Episcopal Church in
        Philadelphia with Richard Allen as first bishop.

        Death of Francis Asbury.

1817    Beginning of Methodist missions in India.

        Mission to Wyandot Indians in Ohio established.

        Jarena Lee, first African Methodist Episcopal female preacher,
        begins her preaching career.

1820    General Conference confirms the foundation of the Methodist
        Missionary Society in America.

        Reformers debate the role of bishops and laity in the Methodist
        Episcopal Church.

        Wesleyan Methodists establish mission to Gambia.

1821    African Methodist Episcopal Zion Church formed.

1822    Daniel Coker organizes freed slaves en route to Liberia into a
        Methodist society.

| 1823 | First Methodist weekly newspaper, *Zion's Herald*, begins publication. |
|------|---|
| 1824 | African Methodist Episcopal Church begins mission work in Haiti and the Dominican Republic. |
| 1825 | Reverend Timothy Merritt publishes his *Christian's Manual*, a treatise on Christian perfection. |
| 1827 | Dispute over the purchase of an organ for Brunswick Chapel, Leeds, results in secession and the formation of the Protestant Methodist Connection the following year. |
| 1828 | Methodist Episcopal Church "Reformers" leave to form the associated Methodist Churches. |
| 1829 | Primitive Methodists begin mission to America. |
| 1830 | Methodist Protestant Church founded in the United States. |
| 1832 | Beginning of mission to Fiji Islands. |
| 1833 | Melville Cox, first American Methodist missionary overseas, is sent to Liberia. |
|      | Jason Lee travels west to establish a mission in Oregon. |
| 1834 | Dispute among English Methodists over the formation of a theological institution with Jabez Bunting as president leads to the formation of the Wesleyan Methodist Association. |
|      | Sophronia Farrington becomes the first unmarried Methodist woman missionary to arrive in Liberia. |
| 1835 | Methodist mission in South America established in Brazil. |
|      | Methodist church established in Fiji. |
|      | Methodist mission activity begins in Ghana. |
| 1836 | Sarah Lankford, sister of Phoebe Palmer, begins the Tuesday Prayer Meeting in her New York City residence, an event most commonly associated with Palmer. |
| 1837 | Ann Wilkins goes to Liberia as a missionary. |
| 1839 | Methodists in New England establish the first "Biblical Institute" for the training of preachers (later to become the Boston University School of Theology). |
|      | The Methodist Episcopal Church acquires Wesleyan Female College, Macon, Georgia, the first institution to grant full collegiate degrees to women. |
|      | Timothy Merritt begins publishing *Guide to Christian Perfection*, a key holiness publication. |
|      | Methodist missions in Switzerland begin. |
| 1841 | *The Ladies' Repository*, the first Methodist periodical for women, commences publication. |

| 1842 | Orange Scott and other abolitionists secede from the Methodist Episcopal Church, leading to the formation of the Wesleyan Methodist Connection the following year. |
| | First Methodist church built in Argentina. |
| 1843 | Methodism introduced into Hong Kong. |
| | Phoebe Palmer publishes *The Way of Holiness*. |
| 1844 | Schism between northern and southern Methodists in the United States over the issue of slavery leads to the Plan of Separation. |
| | The New York Ladies' Home Missionary Society is organized. |
| | Indian Mission to the Oklahoma Territory is formed. |
| 1845 | Methodist Episcopal Church, South (MECS) is organized. |
| 1846 | First annual conference of the Methodist Episcopal Church, South. |
| 1846–49 | Flysheets controversy leads to expulsion of several ministers and schism with English Wesleyan Methodist Connection. |
| 1847 | Methodist missions established in China. |
| | The Methodist Episcopal Church, South, commences publishing *Southern Ladies' Companion*. |
| 1848 | The Ladies' China Missionary Society of Baltimore is organized. |
| | The Methodist Episcopal Church, South, begins mission work in China. |
| 1849 | Establishment of Methodist German mission in Bremen. |
| | Jarena Lee's *Journal* is published. |
| 1850 | Five Points Mission is established in New York City. |
| 1853 | Beginning of Methodist missions in Norway. |
| | First Methodist class meetings in Portugal. |
| | Benigno Cardenas preaches the first Methodist sermon in Spanish in Santa Fe, New Mexico. |
| 1855 | Australasian Conference formed. |
| 1856 | American Methodist missions established in India. |
| 1857 | United Methodist Free Churches formed. |
| 1858 | Women's Missionary Auxiliary established in England. |
| 1859 | First Methodist society organized in Denmark. |
| 1860 | Free Methodist Church formed by those who seceded from the Methodist Episcopal Church over issues of Christian perfection, episcopal authority, and free pews. |
| | British Methodists inaugurate missions to Italy. |
| 1861 | Methodist missions to Kenya begin. |

1861–65   American Civil War.

1864   Full clergy rights extended to black preachers in the Methodist Episcopal Church.

1865   William and Catherine Booth begin work in London slums, leading to the foundation of the Salvation Army.

1866   Methodist Protestant Church ordains Helenor M. Davison as a deacon, probably the first woman ordained in the American Methodist tradition.

Methodist Episcopal Church, South, inaugurates lay representation at Annual and General Conferences.

1867   African Methodist Episcopal Church opens Wilberforce University in Ohio.

National Campmeeting Association for the Promotion of Holiness formed by Methodist Episcopal Church ministers in the United States.

Otis Gibson begins work with Chinese immigrants in California (account published in 1870).

1868   Annie Whitmeyer establishes the Ladies and Pastors Christian Union.

1869   Woman's Foreign Missionary Society founded by the Methodist Episcopal Church.

Isabella Thoburn and Clara Swain leave for missionary work in India.

1870   Methodist preaching in Austria begins.

Colored Methodist Episcopal Church organized (name changed to Christian Methodist Episcopal Church in 1952).

1871   Alejo Hernendez becomes the first Mexican ordained by a Methodist body, the Methodist Episcopal Church, South.

1872   The Methodist Episcopal Church adopts lay representation at General Conference.

1873   William and Clementina Butler begin Methodist mission in Mexico.

American and Canadian Methodists begin missionary work in Japan.

1874   The Women's Christian Temperance Union is formed.

1875   Methodist worship begins in New Guinea.

1876   Anna Oliver is the first woman to receive a degree from Boston University School of Theology.

1877   William Taylor brings Methodism to Chile and Peru.

1879   Bishop James M. Thoburn begins mission work in Burma.

1880    Anna Howard Shaw and Anna Oliver denied ordination by
        General Conference of the Methodist Episcopal Church. Shaw is
        ordained later that year by the New York Conference of the
        Methodist Protestant Church.

1882    Board of Church Extension is started by the Methodist Episcopal
        Church.

1884    Methodist Episcopal Church establishes missions in Korea.

        General Conference of the African Methodist Episcopal Church
        begins licensing women as local preachers for evangelistic work.

1885    William Taylor establishes Methodist missions in Angola and
        Congo.

        James Thoburn begins Methodist missions in Singapore and
        Malaysia.

        The Spanish Mission Conference of the Methodist Episcopal
        Church is organized.

        The Mexican Frontier Conference of the Methodist Episcopal
        Church, South, is organized.

# Notes

## INTRODUCTION

1. The story is recounted in Dorothea Price Hughes, *The Life of Hugh Price Hughes* (London: Hodder and Stoughton, 1904). It should be pointed out that in 2003 Oxford University finally unveiled a memorial to John Wesley in Lincoln College to celebrate the three-hundredth anniversary of his birth. See also *Essays and Reviews* (London: Longman, Green, Longman, and Roberts, 1861). The other contributors were Frederick Temple, Rowland Williams, Baden Powell, Henry Bristow Wilson, C. W. Goodwin, and Benjamin Jowett.

2. W. J. Townsend, H. B. Workman, and George Eayrs, eds., *A New History of Methodism*, 2 vols. (London: Hodder and Stoughton, 1909); David Martin, *Pentecostalism: The World Their Parish* (Oxford: Blackwell, 2001); Grant Wacker, *Heaven Below: Early Pentecostals and American Culture* (Cambridge: Harvard University Press, 2001); Philip Jenkins, *The Next Christendom: The Coming of Global Christianity* (New York: Oxford University Press, 2002), 7–8.

3. Townsend, Workman, and Eayrs, eds., *A New History*, v; Mark Pattison, "Tendencies of Religious Thought in England, 1688–1750," in *Essays and Reviews*, 255. Excellent histories of the rise of Methodism exist for most of the countries and regions in which it took root. Among the most recent and best researched are Neil Semple, *The Lord's Dominion: The History of Canadian Methodism* (Montreal: McGill-Queen's University Press, 1996); William Westfall, *Two Worlds: The Protestant Culture of Nineteenth-Century Ontario* (Montreal: McGill-Queen's University Press, 1989); A. D. Gilbert, *Religion and Society in Industrial England: Church, Chapel, and Social Change, 1740–1914* (New York: Longman, 1976); Dee E. Andrews, *The Methodists and Revolutionary America, 1760–1800: The Shaping of an Evangelical Culture* (Princeton: Princeton University Press, 2000); John H. Wigger, *Taking Heaven by Storm: Methodism and the Rise of Popular Christianity in America* (New York: Oxford University Press, 1998); Nathan O. Hatch, *The Democratization of American Christianity* (New Haven: Yale University Press, 1989); Nathan O. Hatch and John H. Wigger, eds., *Methodism and the Shaping of American Culture* (Nashville: Kingswood, 2001); Arnold D. Hunt, *This Side of Heaven: A History of Methodism in South Australia* (Adelaide: Lutheran Publishing, 1985); W. R. Ward, *The Protestant Evangelical Awakening* (Cambridge: Cambridge University Press, 1992); and David Hempton, *The Religion of the People: Methodism and Popular Religion, c. 1750–1900* (New York: Routledge,

1996). For an influential recent account of African-American Methodism see Sylvia R. Frey and Betty Wood, *Come Shouting to Zion: African American Protestantism in the American South and British Caribbean to 1830* (Chapel Hill: University of North Carolina Press, 1998).

4. E. P. Thompson, *The Making of the English Working Class,* new ed. (Harmondsworth: Penguin, 1968). For a recent analysis of E. P. Thompson's views on Methodism see David Hempton and John Walsh, "E. P. Thompson and Methodism," in *God and Mammon: Protestants, Money, and the Market, 1790–1860,* ed. Mark A. Noll (New York: Oxford University Press, 2001), 99–120.

5. See David D. Hall, ed., *Lived Religion in America: Toward a History of Practice* (Princeton: Princeton University Press, 1997).

## CHAPTER 1: COMPETITION AND SYMBIOSIS

1. Margaret J. Wheatley, *Leadership and the New Science: Discovering Order in a Chaotic World* (San Francisco: Berrett-Koehler, 1999). Good examples of Methodist history written largely from within the tradition include Richard P. Heitzenrater, *Wesley and the People Called Methodists* (Nashville: Abingdon, 1995), and John C. Bowmer, *Pastor and People: A Study of Church and Ministry in Wesleyan Methodism from the Death of John Wesley (1791) to the Death of Jabez Bunting (1858)* (London: Epworth, 1975).

2. Ronald Arbuthnott Knox, *Enthusiasm: A Chapter in the History of Religion, with Special Reference to the Seventeenth and Eighteenth Centuries* (Oxford: Clarendon, 1950); E. P. Thompson, *The Making of the English Working Class* (Harmondsworth: Penguin, 1968); John Kent, *Wesley and the Wesleyans* (Cambridge: Cambridge University Press, 2001); Bernard Semmel, *The Methodist Revolution* (New York: Basic, 1973).

3. W. R. Ward, *Christianity Under the Ancien Régime, 1648–1789* (Cambridge: Cambridge University Press, 1999), 250. See also W. R. Ward, *Faith and Faction* (London: Epworth, 1993); W. R. Ward, *The Protestant Evangelical Awakening* (Cambridge: Cambridge University Press, 1992); John Walsh, " 'Methodism' and the Origins of English-Speaking Evangelicalism," in *Evangelicalism: Comparative Studies in Popular Protestantism in North America, the British Isles, and Beyond, 1700–1990,* ed. Mark A. Noll, David W. Bebbington, and George A. Rawlyk (New York: Oxford University Press, 1994); John Walsh, Colin Haydon, and Stephen Taylor, *The Church of England, c. 1689–c. 1833: From Toleration to Tractarianism* (Cambridge: Cambridge University Press, 1993).

4. Colin Podmore, *The Moravian Church in England, 1728–1760* (Oxford: Clarendon, 1998); Frederick A. Dreyer, *The Genesis of Methodism* (London: Associated University Presses, 1999). See also J. C. S. Mason, *The Moravian Church and the Missionary Awakening in England* (London: The Royal Historical Society, Boydell, 2001); Susan O'Brien, "A Transatlantic Community of Saints: The Great Awakening and the First Evangelical Networks, 1735–1755," *American Historical Review* 91 (October 1986): 811–32; Richard Carwardine, *Transatlantic Revivalism: Popular Evangelicalism in Britain and America, 1790–1865* (Westport, Conn.: Greenwood, 1978). A more thorough analysis of the Methodist message follows in Chapter 3.

5. The best treatment of the early meetings of the Fetter Lane Society is Podmore, *The Moravian Church in England.* See also Arthur J. Freeman, *An Ecumeni-*

*cal Theology of the Heart: The Theology of Count Nicholas Ludwig von Zinzendorf* (Bethlehem, Pa.: The Moravian Church in America, 1998). Good introductions to Wesley's theology include Randy L. Maddox, *Responsible Grace: John Wesley's Practical Theology* (Nashville: Abingdon, 1994), and Albert C. Outler, ed., *John Wesley* (New York: Oxford University Press, 1964). For most aspects of Wesley's theology, the best approach is to consult the original texts and the excellent introductions in the new Abingdon edition of Wesley's *Works*.

6. Benjamin Ingham and Richard P. Heitzenrater, *Diary of an Oxford Methodist, Benjamin Ingham, 1733–1734* (Durham: Duke University Press, 1985); Simon Ross Valentine, *John Bennet and the Origins of Methodism and the Evangelical Revival in England* (Lanham, Md.: Scarecrow, 1997).

7. E. A. Wrigley and R. S. Schofield, *Population History of England, 1541–1870: A Reconstruction* (London: Edward Arnold, 1981); Maxine Berg, *The Age of Manufactures: Industry, Innovation, and Work in Britain, 1700–1820* (Oxford: Blackwell in association with Fontana, 1985); Charles Sellers, *Market Revolution: Jacksonian America, 1815–1846* (New York: Oxford University Press, 1991); Neil McKendrick, John Brewer, and J. H. Plumb, *The Birth of a Consumer Society: The Commercialization of Eighteenth-Century England* (Bloomington: Indiana University Press, 1982); David Cannadine, *Ornamentalism: How the British Saw Their Empire* (London: Allen Lane, 2001); Peter J. Marshall, ed., *The Oxford History of the British Empire: The Eighteenth Century* (London: Oxford University Press, 1998); R. R. Palmer, *The Age of the Democratic Revolution: A Political History of Europe and America, 1760–1800* (Princeton: Princeton University Press, 1959); and Bret E. Carroll, *The Routledge Historical Atlas of Religion in America* (New York: Routledge, 2000).

8. Sellers, *Market Revolution*. See Richard Carwardine, "'Antinomians' and 'Arminians': Methodists and the Market Revolution," in *The Market Revolution in America*, ed. Melvyn Stokes and Stephen Conway (Charlottesville: University of Virginia Press, 1996), 282–307.

9. Some of the best local studies of Methodist growth from different ideological perspectives are James Obelkevich, *Religion and Rural Society: South Lindsey, 1825–1875* (Oxford: Clarendon, 1976); William Henry Williams, *The Garden of American Methodism: The Delmarva Peninsula, 1769–1820* (Wilmington, Del.: Published for the Peninsula Conference of the United Methodist Church by Scholarly Resources, 1984); and Curtis D. Johnson, *Islands of Holiness: Rural Religion in Upstate New York, 1790–1860* (Ithaca: Cornell University Press, 1989).

10. Frank Baker, *John Wesley and the Church of England* (New York: Abingdon, 1970); William H. Williams, "The Attraction of Methodism: The Delmarva Peninsula as a Case Study, 1769–1820," in *Perspectives on American Methodism: Interpretive Essays*, ed. Russell E. Richey, Kenneth E. Rowe, and Jean Miller Schmidt (Nashville: Abingdon, 1993), 31–45; David Hempton, *The Religion of the People: Methodism and Popular Religion, c. 1750–1900* (New York: Routledge, 1996), 29–48; and Neil Semple, *The Lord's Dominion: The History of Canadian Methodism* (Montreal: McGill-Queen's University Press, 1996), 42–52.

11. Geraint H. Jenkins, *The Foundations of Modern Wales: Wales, 1642–1780* (Oxford: Clarendon, 1987); Geraint H. Jenkins, *Literature, Religion, and Society in Wales, 1660–1730* (Cardiff: University of Wales Press, 1978); I. M. Green, *The Christian's Abc: Catechism and Catechizing in England, c. 1530–1740* (Oxford: Clarendon, 1996); I. M. Green, *Print and Protestantism in Early Modern England* (Oxford:

Clarendon, 2000); Peter Virgin, *The Church in an Age of Negligence: Ecclesiastical Structure and Problems of Church Reform, 1700–1840* (Edinburgh: James Clarke, 1989); David Hempton and Myrtle Hill, *Evangelical Protestantism in Ulster Society, 1740–1890* (London: Routledge, 1992); James C. Deming, "Protestantism and Society in France: Revivalism and the French Reformed Church in the Department of the Gard, 1815–1848" (Ph.D. diss., University of Notre Dame, 1989); and A. J. Hayes and D. A. Gowland, eds., *Scottish Methodism in the Early Victorian Period* (Edinburgh: Edinburgh University Press, 1981).

12. Robert Currie, Alan Gilbert, and Lee Horsley, *Churches and Churchgoers: Patterns of Church Growth in the British Isles Since 1700* (Oxford: Clarendon, 1977); John Dennis Gay, *The Geography of Religion in England* (London: Duckworth, 1971). For a detailed study of how this worked out in practice see Judith Jago, *Aspects of the Georgian Church: Visitation Studies of the Diocese of York, 1761–1776* (London: Associated University Presses, 1997); Semple, *The Lord's Dominion*, 28–29.

13. Dee E. Andrews, *The Methodists and Revolutionary America, 1760–1800: The Shaping of an Evangelical Culture* (Princeton: Princeton University Press, 2000), 35–38; W. J. Townsend, H. B. Workman, and George Eayrs, eds., *A New History of Methodism* (London: Hodder and Stoughton, 1909), 2:237–81; and Ian Breward, *A History of the Churches in Australasia* (Oxford: Oxford University Press, 2001).

14. Wesley's patriotic *A Calm Address to Our American Colonies* sold more than forty thousand copies within a month of its publication. See Andrews, *The Methodists and Revolutionary America*, 49–50. For an authoritative treatment of this much-misunderstood aspect of Wesley's thought see John Walsh, "John Wesley and the Community of Goods," in *Protestant Evangelicalism: Britain, Ireland, Germany, and America, c. 1750–1950*, ed. Keith Robbins (Oxford: Basil Blackwell, 1990). For an excellent treatment of Wesley's ideological polarity between enthusiasm and enlightenment see Henry D. Rack, *Reasonable Enthusiast: John Wesley and the Rise of Methodism*, 2nd ed. (Nashville: Abingdon, 1992).

15. Peter J. Yalden, "Nonconformity in North Shropshire: The Evolution of Chapel Communities in a Rural Society, c. 1650–1900," 2 vols. (Ph.D. diss., University of New South Wales, 1997).

16. Paul Gustaf Faler, "Workingmen, Mechanics, and Social Change: Lynn, Massachusetts, 1800–1860" (Ph.D. diss., University of Wisconsin, 1971), 64–123; James Mudge, *The New England Conference of the Methodist Episcopal Church* (Boston: Published by the Conference, 1910), 35–42.

17. Faler, "Workingmen, Mechanics, and Social Change," 474.

18. The painting is in the New York Metropolitan Museum of Art, Rogers Fund, 1942. The name of the artist is not entirely certain. The painting is probably by Svinin (ca. 1811–13), but may possibly have been painted by a young German artist called John Lewis Krimmel, who also painted satirical street scenes of Philadelphia. The past decade has seen the appearance of a number of fine studies of African-American Methodism, a subject that was once a historiographical lacuna of serious proportions. See Cynthia Lynn Lyerly, *Methodism and the Southern Mind, 1770–1810* (New York: Oxford University Press, 1998); Sylvia R. Frey and Betty Wood, *Come Shouting to Zion: African American Protestantism in the American South and British Caribbean to 1830* (Chapel Hill: University of North Carolina Press, 1998); Milton C. Sernett, ed., *African American Religious History: A Documentary Witness*, 2nd ed. (Durham: Duke University Press, 1999); John H. Wigger, *Taking Heaven by*

*Storm: Methodism and the Rise of Popular Christianity in America* (New York: Oxford University Press, 1998); Andrews, *The Methodists and Revolutionary America*. Some older works still retain their value, however. See Albert J. Raboteau, *Slave Religion: The "Invisible Institution" in the Antebellum South* (New York: Oxford University Press, 1978).

19. Lawrence W. Levine, "Slave Songs and Slave Consciousness: An Exploration in Neglected Sources," in *African-American Religion: Interpretive Essays in History and Culture*, ed. Timothy Earl Fulop and Albert J. Raboteau (New York: Routledge, 1997).

20. Ann Taves, *Fits, Trances, and Visions: Experiencing Religion and Explaining Experience from Wesley to James* (Princeton: Princeton University Press, 1999), 116–17.

21. Thomas Shaw, *A History of Cornish Methodism* (Truro, U.K.: D. Bradford Barton, 1967), 65–66.

22. David Luker, "Revivalism in Theory and Practice: The Case of Cornish Methodism," *Journal of Ecclesiastical History* 37, no. 4 (1986): 605. For a helpful survey of the results of the 1851 religious census in England and Wales see Bruce I. Coleman, *The Church of England in the Mid-Nineteenth Century* (London: The Historical Association, 1980).

23. See Lambeth Palace Library Mss, Secker Papers, 8 (Methodists), folios 4–5. Much of this correspondence has been reproduced in Oliver A. Beckerlegge, "The Lavington Correspondence," *Proceedings of the Wesley Historical Society* 42 (1980): 101–11, 139–49, and 167–80. See also John Rule, "Methodism, Popular Beliefs, and Village Culture in Cornwall, 1800–1850," in *Popular Culture and Custom in Nineteenth-Century England*, ed. Robert D. Storch (London: Croom Helm, 1982); Edward P. Thompson, "Anthropology and the Discipline of Historical Context," *Midland History* 1, no. 3 (1972): 41–55, and "Patrician Society, Plebeian Culture," *Journal of Social History* 7, no. 4 (1974): 382–405.

24. W. R. Ward, ed., *The Early Correspondence of Jabez Bunting, 1820–1829* (London: Royal Historical Society, 1972), 181–82.

25. Shaw, *A History of Cornish Methodism*, 68–75; Arnold D. Hunt, *This Side of Heaven: A History of Methodism in South Australia* (Adelaide: Lutheran Publishing, 1985), 117–30.

26. For a fuller treatment of Irish Methodism than is possible here see Hempton, *The Religion of the People*, 29–48; John Vickers, *Thomas Coke: Apostle of Methodism* (London: Epworth, 1969), 307; University of London School of Oriental and African Studies, Methodist Missionary Mss, boxes 1–3 and 74–75. Additional missionary correspondence is to be found in the Irish Wesley Historical Society Mss, currently located in the Public Records Office of Northern Ireland; Charles H. Crookshank, *History of Methodism in Ireland*, vol. 2, *The Middle Age* (London: T. Woolmer, 1886), 159–236. Crookshank's account is virtually an extended paraphrase of the letters sent by the Irish missioners to headquarters in London; Public Records Office of Northern Ireland Mss, Ouseley Collection CR 6/3 ACC 13019, VII folio 12. The phrase "the psychic process of counter revolution" is taken from Thompson, *The Making of the English Working Class*.

27. Norman W. Taggart, *The Irish in World Methodism, 1760–1900* (London: Epworth, 1986), 142. During his earlier sojourn in Cape Colony, McKenny wrote, "long before I left the Cape I was convinced that the interior of Africa is not likely

to be a good soil for Methodism, as it is already almost overrun with Calvinism"; ibid., 130.

28. Robert Samuel Moore, *Pit-Men, Preachers, and Politics: The Effects of Methodism in a Durham Mining Community* (Cambridge: Cambridge University Press, 1974).

29. Townsend, Workman, and Eayrs, eds., *A New History of Methodism*, 2:283–360.

30. David Martin, *Pentecostalism: The World Their Parish* (Oxford: Blackwell, 2001). See the gender proportions of Methodist societies in New York, Philadelphia, and Baltimore in Andrews, *The Methodists and Revolutionary America*, 247–48. See also Clive D. Field, "The Social Composition of English Methodism to 1830: A Membership Analysis," *Bulletin of the John Rylands University Library of Manchester* 76, no. 1 (1994): 153–69. Based on a large sample of Methodist members, Field estimated a female mean of 57.7 percent. Dickson D. Bruce, Jr., *And They All Sang Hallelujah: Plain-Folk Camp-Meeting Religion, 1800–1845* (Knoxville: University of Tennessee Press, 1974). The extent of millenarian ideas within Methodism is the source of some disagreement. For a contrary view to the one expressed here, see Kenneth G. C. Newport, *Apocalypse and Millennium: Studies in Biblical Eisegesis* (Cambridge: Cambridge University Press, 2000).

31. Sellers, *Market Revolution*, 202–36; Arnold Bennett, *The Old Wives' Tale* (New York: Hodder and Stoughton, 1909). See the analysis of Methodist consolidation and decline in Chapter 8.

## Chapter 2: Enlightenment and Enthusiasm

1. See for example David Hempton, "Enlightenment and Faith," in *The Oxford History of the British Isles: The Eighteenth Century*, ed. Paul Langford (Oxford: Oxford University Press, 2002). Methodism is conspicuous by its absence in most of the standard histories of religion during the Enlightenment. See Knud Haakonssen, *Enlightenment and Religion: Rational Dissent in Eighteenth-Century Britain* (Cambridge: Cambridge University Press, 1996). See also Peter Harrison, *"Religion" and the Religions in English Enlightenment* (Cambridge: Cambridge University Press, 1990). This is the view in E. P. Thompson, *The Making of the English Working Class* (Harmondsworth: Penguin, 1968). For a helpful analysis of contemporary satire against Methodist enthusiasm see Albert M. Lyles, *Methodism Mocked: The Satiric Reaction to Methodism in the Eighteenth Century* (London: Epworth, 1960).

2. Edmund Gibson, *Observations Upon the Conduct and Behaviour of a Certain Sect Usually Distinguished by the Name of Methodists* (London, 1744), 4–13; George Lavington, *The Enthusiasm of Methodists and Papists Compar'd* (London, 1749–51). For the full text of Wesley's reply see G. R. Cragg, ed., *The Works of John Wesley* (Oxford: Clarendon, 1975), 11:353–436.

3. Ronald A. Knox, *Enthusiasm: A Chapter in the History of Religion* (Oxford: Clarendon, 1950), 452; Henry D. Rack, *Reasonable Enthusiast: John Wesley and the Rise of Methodism*, 2nd ed. (Nashville: Abingdon, 1992).

4. Lyles, *Methodism Mocked*, 32–43.

5. In his *Advice to People Called Methodists*, John Wesley urged his followers to "carefully avoid enthusiasm." For the fullest and most clearly argued of Wesley's writings on enthusiasm see his sermon "The Nature of Enthusiasm."

6. I owe this refinement of Wesley's position in relation to mainstream Anglicanism to John Walsh.

7. John Wesley, *Journal*, May 17, 1752, and May 29, 1743. See also John Wesley, *An Answer to the Rev. Mr. Church's Remarks on the Rev. Mr. Wesley's Last Journal, in a Letter to that Gentleman* (London, 1745), 8.

8. Wesley, *Journal*, January 17, 1739, July 13, 1741. See also Wesley, *Journal*, December 4, 1742; Wesley, "The Nature of Enthusiasm," 12; John Wesley, *The Complete English Dictionary, Explaining most of the Hard Words which are found in the Best English Writers* (London: R. Hawes, 1777); Wesley, *Journal*, December 4, 1742, December 22, 1762, February 10, 1766, and August 25, 1789.

9. W. Briggs to Charles Wesley, London, October 28, 1762. The letter is reproduced in full and with excellent textual apparatus in Gareth Lloyd and Kenneth G. C. Newport, "George Bell and Early Methodist Enthusiasm: A New Manuscript Source from the Manchester Archives," *Bulletin of the John Rylands University Library of Manchester* (1998): 89–101. To follow Wesley's responses to this challenge to Methodist discipline see W. R. Ward and Richard P. Heitzenrater, eds., *The Works of John Wesley: Journals and Diaries, The Bicentennial Edition of the Works of John Wesley*, vols. 18–23 (Nashville: Abingdon, 1988–95), vol. 21.

10. Lloyd and Newport, "George Bell," 89.

11. Gareth Lloyd, " 'A Cloud of Perfect Witnesses': John Wesley and the London Disturbances, 1760–1763," *Asbury Theological Journal* 56 (Fall 2001–Spring 2002): 117–36; Kenneth Newport, "George Bell: Prophet and Enthusiast," *Methodist History* 35:2 (January 1997); Bruce Hindmarsh, *John Newton and the English Evangelical Tradition Between the Conversions of Wesley and Wilberforce* (Oxford: Clarendon, 1996), 126–35; and W. Stephen Gunter, *The Limits of Love Divine: John Wesley's Response to Antinomianism and Enthusiasm* (Nashville: Kingswood, 1989).

12. Wesley, *Journal*, January 28, 1739; Wesley, *An Answer to the Rev. Mr. Church*.

13. For a sample of such stories see New England United Methodist Historical Society Mss., Howard Cary Dunham, "Methodists of the Olden Times" (November 19, 1888). Dunham tells the story of Benjamin Keith, a Methodist preacher on Cape Cod who soared towards heaven and was brought down to earth by his wife.

14. Frederick Dreyer, *The Genesis of Methodism* (London: Associated University Presses, 1999), 78–105; Richard E. Brantley, *Locke, Wesley, and the Method of English Romanticism* (Gainesville: University Presses of Florida, 1984); J. W. Haas, Jr., "John Wesley's Views on Science and Christianity: An Examination of the Charge of Antiscience," *Church History* 63 (1994): 378–92; and Ken MacMillan, "John Wesley and the Enlightened Historians," *Methodist History* 38 (January 2000): 121–32. See also Ted A. Campbell, "John Wesley and Conyers Middleton on Divine Intervention in History," *Church History* 55 (1986): 39–49; Joseph William Seaborn, Jr., "Wesley's Views on the Uses of History," *Wesleyan Theological Journal* 21 (1986): 129–36; Bernard Semmel, *The Methodist Revolution* (London: Heinemann, 1974); and D. W. Bebbington, *Evangelicalism in Modern Britain: A History from the 1730s to the 1980s* (London: Unwin Hyman, 1989), 20–74.

15. See Roger Anstey, *The Slave Trade and British Abolition, 1760–1810* (Atlantic Highlands, N.J.: Humanities, 1975), 240–41. I survey Methodist petitioning against slavery in "Evangelicalism and Reform, c. 1780–1832," in *Evangelical Faith and Public Zeal: Evangelicals and Society in Britain, 1780–1980*, ed. John Wolffe (London: SPCK, 1995), 17–37. See also Maldwyn Edwards, *John Wesley and the Eighteenth*

*Century* (London: Allen and Unwin, 1933), 112. For the basis of Wesley's opposition to slavery see John Wesley, *Thoughts Upon Slavery* (London, 1772). Irv Brendlinger is preparing an authoritative treatment of evangelicalism and slavery in which Wesley's emphasis on holiness is seen to be crucial to his opposition to slavery. In contrast, many Calvinists were either silent on the question of slavery or in favor of its continued existence. For a more expansive discussion of Wesley's views on society, see John Walsh, *John Wesley, 1703–1791: A Bicentennial Tribute* (Inverness: Friends of Dr. Williams's Library, 1993), 7.

16. Adam Smith, *An Inquiry into the Nature and Causes of the Wealth of Nations,* ed. Edwin Cannan (New York: Random House, 1937), 741–42.

17. Ibid., introduction by Max Lerner, viii. For an excellent treatment of Smith's views on religion see Charles L. Griswold, *Adam Smith and the Virtues of Enlightenment* (New York: Cambridge University Press, 1999); Smith, *Wealth of Nations,* 745.

18. Smith, *Wealth of Nations,* 748.

19. W. R. Ward, *Christianity Under the Ancien Régime, 1648–1789* (Cambridge: Cambridge University Press, 1999), 250. See also Andrew F. Walls, *The Missionary Movement in Christian History* (Orbis, 1996), 241.

20. W. R. Ward, *The Protestant Evangelical Awakening* (Cambridge: Cambridge University Press, 1992). See also W. R. Ward, *Faith and Faction* (London: Epworth, 1993); and W. R. Ward, "The Relations of Enlightenment and Religious Revival in Central Europe and in the English-Speaking World," in *Reform and Reformation: England and the Continent, c. 1500–c. 1750,* ed. Derek Baker, 281–305.

21. These ideas were worked out with great skill by the late Professor John Clayton in his inaugural address as Professor of Religion at Boston University. I am grateful to him for allowing me access to his address and to make use of his insights.

22. Thomas Jefferson to James Smith, Monticello, December 8, 1822. H. A. Washington, ed., *The Writings of Thomas Jefferson* (Philadelphia, 1871), 7:269–70.

23. Thomas Jefferson to Dr. Benjamin Waterhouse, Monticello, July 26, 1822, ibid., 7:252–53.

24. See Roy Porter and Mikulas Teich, *The Enlightenment in National Context* (Cambridge: Cambridge University Press 1981); Margaret Jacob, *The Radical Enlightenment: Pantheists, Freemasons, and Republicans* (London: Allen and Unwin, 1981); Dorinda Outram, *The Enlightenment* (Cambridge: Cambridge University Press, 1995); Charles Withers, "Geography, Natural History, and the Eighteenth-Century Enlightenment: Putting the World in Place," *History Workshop Journal* 39 (1995): 136–63; and David N. Livingstone and Charles W. J. Withers, eds., *Geography and Enlightenment* (Chicago: University of Chicago Press, 1999).

25. Dreyer, *Genesis of Methodism,* 78–105.

26. Ibid., 82.

27. Ibid., 104.

28. Peter Clark, *British Clubs and Societies, 1580–1800: The Origins of an Associational World* (Oxford: Clarendon, 2000), 2.

29. New England United Methodist Historical Society, Manuscript Collection, William J. Hambledon, "The Life and Labors of Rev. David Niles Bently, 1785–1884." See also Ann Taves, *Fits, Trances, and Visions: Experiencing Religion and Explaining Experience from Wesley to James* (Princeton: Princeton University Press, 1999).

## CHAPTER 3: THE MEDIUM AND THE MESSAGE

1. E. P. Thompson, *The Making of the English Working Class* (Harmondsworth: Penguin, 1968), 917–18.

2. James A. Secord, *Victorian Sensation: The Extraordinary Publication, Reception, and Secret Authorship of Vestiges of the Natural History of Creation* (Chicago: University of Chicago Press, 2000).

3. Leigh Eric Schmidt, *Hearing Things: Religion, Illusion, and the American Enlightenment* (Cambridge: Harvard University Press, 2000), 15, 56, and 57.

4. Randy L. Maddox, *Responsible Grace: John Wesley's Practical Theology* (Nashville: Abingdon, 1994).

5. According to the preliminary survey carried out by Isobel Rivers, Wesley's favorite lives for republication were David Brainerd (1718–1747), J. W. Fletcher (1729–1785), Thomas Halyburton (1674–1712), Gregory Lopez (1542–1596), and Gaston de Renty (1611–1649). Isobel Rivers, "John Wesley and Religious Biography," distributed at the tercentenary conference on John Wesley at the University of Manchester, June 2003. Dr. Rivers was primarily investigating multivolume collections of religious biographies and autobiographies in the eighteenth century. All inferences from her work are my responsibility. This section is also based upon the work of Vicki Tolar Burton, who distributed a "Summary of John Wesley's Book Inventory (1791)" at the same tercentenary conference. The inventory contained 362 titles, 254,512 books, and 14,831 Arminian magazines. Dr. Tolar Burton also supplied a careful delineation of how domain (the kind of space works were to be consumed in), genre (types of instruction), and examples of published works lined up in an all-inclusive paradigm for the pursuit of holy living.

6. New England United Methodist Historical Society Manuscripts (hereinafter NEUMHS Mss.), John Edwards Risley, "Autobiography."

7. Fanny Newell, *Diary of Fanny Newell with a Sketch of her Life* (Boston: Charles H. Peirce, 1848), 67, 79.

8. Conversion narratives are, of course, not unique to Methodism. For an earlier pattern of Puritan narratives see Patricia Caldwell, *The Puritan Conversion Narrative: The Beginnings of American Expression* (Cambridge: Cambridge University Press, 1983), and Owen C. Watkins, *The Puritan Experience: Studies in Spiritual Autobiography* (New York: Schocken, 1972).

9. Hannah Syng Bunting, *Memoir, Diary, and Letters of Miss Hannah Syng Bunting compiled by Rev. T. Merritt* (New York: T. Mason and G. Lane, 1837), 42, 56, 64, and 173–77.

10. For some of the ideas in this paragraph I am grateful to Rick Bell for access to his fine paper on deathbed scenes in Methodist magazines in eighteenth-century Britain, presented to the American Colloquium of Harvard Divinity School, October 30, 2001. Bell calculated that about one-third of deathbed accounts were written by itinerant preachers and the rest were mostly written by the Methodist laity.

11. The most authoritative volume on the content and practice of Methodist worship in the United States is Karen B. Westerfield Tucker, *American Methodist Worship* (New York: Oxford University Press, 2001). The best critical edition of Wesleyan hymns is now Franz Hildebrandt and Oliver A. Beckerlegge, eds., *A Collection of Hymns for the Use of the People Called Methodists*, vol. 7 of *The Works of John Wesley* (Nashville: Abingdon, 1983). See Bernard Lord Manning, *The Hymns of*

*Wesley and Watts* (London: Epworth, 1943); R. Newton Flew, *The Hymns of Charles Wesley: A Study of Their Structure* (London: Epworth, 1953), 10; J. Ernest Rattenbury, *The Evangelical Doctrines of Charles Wesley's Hymns* (London: Epworth, 1941), 72–74; and Carlton R. Young, *Music of the Heart: John and Charles Wesley on Music and Musicians* (Carol Stream, Ill.: Hope, 1995), 191. For a fine modern collection of essays on Charles Wesley's manifold writings see S. T. Kimbrough, Jr., *Charles Wesley: Poet and Theologian* (Nashville: Abingdon, 1992).

12. Young, *Music of the Heart*, 38; Frederick C. Gill, *Charles Wesley: The First Methodist* (Nashville: Abingdon, 1964), 52.

13. Hildebrandt and Beckerlegge, eds., *A Collection of Hymns*, 73–74.

14. Young, *Music of the Heart*, 113.

15. Hildebrandt and Beckerlegge, eds., *A Collection of Hymns*, 63.

16. James Obelkevich, Lyndal Roper, and Raphael Samuel, eds., *Disciplines of Faith: Studies in Religion, Politics, and Patriarchy* (London: Routledge, 1987); Stephen Marini, "Hymnody as History: Early Evangelical Hymns and the Recovery of American Popular Religion," *Church History* 71 (June 2002): 273–306; and Clifford Geertz, "Religion as a Cultural System," in *The Interpretation of Cultures: Selected Essays* (New York: Basic, 1973), 87–125.

17. NEUMHS Mss., Enoch Mudge (1776–1850), "Sermon Outlines"; Sarah Murch, "Book of Texts, 1817–1835"; and Daniel Webb (1778–1867), "Plans of Sermons, 1806–1807." See also the manuscript sermons of John G. Dow, "A Sketch of religious experience, call to the ministry and field of labour occupied by John G. Dow."

18. NEUMHS Mss., Daniel Webb, "Plans of Sermons" (1806).

19. NEUMHS Mss., Thomas Marcy, "Semi-Centennial Address delivered before the New England Conference at Springfield Mass. April 9 1885."

20. Ibid.; Ralph Willard Allen, "Rev. Ira M. Bidwell, 1803–1880"; Enoch Mudge, "Sermon Outlines"; and George M. Steele, "The Builders of Methodism in New England," Centennial Address, New England Conference, Springfield, 1896. Mark Noll, "The Evangelical Surge and the Significance of Religion in the Early United States, 1783–1865" (unpublished paper). I am grateful to Professor Noll for this information.

21. John H. Wigger, *Taking Heaven by Storm: Methodism and the Rise of Popular Christianity in America* (New York: Oxford University Press, 1998), 80–103; Frank Baker, "The People Called Methodists: Polity," in *A History of the Methodist Church in Great Britain* (London: Epworth, 1965), 1:218–26; Simon Ross Valentine, *John Bennet and the Origins of Methodism and the Evangelical Revival in England* (Lanham, Md.: Scarecrow, 1997), 89–91; John Wesley, *The Nature, Design, and General Rules of the United Societies* (1743); and John Wesley, *A Plain Account of the People called Methodists* (1749), 266.

22. Dee E. Andrews, *The Methodists and Revolutionary America, 1760–1800: The Shaping of an Evangelical Culture* (Princeton: Princeton University Press, 2000), 247–54; Wigger, *Taking Heaven by Storm*, 84–85.

23. NEUMHS Mss., Fanny L. Bartlett to G. F. Cox, Lima, N.Y., July 16, 1849. I am grateful to my research assistant Glen Messer for bringing this letter to my attention.

24. W. R. Ward, "Was There a Methodist Evangelistic Strategy in the Eigh-

teenth Century?" in *England's Long Reformation, 1500–1800,* ed. Nicholas Tyacke (London: UCL Press, 1998).

25. Julia Stewart Werner, *The Primitive Methodist Connexion: Its Background and Early History* (Madison: University of Wisconsin Press, 1984); Bernard A. Weisberger, *They Gathered at the River* (Boston: Little, Brown, 1958).

26. *Minutes of the Methodist Conference* (London, 1812–54), 1:9; G. F. Nuttall, "Howell Harris and the 'Grand Table': A Note on Religion and Politics, 1744–1750," *Journal of Ecclesiastical History* 39 (1988): 531–44. See also W. R. Ward, *The Protestant Evangelical Awakening* (Cambridge: Cambridge University Press, 1992); and Ward, "Was There a Methodist Evangelistic Strategy?"

27. Ward, "Was There a Methodist Evangelistic Strategy?"

28. This paragraph is based on the splendid insights in Tucker, *American Methodist Worship,* 270–81.

29. Andrews, *The Methodists and Revolutionary America,* 73–96; Cynthia Lynn Lyerly, *Methodism and the Southern Mind, 1770–1810* (New York: Oxford University Press, 1998), 27–46.

30. James Obelkevich, *Religion and Rural Society: South Lindsey, 1825–1875* (Oxford: Clarendon, 1976), 220–58; David Hempton, *Methodism and Politics in British Society, 1750–1850* (Stanford: Stanford University Press, 1984), 55–115; David Hempton, *Religion and Political Culture in Britain and Ireland: From the Glorious Revolution to the Decline of Empire* (Cambridge: Cambridge University Press, 1996), 49–71; and David Hempton and Myrtle Hill, *Evangelical Protestantism in Ulster Society, 1740–1890* (London: Routledge, 1996).

31. See for example, Nathan Bangs, *The Errors of Hopkinsianism* (New York: John Totten, 1815); Nathan Bangs, *An Original Church of Christ* (New York: Mason and Lane, 1837); Wilbur Fisk, *Calvinist Controversy* (1835); and E. Brooks Holifield, *Theology in America: Christian Thought from the Age of the Puritans to the Civil War* (New Haven: Yale University Press, 2003), 260. Chapter 12 of Holifield's book on Methodist Perfection serves as a fine introduction to Methodist theology between the Revolutionary and Civil Wars.

32. See Timothy Merritt, *The Christian's Manual: A Treatise on Christian Perfection* (New York: Emory and Waugh, 1828), and Phoebe Palmer, *The Way of Holiness* (1843).

## CHAPTER 4: OPPOSITION AND CONFLICT

1. For an excellent account of George Eliot's early religious convictions and their influence on her fiction see Gordon S. Haight, *George Eliot: A Biography* (Oxford: Oxford University Press, 1968).

2. The best treatments of anti-Methodist sentiment and action are John Walsh, "Methodism and the Mob in the Eighteenth Century," *Studies in Church History* 8 (1972): 213–27; David Hempton, *The Religion of the People: Methodism and Popular Religion, c. 1750–1900* (London: Routledge, 1996), 145–61; and Michael Francis Snape, "Anti-Methodism in Eighteenth-Century England: The Pendle Forest Riots of 1748," *Journal of Ecclesiastical History* 49, no. 2 (1998): 257–81. For a discussion of the legal issues at stake in the opposition to Methodism, see David Hempton, "Methodism and the Law," *Bulletin of the John Rylands University Library of*

*Manchester* 70 (1988): 93–107, and J. S. Simon, "The Conventicle Act and Its Relation to the Early Methodists," *Proceedings of the Wesley Historical Society* 11 (1918): 82–93.

3. A. Warne, *Church and Society in Eighteenth-Century Devon* (Newton Abbott: David and Charles, 1969), 111. For a revealing account of the issues Methodism posed for Church and State, see the Lavington Correspondence in Lambeth Palace Library Mss, Secker Papers 8 (Methodists) folios 4–5: West Austell JPs to G. Lavington, Bishop of Exeter, 23 May 1747. Much of this correspondence has been reproduced in Oliver A. Beckerlegge, "The Lavington Correspondence," *Proceedings of the Wesley Historical Society* 42 (1980): 101–11, 139–49, and 167–90. For a wider social context, see Robert W. Malcolmson, " 'A Set of Ungovernable People': The Kingswood Colliers in the Eighteenth Century," in *An Ungovernable People: The English and Their Law in the Seventeenth and Eighteenth Centuries,* ed. John Brewer and John Styles (London: Hutchinson, 1980), 85–127.

4. For more general interpretations of the social conservatism of popular protest in England in the eighteenth century see John Stevenson, *Popular Disturbances in England, 1700–1870* (London: Longman, 1979), 301–23; E. P. Thompson, "The Moral Economy of the English Crowd in the Eighteenth Century," *Past and Present* 50 (1971): 76–136; and Jan Albers, " 'Papist Traitors' and 'Presbyterian Rogues': Religious Identities in Eighteenth-Century Lancashire," in *The Church of England, c. 1689–c. 1833: From Toleration to Tractarianism,* ed. John Walsh, Colin Haydon, and Stephen Taylor (Cambridge: Cambridge University Press, 1993), 317–33.

5. On the wider framework of English anti-Catholicism see David Hempton, *Methodism and Politics in British Society, 1750–1850* (London: Hutchinson, 1984), 31–34; Walsh, "Methodism and the Mob," 226–27; and Colin Haydon, *Anti-Catholicism in Eighteenth-Century England: A Political and Social Study* (Manchester: Manchester University Press, 1993), 63–66. The intriguing presentment brought against Williamson and its subsequent legal outcome can be followed through the Borthwick Institute Mss. (York, England), D/C CP. 1755/2, 3 and Trans. CP. 1756/1. The original presentment is preserved at York Minster Library, C3a, visitation papers, 1755.

6. Simon Ross Valentine, *John Bennet and the Origins of Methodism and the Evangelical Revival in England* (Lanham, Md.: Scarecrow, 1997), 153.

7. The best treatment of the Pendle Forest riots and their social, religious, and economic backgrounds is Snape, "Anti-Methodism in Eighteenth-Century England."

8. Ibid., 281.

9. John Wesley, *Letters,* 2 vols., ed. Frank Baker (Oxford: Clarendon, 1982, vol. 26 of *The Works of John Wesley*), 2:324–27, 335–37, 340–41, and 474–75. For the judgment of King's Bench in favor of Wesley and the Methodists see Public Record Office (London), KB 122, Great Dogget of Trinity term in the 24th of George II, 240. For an account of the anti-Methodist riots in Cork see Hempton, *The Religion of the People,* 152–54. The most revealing contemporary account of the riots can be found in the Cork Baptist Church Book, 1653–1875 (Ms.) still in the possession of the Cork Baptist Church.

10. Dee E. Andrews, *The Methodists and Revolutionary America, 1760–1800: The*

*Shaping of an Evangelical Culture* (Princeton: Princeton University Press, 2000), 52–55. See also Arthur Bruce Ross, *Thomas Webb: A Founder of American Methodism* (Lake Janaluska, N.C., 1975), and Frank Baker, *From Wesley to Asbury: Studies in Early American Methodism* (Durham: Duke University Press, 1976).

11. Christine Leigh Heyrman, *Southern Cross: The Beginnings of the Bible Belt* (New York: Alfred A. Knopf, 1998), 229–30.

12. Andrews, *The Methodists and Revolutionary America,* 61; Heyrman, *Southern Cross,* 234.

13. David R. Kasserman, *Fall River Outrage: Life, Murder, and Justice in Early Industrial New England* (Philadelphia: University of Pennsylvania Press, 1986). See, for example, Richard Hildreth, *Report of the Trial of the Rev. Ephraim K. Avery before the Supreme Judicial Court of Rhode Island on an Indictment for the Murder of Sarah Maria Cornell, containing a Full Statement of the Testimony, together with the Arguments of Counsel and the Charge to the Jury* (Boston: Russell, Odiorne, 1833). See also *Report of the Examination of Ephraim K. Avery, of Bristol, charged with the Murder of Sarah M. Cornell, in Tiverton, R.I. on 20 December 1832.*

14. *Report of a Committee of the New England Annual Conference of the Methodist Episcopal Church, on the Case of Rev. Ephraim K. Avery, Member of said Conference* (Boston: David H. Ela, 1833).

15. Kasserman, *Fall River Outrage,* 218–20.

16. Ibid., 233–39.

17. Catharine Williams, *Fall River: An Authentic Narrative,* edited by Patricia Caldwell (New York: Oxford University Press, 1993), 5–6.

18. Ibid., 148–49.

19. Ibid., 161.

20. New England United Methodist Historical Society Manuscripts (NEUMHS Mss.), Asa Kent, Report to the members of the New England Conference concerning the collection of funds and the payment of expenses associated with the case of Ephraim K. Avery, July 19, 1836.

21. For some examples of the kind of violence directed against itinerant preachers see Billy Hibbard, *Memoirs of the Life and Travels of B. Hibbard, Minister of the Gospel* (New York: Percy and Reed, 1843); Abel Stevens, *Memorials of the Introduction of Methodism into the Eastern States* (Boston: Charles H. Pierce, 1848); and David Hempton, "Gideon Ouseley: Rural Revivalist, 1791–1839," *Studies in Church History* 25 (1988): 203–14. For the campaign against itinerancy in England during the French Revolutionary Wars see Hempton, *Methodism and Politics,* 77–115. See also W. R. Ward, *Religion and Society in England, 1790–1850* (London: Batsford, 1972).

22. I survey the historiography of the British side of this story in Hempton, *The Religion of the People,* 162–78. The most influential treatment of the American side remains Nathan O. Hatch, *The Democratization of American Christianity* (New Haven: Yale University Press, 1989).

23. Hempton, *Methodism and Politics,* 64–73. See also Ward, *Religion and Society in England.* Alexander Kilham (Paul and Silas, pseud.), *An Earnest Address to the Preachers Assembled in Conference* (n.p., 1795); Alexander Kilham, *The Progress of Liberty Amongst the People Called Methodists: To which is added the Out-lines of a Constitution* (Alnwick, 1795); Alexander Kilham, *A Candid Examination of the London Methodistical Bull* (Alnwick, 1796); Alexander Kilham, *An Account of the Trial of Alexan-*

*der Kilham, Methodist Preacher, before the General Conference in London* (Nottingham, 1796); and Alexander Kilham (with William Thom), *Out-lines of a Constitution proposed for the examination, amendment and acceptance of the Members of the Methodist New Itinerancy* (Leeds, 1797).

24. There is a good account of O'Kelly's complaints in Andrews, *The Methodists and Revolutionary America,* 196–207. Andrews describes the language as "a unique blend of Old Testament and antifederalist rhetoric," 203. See also the insightful discussion of O'Kelly's "Republican language" in Russell E. Richey, *Early American Methodism* (Bloomington: Indiana University Press, 1991), 88–91; James O'Kelly, *The Author's Apology for Protesting against the Methodist Episcopal Government* (Richmond: John Dixon, 1798). For the wider religious and social context of O'Kelly's views see Hatch, *Democratization of American Christianity,* 67–122.

25. The most insightful essays on how these processes were worked out are to be found in W. R. Ward, *Faith and Faction* (London: Epworth, 1993).

26. Andrews, *The Methodists in Revolutionary America,* 206–7; Mark A. Noll, *America's God: From Jonathan Edwards to Abraham Lincoln* (New York: Oxford University Press, 2002), 340–41.

27. Richey, *Early American Methodism,* 91; see the letters in W. R. Ward, ed., *The Early Correspondence of Jabez Bunting, 1820–1829* (London: Royal Historical Society, 1972).

28. These issues can be followed in W. R. Ward, "The Religion of the People and the Problem of Control," *Studies in Church History* 8 (1972): 237–57. See also Ward, *Religion and Society in England,* and Hempton, *Methodism and Politics.* I survey the complex historiography of religion and social class in early industrial England in a more extensive way than is possible here in Hempton, *The Religion of the People,* 162–78.

29. William R. Sutton, *Journeymen for Jesus: Evangelical Artisans Confront Capitalism in Jacksonian Baltimore* (University Park: Pennsylvania State University Press, 1998), 76–77 and 108. Clause II of Stilwell's pamphlet stated, "Each member, male and female, shall have a vote in the choice of preachers, and the allowance to be made for their services." Clause VI stated, "The members, having equal rights, may form such rules for regulating and promoting the good of the society as may be thought expedient by a majority of the members."

30. Hempton, *Methodism and Politics,* 179–223; Jabez Bunting to Joseph Entwistle, Salford, December 22, 1827, in *The Early Correspondence of Jabez Bunting,* ed. Ward, 164.

31. The best account of "Free Methodism" is supplied by D. A. Gowland, *Methodist Secessions: The Origins of Free Methodism in Three Lancashire Towns* (Manchester: Manchester University Press, 1979).

32. Benjamin Gregory, *Side Lights on the Conflicts of Methodism During the Second Quarter of the Nineteenth Century, 1827–1852* (London: Casell, 1898).

33. Richard Allen, *The Life Experience and Gospel Labors of the Rt. Rev. Richard Allen,* with an introduction by George A. Singleton (Nashville: Abingdon, 1983). See also John G. McEllhenney, ed., *United Methodism in America: A Compact History* (Nashville: Abingdon, 1992), 57–60; Will B. Gravely, "African Methodisms and the Rise of Black Denominationalism," in *Perspectives on American Methodism: Interpretive Essays,* ed. Russell E. Richey, Kenneth E. Rowe, and Jean Miller Schmidt (Nashville: Kingswood, 1993), 108–26.

34. I have taken this account of Douglass's experience from the NEUMHS archives, Leonard B. Ellis, "Centennial Account of New Bedford Methodism" (1895).

35. Richard Carwardine, "Trauma in Methodism: Property, Church Schism, and Sectional Polarization in Antebellum America," in *God and Mammon: Protestants, Money, and the Market, 1790–1860,* ed. Mark A. Noll (New York: Oxford University Press, 2001), 195–216; Richard Carwardine, "Methodists, Politics, and the Coming of the American Civil War," in *Methodism and the Shaping of American Culture,* ed. Nathan O. Hatch and John H. Wigger (Nashville: Kingswood, 2001), 331. See also Richard Carwardine, *Evangelicals and Politics in Antebellum America* (New Haven: Yale University Press, 1993).

36. See, for example, the rise of Primitive Methodism in England as described by Julia Stewart Werner, *The Primitive Methodist Connexion: Its Background and Early History* (Madison: University of Wisconsin Press, 1984).

## CHAPTER 5: MONEY AND POWER

1. Robert Currie, Alan Gilbert, and Lee Horsley, *Churches and Churchgoers: Patterns of Church Growth in the British Isles Since 1700* (Oxford: Clarendon, 1977); John H. Wigger, *Taking Heaven by Storm: Methodism and Popular Christianity in America* (New York: Oxford University Press, 1998), 3–7; John H. Wigger, "Taking Heaven by Storm: Enthusiasm and Early American Methodism, 1770–1820," *Journal of the Early Republic* 14, no. 2 (1994), 167–94; Bernard Semmel, *The Methodist Revolution* (London: Heinemann, 1974), 152–66. See also Stuart Piggin, "Halévy Revisited: The Origins of the Wesleyan Methodist Missionary Society: An Examination of Semmel's Thesis," *Journal of Imperial and Commonwealth History* 9, no. 1 (1980): 17–37; Roger H. Martin, "Missionary Competition Between Evangelical Dissenters and Wesleyan Methodists in the Early Nineteenth Century: A Footnote to the Founding of the Methodist Missionary Society," *Proceedings of the Wesley Historical Society* 42 (1979): 81–86; Roger H. Martin, *Evangelicals United: Ecumenical Stirrings in Pre-Victorian Britain, 1795–1830* (Metuchen, N.J.: Scarecrow, 1983); and Wade Crawford Barclay, *History of Methodist Missions,* vol. 1, *Missionary Motivation and Expansion* (New York: Board of Missions and Church Extension of the Methodist Church, 1949).

2. For an excellent treatment of John Wesley's economic teaching see John Walsh, "John Wesley and the Community of Goods," in *Protestant Evangelicalism: Britain, Ireland, Germany, and America, c. 1750–1950,* ed. Keith Robbins (Oxford: Basil Blackwell, 1990); John Walsh, "Methodism and the Common People," in *People's History and Socialist Theory,* ed. Raphael Samuel (London: Routledge, 1981), 354–62. For a wider discussion of these issues see David Hempton, *The Religion of the People: Methodism and Popular Religion, c. 1750–1900* (New York: Routledge, 1996), 85–87. See also John Wesley, *Letters,* 2 vols., ed. Frank Baker (Oxford: Clarendon, 1982, vol. 26 of *The Works of John Wesley*), 2:544–45. For a splendid example of Methodist bookkeeping, which can stand for the rest, see the meticulous account books relating to the first Methodist society and church (Methodist Alley Church) in Boston: New England United Methodist Historical Society Manuscripts (NEUMHS Mss.), Stewards' books 1792–95 and 1795–97, which contain daily entries of income (male and female class, quarterly and Sunday collections)

and expenditure (preachers' room and board, quarterage, and candles). Nevertheless, allegations of financial malpractice within Methodism are almost as frequent as those dealing with sexual impropriety. See Oliver A. Beckerlegge, "The Lavington Correspondence," *Proceedings of the Wesley Historical Society* 42 (1980): 101–11, 139–49, and 167–80.

3. For a more detailed account of these allegations see David Hempton, *Methodism and Politics in British Society, 1750–1850* (London: Hutchinson, 1984), 67–73. See also Alexander Kilham, *The Progress of Liberty, Amongst the People called Methodists* (Alnwick, 1795); *A Candid Examination of the London Methodistical Bull* (Alnwick, 1796); *A Short Account of the Trial of Alexander Kilham, Methodist minister Preacher, at a special district meeting held at Nexcastle* (Alnwick, 1796); *An Appeal to the Methodists of the Alnwick Circuit* (Alnwick, 1796); *An Account of the Trial of Alexander Kilham, Methodist Preacher, before the General Conference in London* (Nottingham, 1796). For the official defense against these allegations see Jonathan Crowther, *Christian Order: or Liberty Without Tyranny and Every Man in his Proper Place* (Bristol, 1796); Thomas Hanby, *An Explanation of Mr Kilham's Statement of the Preachers' Allowance* (Nottingham, 1796).

4. John Rylands Library, Manchester: Methodist Archives and Research Center (hereinafter MARC), Bunting Mss, Martindale to Bunting, July 9, 1816.

5. For the clearest delineation of the issues involved in funding preachers and their dependents see MARC, Bunting Mss, Robert Miller to Jabez Bunting, April 1, 1819.

6. MARC, Bunting Mss, Miles Martindale to Jabez Bunting, July 9, 1816.

7. Ibid.

8. W. R. Ward, *Religion and Society in England, 1790–1850* (London: Batsford, 1972), 97. See also the following letters: MARC, Bunting Mss, John Gaulter to Jabez Bunting, April 6, 1809; Thomas Allan to Jabez Bunting, July 28, 1810; Matthew Lamb to Jabez Bunting, June 13, 1812; Joseph Entwistle to Jabez Bunting December 18, 1812; Joseph Butterworth to Jabez Bunting, November 9, 1814; Joseph Entwistle to Jabez Bunting, December 15, 1814; and Edward Hare to Jabez Bunting, January 9, 1815. Deciding on the appropriate number of preachers to meet the needs of a circuit caused much debate. The issue was that poorer and more distant circuits needed extra help but could not raise sufficient money to pay for it. These internal transfers of resources from wealthier to poorer circuits could, depending on circumstances, produce both magnanimity and great resentment. See MARC, Bunting Mss, Theophilus Lessey Snr. to Jabez Bunting, June 7, 1811. Financing itinerant preaching was a particularly thorny issue. Since itinerant preachers were the chief beneficiaries of class and society collections, it was difficult for them publicly to criticize either the level or the administration of the giving. See MARC, Bunting Mss, E. Hare to Jabez Bunting, November 12, 1810; Thomas Coke to Jabez Bunting, April 21, 1812; and John Barber to Jabez Bunting, April 24, 1812. It was also difficult for connectional leaders at the time, and difficult for historians since, to estimate with any degree of accuracy the average cost of maintaining single and married itinerant preachers. When asked by the Property Commissioners in 1810 for an official estimate, Bunting replied that "as the ministers in that Connexion have no regular salaries, but are maintained by different small allowances made to them by their Societies, which vary considerably according to circumstances, there is some difficulty in determining our proper annual income.

But I am informed that some years ago, when the whole case was laid before the Commissioners, & left to their decision, they were pleased to fix on the sum of Sixty Pounds per annum as the sum for which the Methodist ministers of this town should be chargeable to the duty of professions." A decade later some careful calculations by Robert Miller estimated the cost at £103 per annum. To what extent this represents a real increase in the early decades of the nineteenth century, or is merely the result of different calculations for different audiences, is difficult to determine with any precision, but the sheer volume of correspondence complaining of increased allowances for preachers indicates that something was happening. See MARC, Bunting Mss, Robert Miller to Jabez Bunting, April 1, 1819.

9. MARC, Bunting Mss, William Williams to Jabez Bunting, February 17, 1809; E. Hare to Jabez Bunting, November 12, 1812; W. Midgley to Jabez Bunting, May 22, 1812; Walter Griffith to Jabez Bunting, February 4, 1814; Thomas Hutton to Jabez Bunting, March 17, 1815; and W. Worth to Jabez Bunting, January 23, 1818. See also United Methodist Church Archives, Lake Junaluska, Jabez Bunting to James Wood, late August or early September, 1811.

10. MARC, Bunting Mss, Jabez Bunting to Joseph Dutton, December 27, 1813.

11. Complaints were legion about the administrative frailties of Methodist giving and fund-raising. See MARC, Bunting Mss, Edward Hare to Jabez Bunting, November 12, 1810; Thomas Hutton to Jabez Bunting, February 4, 1811; John Barber to Jabez Bunting, April 24, 1812; Joseph Entwistle to Jabez Bunting, December 18, 1812; Joseph Cusworth to Jabez Bunting, April 14, 1815; George Morley to Jabez Bunting, October 28, 1815; Edward Hare to Jabez Bunting, May 30, 1816, Jonathan Roberts to Jabez Bunting, July 17, 1818. See also W. R. Ward, ed., *The Early Correspondence of Jabez Bunting, 1820–1829* (London: Royal Historical Society, Camden 4th Series, 1972). See letter from John Mercer to Jabez Bunting, March 14, 1820, detailing the privations of laboring in the debt-ridden societies of the Isle of Man.

12. Edward Royle, *Queen Street Chapel and Mission Huddersfield* (Huddersfield: The Local History Society, 1994). This huge chapel built in 1819 to accommodate some two thousand people cost about ten thousand pounds sterling. Similar-sized chapels were constructed in other northern towns in this period. See also MARC, Bunting Mss, R. Smith to Jabez Bunting, March 30, 1809; Jabez Bunting to James Wood, January 7, 1815; Theophilus Lessey Snr. to Jabez Bunting, May 6, 1815; and Jabez Bunting to Isaac Clayton, July 14, 1815. Bunting stated: "I do not think it desirable that any *large or considerable* portion of the supplies necessary for the maintenance of our ministry should come from the chapels. This, I know, is the dissenting plan. But the longer I live, the less I am disposed to assimilate our plan to theirs. *Our* plan is to support our ministry by the voluntary subscriptions of our *societies*. This I think is almost infinitely preferable."

13. MARC, Bunting Mss, Thomas Allan to Jabez Bunting, July 28, 1810.

14. MARC, Bunting Mss, Joseph Entwistle to Jabez Bunting, December 15, 1814.

15. MARC, Bunting Mss, Jabez Bunting to Samuel Taylor, March 10, 1814

16. The key years in the transformation of missionary funding were 1814 and 1815. For accounts of what was going on up and down the country see MARC, Bunting Mss, Walter Griffith to Jabez Bunting, February 4, 1814; John Furness to Jabez Bunting, February 28, 1814; Jabez Bunting to Samuel Taylor, March 10,

1814; Jabez Bunting to James Everett, March 29, 1814; George Morley to Jabez Bunting, September 22, 1814; Joseph Butterworth to Jabez Bunting, September 27, 1814; John Beaumont to Jabez Bunting, October 18, 1814; Thomas Kelk to Jabez Bunting, October 25, 1814; George Morley to Jabez Bunting, October 29, 1814; Jabez Bunting to T. S. Swale, November 19, 1814; Thomas Kelk to Jabez Bunting, December 14, 1814; Joseph Entwistle to Jabez Bunting, December 15, 1814; George Morley to Jabez Bunting, December 30, 1814; Jabez Bunting to James Wood, January 7, 1815; Edward Hare to Jabez Bunting, January 9, 1815; Richard Watson to Jabez Bunting, January 17, 1815; Robert Newton to Jabez Bunting, January 18, 1815; Jabez Bunting to George Morley, January 25, 1815; Thomas Hutton to Jabez Bunting, March 17, 1815; J. Shipman to Jabez Bunting, April 22, 1815; John Barber to Jabez Bunting, April 27, 1815; Jabez Bunting to George Marsden, June 24, 1815; and Walter Griffith to Jabez Bunting, September 21, 1815.

17. MARC, Bunting Mss, Jabez Bunting to George Morley, January 25, 1815.

18. MARC, Bunting Mss, Robert Miller to Jabez Bunting, April 1, 1819. The precise figures were 501 families and 154 single men.

19. Whatever the alleged contribution of industrial conflict, economic destitution, political excitement, and social instability to the success of Methodist revivalism, they all had disastrous consequences for Methodist finances. See MARC, Bunting Mss, Theophilus Lessey Snr. to Jabez Bunting, January 17, 1811; Thomas Hutton to Jabez Bunting, February 4, 1811; Joseph Butterworth to Jabez Bunting, May 23, 1812; George Morley to Jabez Bunting, October 29, 1814; Richard Waddy to Jabez Bunting, January 31, 1816. One of the most radical solutions for financing the Methodist system, proposed partly tongue-in-cheek, was "to raise money not by begging but by *borrowing*." See MARC, Bunting Mss, Jonathan Roberts to Jabez Bunting, July 17, 1818. The proposal was based on the assumption that Methodist "begging" was beginning to obey a law of diminishing returns and that some form of graduated loan system would deliver enough in interest payments to keep the connection ticking over.

20. Ward, *Religion and Society*, 101.

21. Ward, ed., *Early Correspondence of Jabez Bunting*, 4–8. For the wider economic background see Roderick Floud and Donald McLoskey, eds., *The Economic History of Britain Since 1700* (Cambridge: Cambridge University Press, 1994), 1:368–72. Their estimates suggest that real wages were probably stagnant between 1750 and 1815 and then improved substantially between 1815 and 1850.

22. Wigger, *Taking Heaven by Storm*, 49.

23. William H. Williams, *The Garden of American Methodism: The Delmarva Peninsula, 1769–1820* (Wilmington, Del.: Scholarly Resources, 1984), 127–28.

24. David Sherman, *History of the Revisions of the Discipline of the Methodist Episcopal Church* (New York: Nelson and Phillips, 1874), 363.

25. Michael G. Nickerson, "Historical Relationships of Itinerancy and Salary," *Methodist History* 21, no. 1 (1982): 43–59; Wigger, *Taking Heaven by Storm*, 49; *Journals of the General Conference of the Methodist Episcopal Church*, 1:35 (the majority for voting a salary increase in 1800 was only five). See also NEUMHS Mss., John Edwards Risley, Autobiography, Providence, R.I., April 1883, and NEUMHS Mss., Samuel Kelley (1802–1883), "Semicentennial discourse delivered in the Methodist chapel at Quincy Point, Mass., March 17, 1872," 59 pages. Kelley gives a short

account of the fate of all thirty-seven preachers received into conference with him in 1822. For an introduction to the early history of Methodism in New England see Abel Stevens, *Memorials of the Early Progress of Methodism in the Eastern States* (Boston: C. H. Peirce, 1852), and George C. Baker, *An Introduction to the History of Early New England Methodism, 1789–1839* (Durham: Duke University Press, 1941).

26. *Journals of the General Conference*, 20–22 and 41–42.

27. *Journals of the General Conference* (1816), 148–49.

28. *An Account shewing the amount of Collections and Disbursements in the New England Conference for the year ending June 20, 1821* (Boston, 1821). A sum of $893 was received from central funds, made up of contributions from the book concern, the chartered fund, the widow's mite society, and conference collections. The modesty of this sum indicates the extent of the decentralization of Methodist fund-raising. See also *An Account shewing the amount of Collections and Disbursements in the New England Conference for the year ending June 7 1825* (Boston 1825) and *Minutes of the New England Annual Conference of the Methodist Episcopal Church for the year 1835* (Boston, 1835).

29. NEUMHS Mss., William Gordon (1810–1895), autobiography (copied and read before the society) and "Historical incidents; recollections of Methodism during a half-century." Gordon's reminiscences are remarkably frank and unpretentious, especially concerning the subject of money. See also NEUMHS Mss., Samuel Kelley (1802–1883), "Semi-centennial discourse." Kelley clearly found it hard to make ends meet in the first fifteen years of his ministry. According to his own account what sustained him, both in terms of money and morale, were odd jobs, hospitality in kind, and regular divisions of preachers' modest surpluses on the strict principle of equality. Brotherhood and benevolence more than made up for want and deficiency.

30. *Journals of the General Conference*, 34; Nathan O. Hatch, *The Democratization of American Christianity* (New Haven: Yale University Press, 1989), appendix.

31. *A Phonographic Report of the Debates and Addresses together with the Essays and Resolutions of the New England Methodist Centenary Convention held in Boston, June 5–7, 1866* (Boston, 1866), 31, 85, 171–74, and 231–39. The closing address by Bishop Simpson focused on the prophetic significance of the year 1866 as the date of the American Methodist Centenary, the collapse of papal power in Italy, and the demise of "Mohammedan power."

32. E. C. E. Dorion, *New England Methodism: The Story of the New England Convention of Methodist Men held in Tremont Temple, Boston, Mass., November 11–13, 1914* (New York: The Methodist Book Concern, 1915), 95–96. See also G. A. Crawford, ed., *The Centennial of New England Methodism* (Boston, 1891), 16–17, in which are presented eulogies of early Methodist itinerants who were not great in learning, but who had "the tongue of fire."

33. Crawford, ed., *The Centennial of New England Methodism*, 16–17.

34. It must be borne in mind that the reminiscences upon which this section is based are from old and relatively successful itinerant preachers eager to hold the attention of a later generation. Picaresque tales of heroic adventures mingle with more sober accounts of Methodist trials and tribulations in this literature. The accounts most bearing on the subject of money are those by William Robert Clark, Daniel Dorchester (recounting the life of Moses Hill), William Gordon, Samuel Kelley, Daniel Clark Knowles (memoir of Nathaniel G. Ladd), Thomas Marcy, and

John Edwards Risley. For published versions of the kind of attitudes found among old New England itinerants in the 1880s see Henry Boehm, *Reminiscences, Historical and Biographical of Sixty-Four Years in the Ministry* (New York, 1866), and James Jenkins, *Experience, Labours, and Sufferings of the Rev. James Jenkins of the South Carolina Conference* (n.p., 1842). I am grateful to Dr. John Wigger for these references and for his comments on an earlier version of this chapter.

35. *Journal of General Conference* (1820), 210–11. Resolution 4 stated "that the practice of building houses with pews, and the renting or selling said pews, is contrary to our economy; and that it be the duty of the several annual conferences to use their influence to prevent such houses from being built in future, and as far as possible to make those houses free which have already been built with pews." For an insightful record of how pew rents were in fact operational in Methodist churches, see the pew rental records of the first Methodist church in Lynn, Massachusetts, in Boston University School of Theology Manuscripts. See also the church account book for the Methodist Alley Church in Boston, which reveals that about half the money raised for the church building came from donations made to Jesse Lee in the southern states. The rest came from subscriptions, collections, and borrowing. See also Jesse Lee, *A Short History of the Methodists in the United States of America* (Baltimore, 1810), 164–65. For English parallels see Mark Smith, *Religion in Industrial Society: Oldham and Saddleworth, 1740–1865* (Oxford: Clarendon, 1994).

36. For insightful discussions of these processes at work in Canada and Australia see William Westfall, *Two Worlds: The Protestant Culture of Nineteenth-Century Ontario* (Montreal: McGill-Queen's University Press, 1989), and Arnold D. Hunt, *This Side of Heaven: A History of Methodism in South Australia* (Adelaide: Lutheran Publishing, 1985). See also Mark Noll, "Christianity in Canada: Good Books at Last," a review essay in *Fides et Historia* 23, no. 2 (1991): 80–104.

37. Hempton, *The Religion of the People*, 162–78.

38. William R. Sutton, *Journeymen for Jesus: Evangelical Artisans Confront Capitalism in Jacksonian Baltimore* (University Park: Pennsylvania State University Press, 1998). For Wesley's views see Richard P. Heitzenrater, *The Elusive Mr. Wesley*, 2 vols. (Nashville: Abingdon, 1984), and Henry D. Rack, *John Wesley and the Rise of Methodism* (London: Epworth, 1989). Only much more detailed research, society by society and occupation by occupation, would be able to determine if Methodists became more or less generous with their resources (as a percentage of their family incomes) as their material stock in the world improved over time.

## Chapter 6: Boundaries and Margins

1. Sylvia R. Frey and Betty Wood, *Come Shouting to Zion: African American Protestantism in the American South and British Caribbean to 1830* (Chapel Hill: University of North Carolina Press, 1998), 83–88.

2. See Milton C. Sernett, ed., *African American Religious History: A Documentary Witness* (Durham: Duke University Press, 1999); Christine Leigh Heyrman, *Southern Cross: The Beginnings of the Bible Belt* (New York: Alfred A. Knopf, 1998), 5. Even by the most generous estimate, she reckons that by the 1810s "fewer than one tenth of all African Americans had joined Baptist, Methodist, or Presbyterian churches," though of course the numbers affected by evangelical preaching may have been considerably higher. See also Michael Gomez, *Exchanging Our Country Marks: The Transformation of African Identities in the Colonial and Antebellum South*

(Chapel Hill: University of North Carolina Press, 1998), 260. Gomez cautions against overestimating the numbers of slaves converted to evangelical Christianity, and has also done some impressive work on tracing connections between African and southern American black cultures.

3. Nathan O. Hatch, *The Democratization of American Christianity* (New Haven: Yale University Press, 1989), 104-5; Henry H. Mitchell, *Black Belief: Folk Beliefs of Blacks in America and West Africa* (New York: Harper and Row, 1975); Mechal Sobel, *Trabelin' On: The Slave Journey to an Afro-Baptist Faith* (Westport, Conn.: Greenwood, 1979); and Frey and Wood, *Come Shouting to Zion.*

4. Heyrman, *Southern Cross,* 46-52.

5. See Cynthia Lynn Lyerly, *Methodism and the Southern Mind, 1770-1810* (New York: Oxford University Press, 1998), 47-72. Lyerly points out that racial separation came earlier and was more complete in indoor than in outdoor meetings. See also John H. Wigger, *Taking Heaven by Storm: Methodism and the Rise of Popular Christianity in America* (New York: Oxford University Press, 1998), 125-50. For a flavor of black Methodist exhorting and preaching see Richard Allen, *The Life Experience and Gospel Labors of the Rt. Rev. Richard Allen* (Philadelphia: Martin and Boston, 1833), and Jarena Lee, *The Life and Religious Experience of Jarena Lee* (Philadelphia: printed and published for the author, 1836). On the American Methodist pullback from slavery the standard work is still Donald G. Mathews, *Slavery and Methodism: A Chapter in American Morality, 1780-1845* (Princeton: Princeton University Press, 1965).

6. For a suggestive, if evangelically slanted, discussion of the issues at stake in coming to terms with some of the theological issues in interpreting African-American religious experience see Jay Riley Case, "Crossin' Over into Theology Land: The Historical Search for African American Ethnic, Racial, and Religious Identities in Early America," *Evangelical Studies Bulletin* 16, no. 1 (1999): 1-5. For more substantial treatments of the roots of black theology in the slave experience see James H. Cone, *A Black Theology of Liberation* (Philadelphia: Lippincott, 1970); Gayraud S. Wilmore, *Black Religion and Black Radicalism* (Maryknoll, N.Y.: Orbis, 1983); Dwight N. Hopkins and George C. L. Cummings, *Cut Loose Your Stammering Tongue: Black Theology in the Slave Narratives* (Maryknoll, N.Y.: Orbis, 1991); Dwight N. Hopkins, *Introducing Black Theology of Liberation* (Maryknoll, N.Y.: Orbis, 1999); and Dwight N. Hopkins, *Black Faith and Public Talk: Critical Essays on James H. Cone's Black Theology and Black Power* (Maryknoll, N.Y.: Orbis, 1999).

7. See the discussion in Jon Michael Spencer, *Protest and Praise: Sacred Music of Black Religion* (Minneapolis: Fortress, 1990), 3-34.

8. Ibid., 135.

9. John Paris, "The Moral and Religious State of the African Race in the Southern States," MS 13 Southern Historical Collection, quoted in ibid., 145.

10. See Gilbert Rouget, *Music and Trance: A Theory of the Relations Between Music and Possession,* trans. Brunhilde Biebuyek (Chicago: University of Chicago Press, 1985). The most influential Marxist interpretation of Methodism is E. P. Thompson, *The Making of the English Working Class* (Harmondsworth: Penguin, 1968).

11. For an excellent introduction to Korean Methodism, more wide-ranging than its title suggests, see Haksun Joo, "The Making of Methodist Worship in Korea (1884-1931)" (Th.D. diss., Boston University, 2002). See also Henry G. Appenzeller, *The Korean Mission of the Methodist Episcopal Church,* 2nd ed. (New York: Open Door Emergency Commission, 1905), and George H. Jones and W.

Arthur Noble, *The Korean Revival: An Account of the Revival of the Korean Churches in 1907* (New York: The Board of Foreign Missions of the Methodist Episcopal Church, 1910).

12. James S. Gale, *Korea in Transition* (New York: Eaton and Mains, 1909), 213.

13. Haksun Joo, "The Making of Methodist Worship in Korea," 51–134.

14. Ronald A. Knox, *Enthusiasm: A Chapter in the History of Religion* (Oxford: Clarendon, 1950), 30.

15. Clive D. Field, "The Social Composition of English Methodism to 1830: A Membership Analysis," *Bulletin of the John Rylands University Library of Manchester* 76, no. 1 (1994): 153–69; Dee E. Andrews, *The Methodists and Revolutionary America, 1760–1800: The Shaping of an Evangelical Culture* (Princeton: Princeton University Press, 2000), 247–48. The figures for Boston are taken from the records of the Methodist Alley MEC class meeting in the Boston University School of Theology archives.

16. Ann Braude, "Women's History *Is* American Religious History," in *Retelling U.S. Religious History*, ed. Thomas A. Tweed (Berkeley: University of California Press, 1997), 87–107. For a good survey of the contribution of women to Methodism see Jean Miller Schmidt, *Grace Sufficient: A History of Women in American Methodism, 1760–1939* (Nashville: Abingdon, 1999), 52–53. For a wider interpretation of the role of women in American Protestantism see Marilyn J. Westerkamp, *Women and Religion in Early America, 1600–1850: The Puritan and Evangelical Traditions* (London: Routledge, 1999). For Wesley's recourse to the device of the "extraordinary call" see Henry D. Rack, *Reasonable Enthusiast: John Wesley and the Rise of Methodism*, 3rd ed. (London: Epworth, 2002), 244. Joan Thirsk enunciated her "law" in a lecture entitled "The History Women" delivered at an international conference on women at Queen's University Belfast.

17. For an insightful treatment of women's voices within Methodism see Diane H. Lobody, " 'That Language Might Be Given Me': Women's Experience in Early Methodism," in *Perspectives on American Methodism: Interpretive Essays*, ed. Russell E. Richey, Kenneth E. Rowe, and Jean Miller Schmidt (Nashville: Abingdon, 1993), 127–44.

18. Catherine A. Brekus, *Strangers and Pilgrims: Female Preaching in America, 1740–1845* (Chapel Hill: University of North Carolina Press, 1998), 158. Chapter 3, "Female Laborers in the Harvest," is especially enlightening on women's role within both black and white Methodism. Brekus identifies at least nine female preachers within the African Methodist tradition: Jarena Lee, Rachel Evans, Zilpha Elaw, Elizabeth ? (last name not known), Juliann Jane Tilmann, Sojourner Truth, Julia Foote, Julia Pell, and Rebecca Jackson.

19. A. Gregory Schneider, *The Way of the Cross Leads Home: The Domestication of American Methodism* (Bloomington: Indiana University Press, 1993), xvi–xxviii.

20. See Charles E. White, *The Beauty of Holiness: Phoebe Palmer as Theologian, Revivalist, Feminist, and Humanitarian* (Grand Rapids, Mich.: Zondervan, 1986).

21. On Methodist women losing a public voice as the movement consolidated see the excellent analysis of Susan Juster, *Disorderly Women: Sexual Politics and Evangelicalism in Revolutionary New England* (Ithaca: Cornell University Press, 1994).

22. Paul Wesley Chilcote, ed., *Her Own Story: Autobiographical Portraits of Early Methodist Women* (Nashville: Kingswood, 2001). The chronological boundaries of Chilcote's selection are 1739 and 1815.

23. Mary Taft, *Memoirs* (1828), quoted in ibid., 167–69.

24. Mrs. Ann Ray to Miss Elizabeth Hurrell, Sept. 2, 1769, in Chilcote, *Her Own Story*, 199–202; Elizabeth Mortimer, *Memoirs*, quoted in ibid., 113; and the Diaries of Sarah Crosby, quoted in ibid., 78–79.

25. These reflections were stimulated by Phyllis Mack's lecture "Does Gender Matter? Salvation and Selfhood in Eighteenth-Century Methodism," delivered at the tercentenary celebration of John Wesley: Life, Legend, and Legacy, in Manchester, England, 2003. The conference proceedings will appear in print in due course.

26. Chilcote, *Her Own Story*, 44, 49, and 59,

27. Joseph Sutcliffe, *The Experience of the late Mrs. Frances Pawson, Widow of the late Rev. John Pawson* (London, 1813), quoted in ibid., 89–90.

28. Chilcote, *Her Own Story*, 99–100.

29. See David Hempton, *Methodism and Politics in British Society, 1750–1850* (London: Hutchinson, 1984), 55–84.

30. Chilcote, *Her Own Story*, 140.

31. Braude, "Women's History *Is* American Religious History." This criticism has been made by feminist scholars both of E. P. Thompson's important book *The Making of the English Working Class* and of Nathan Hatch's influential account in *The Democratization of American Christianity*. The two most significant books on female Methodist leaders and preachers on either side of the Atlantic are Deborah M. Valenze, *Prophetic Sons and Daughters: Female Preaching and Popular Religion in Industrial England* (Princeton: Princeton University Press, 1985), and Brekus, *Strangers and Pilgrims*. See, for example, the excellent chapters in Wigger, *Taking Heaven by Storm*, 151–72, and Lyerly, *Methodism and the Southern Mind*, 94–118.

32. Olwen Hufton, "Women, Gender, and the Fin de Siècle," in *The Routledge Companion to Historiography*, ed. Michael Bentley (London: Routledge, 1997). See also Amanda Vickery, "Golden Age to Separate Spheres? A Review of the Categories and Chronology of English Women's History," *The Historical Journal* 36, no. 2 (1993): 383–414.

33. Chilcote, *Her Own Story*, 169.

34. The incident is recorded in the manuscript Memoirs of William Gordon in the New England Methodist Historical Society collection in the School of Theology Library, Boston University. I am grateful to my research assistant Brian Clark for allowing me to reproduce extracts from his research paper.

35. Brian C. Clark, "The Memoirs of William Gordon," unpublished paper.

## CHAPTER 7: MAPPING AND MISSION

1. Wade Crawford Barclay, *History of Methodist Missions, Early American Methodism, 1769–1844*, vol. 1, *Missionary Motivation and Expansion* (New York: Board of Missions and Church Extension of the Methodist Church, 1949), 166–75. For a useful overview of the mission history of American Methodism see the *History of Methodist Missions* series by Barclay (vols. 1–3) and J. Tremayne Copplestone (vol. 4), published by the Board of Missions of the Methodist Church. For more detailed information on the rise of Methodism in Nova Scotia see Neil Semple, *The Lord's Dominion: The History of Canadian Methodism* (Montreal: McGill-Queen's University Press, 1996), 30–37.

2. Wade Crawford Barclay, *History of Methodist Missions, Methodist Episcopal Church, 1845–1939*, vol. 3, *Widening Horizons, 1845–1895* (New York: Board of

Missions of the Methodist Church, 1957), 156–57. Dana L. Robert, " 'History's Lessons for Tomorrow's Mission': Reflections on American Methodism in Mission," *Boston University School of Theology Focus*, Winter–Spring 1999: 7.

3. For good surveys of the missionary expansion of British Methodism see W. J. Townsend, H. B. Workman, and George Eayrs, eds., *A New History of Methodism*, vol. 2 (London: Hodder and Stoughton, 1909), and N. Allen Birtwhistle, "Methodist Missions," in *A History of the Methodist Church in Great Britain*, ed. Rupert Davies, A. Raymond George, and Gordon Rupp (London: Epworth, 1983), 3:1–116.

4. For a detailed, if not very analytical, account of the westward expansion of Methodism see Barclay, *Widening Horizons*, 194–364. There is some evidence to suggest that in particularly difficult missionary locations, especially in confronting Roman Catholicism, Methodists cooperated with other popular evangelical groups, including the Baptists.

5. James B. Finley, *History of the Wyandott Mission* (Cincinnati: Wright and Swormstedt, 1840); and Donald B. Smith, *Sacred Feathers: The Reverend Peter Jones (Kahkewaquonaby) and the Mississauga Indians* (Lincoln: University of Nebraska Press, 1987). Jones was of mixed race and was converted at a Methodist camp meeting in 1823. For earlier Moravian missions to Native Americans which may have had a bearing on Methodist strategy see Earl P. Olmstead, *David Zeisberger: A Life Among the Indians* (Kent, Ohio: Kent State University Press, 1997); and Joel W. Martin, *Sacred Revolt: The Muskogees' Struggle for a New World* (Boston: Beacon, 1991), 108–10. For a wider interpretation of American Indian identity see Richard A. Grounds, George E. Tinker, and David E. Wilkins eds., *Native Voices: American Indian Identity and Resistance* (Lawrence: University Press of Kansas, 2003).

6. Finley, *History of the Wyandott Mission;* Wade Crawford Barclay, *History of Methodist Missions, Early American Methodism, 1769–1844,* vol. 2, *To Reform the Nation* (New York: Board of Missions and Church Extension of the Methodist Church, 1950), 283–85; Nathan Bangs, *A History of the Methodist Episcopal Church,* 4:294. See also Barclay's judicious general conclusion on the fate of the Methodist mission to Native Americans in *Widening Horizons*, 363–64. There were nevertheless a reasonable number of Native American Methodists who preached to their own people; ibid., 363.

7. *Fourth Annual Report of the Methodist Episcopal Church Missionary Society* (New York, 1823), 8–9, 16–17; *Fifth Annual Report of the Methodist Episcopal Church Missionary Society* (New York, 1824), 22.

8. See, for example, *Fourteenth Annual Report of the Methodist Episcopal Church Missionary Society* (New York, 1833), 7–8; *Twentieth Annual Report of the Methodist Episcopal Church Missionary Society* (New York, 1839), 11–13.

9. Barclay, *Missionary Motivation and Expansion*, 325–44. See also Casely B. Essamuah, "Genuinely Ghanaian: A History of the Methodist Church, Ghana, in Missiological Perspective, 1961–2000" (Th.D. diss., Boston University, 2003), 27–76.

10. Robert, " 'History's Lessons for Tomorrow's Mission,' " 7; Barclay, *Widening Horizons*, 758–868, 932–1060.

11. Barclay, *Missionary Motivation and Expansion*, 205–6; David Hempton, *The Religion of the People: Methodism and Popular Religion, c. 1750–1900* (London: Routledge, 1996), 103–5; T. P. Bunting, *The Life of Jabez Bunting, D.D., with Notices of Contemporary Persons and Events* (London, 1887), 410–12. See also Bernard Semmel, *The Methodist Revolution* (London: Heinemann, 1974), 152–56; Stuart Piggin,

"Halévy Revisited: The Origins of the Wesleyan Methodist Missionary Society: An Examination of Semmel's Thesis," *Journal of Imperial and Commonwealth History* 9, no. 1 (1980): 19–20; R. H. Martin, "Missionary Competition Between Evangelical Dissenters and Wesleyan Methodists in the Early Nineteenth Century: A Footnote to the Founding of the Methodist Missionary Society," *Proceedings of the Wesley Historical Society* 42 (1979): 81–86.

12. Barclay, *Missionary Motivation and Expansion*, 291–94. See also Dana L. Robert, *American Women in Mission: A Social History of Their Thought and Practice* (Macon, Ga.: Mercer University Press, 1997), 125–88.

13. For a table of receipts and expenditures of the first twenty-five years of the American Methodist Missionary Society see Barclay, *Missionary Motivation and Expansion*, 300; Frances J. Baker, *The Story of the Woman's Foreign Missionary Society of the Methodist Episcopal Church, 1869–1895* (New York: Hunt and Eaton, 1896); Robert, *American Women in Mission*, 188; and Dana L. Robert, "The Methodist Struggle over Higher Education in Fuzhou, China, 1877–1883," *Methodist History* 34 (April 1996): 173–89.

14. *Twentieth Annual Report* (1839), 3–5.

15. *Twenty-fifth Annual Report of the Methodist Episcopal Church Missionary Society* (New York, 1844), 86–87; *Fifth Annual Report* (1824), 26–27.

16. *Thirtieth Annual Report of the Methodist Episcopal Church Missionary Society* (New York: Conference Office, 1849), 105–10.

17. *Thirty-fifth Annual Report of the Methodist Episcopal Church Missionary Society* (New York: Conference Office, 1854), 37.

18. Ibid., 42–43; *Fiftieth Annual Report of the Methodist Episcopal Church Missionary Society* (New York: Printed for the Society, 1869), 60–68; and *Fifty-fifth Annual Report of the Methodist Episcopal Church Missionary Society* (New York, 1874), 32.

19. *Twenty-first Annual Report of the Methodist Episcopal Church Missionary Society* (New York: Conference Office, 1840), 82–86.

20. For examples of the rhetoric see the *Thirtieth Annual Report*, 13, in which Catholicism is described as "the galling fetters of Romish superstition."

21. *Thirty-fifth Annual Report* (1854), 86–89; *Thirty-sixth Annual Report*, 130–31, in which Cardenas reported that he had been shot at, and is "everywhere threatened by a fanatical multitude, and publicly denounced by the Roman Catholic bishop." See also *Thirty-fifth Annual Report* (1854), 72–76.

22. His revealing letters from India include Boston University School of Theology Manuscripts (hereinafter BU STh Mss.), William Butler (1818–1899) to Members of the New England Conference, February 12, 1858, and February 1, 1865. On Methodism in Mexico see BU STh Mss., William Butler (1818–1899) to the Members of the New England Conference, March 18, 1878. See also letters dated March 20, 1875, March 18, 1876, March 5, 1877, and February 21, 1879.

23. See, for example, *Fortieth Annual Report* (1859), 37, and *Fiftieth Annual Report* (1869), 107–14

24. See *Fifty-fifth Annual Report* (1874), 74–79, 86–102.

25. The "remorseless pragmatism and sheer optimism" of Methodist missionaries resembles the interpretive framework of Pentecostalism employed in Grant Wacker, *Heaven Below: Early Pentecostals and American Culture* (Cambridge: Harvard University Press, 2001).

26. William Taylor, *Seven Years Street Preaching in San Francisco, California; Embracing Incidents, Triumphant Death Scenes, etc.* (New York: Carlton and Porter, 1856).

For good short accounts of his career see David Bundy, "Bishop William Taylor and Methodist Mission: A Study in Nineteenth Century Social History" (part 1), *Methodist History* 27 (July 1989): 197–210, and part 2, *Methodist History* 28 (October 1989): 2–21. Bundy's bibliography supplies a useful list of Taylor's prolific publications, including *Story of My Life; An account of what I have thought and said and done in my ministry of more than fifty-three years in Christian lands and among the heathen, written by myself* (New York: Eaten and Mains, 1895).

27. Bundy, "Bishop William Taylor" (part 2), 3.

28. Taylor claimed six thousand conversions during his two and half years in Australia. See William Taylor, *Christian Adventures in South Africa* (New York: Nelson and Phillips, 1876), 2–3, 94–98, 451; Daryl M. Balia, "Bridge over Troubled Waters: Charles Pamla and the Taylor Revival in South Africa," *Methodist History,* 30 (January 1992): 78–90.

29. Taylor, *Christian Adventures in South Africa,* 254–56, 474–78, 506–18, and 516–17; Wallace G. Mills, "The Taylor Revival of 1866 and the Roots of African Nationalism in the Cape Colony," *Journal of Religion in Africa* 8 (1976): 121.

30. See Barclay, *Widening Horizons,* 509–35; William Taylor, *Ten Years of Self-Supporting Missions in India* (New York: Phillips and Hunt, 1882), 48–49.

31. David Bundy, "Pauline Methods: The Mission Theory of William Taylor," 14; Walter J. Hollenweger, "Methodism's Past Is Pentecostalism's Present: A Case Study of Cultural Clash in Chile," *Methodist History* 20 (1982): 169–82.

32. Taylor, *Ten Years of Self-Supporting Missions,* 25, 33–40, 49–50.

33. Ibid., 76–77, 353; William Taylor, *Story of My Life: An Account of what I have thought and said and done in my ministry of more than fifty-three years in Christian Lands and among the Heathen,* edited by John Clark Ridpath (New York: Eaton and Mains, 1896).

34. BU STh Mss., Samuel Osgood Wright (1808–1834) to Benjamin H. Barnes, on board the ship Jupiter bound for Liberia, December 30, 1833; and from Monrovia, January 13, 1834. Osgood died soon after. See, for example, Melville B. Cox, *Remains of Melville B. Cox: Late Missionary to Liberia: with a Memoir* (Boston: Light and Horton, 1835); BU STh Mss., Daniel Parish Kidder (1815–1891) to W. C. Russell and Eleanor Russell, Rio de Janeiro, April 20, 1840, informing them of the death of their daughter Cynthia Kidder; BU STh Mss., William Butler (1818–1899) to the Members of the New England Conference, Meerut, India, February 12, 1858. Butler writes, "I need not recapitulate here the 'great fight of afflictions' through which we have passed since your last session. Much of it must be known to you. But I want to assure you my brethren that I am *not discouraged;* far from it. I never had hopes so strong of the Salvation of India as I have *now.*"

CHAPTER 8: CONSOLIDATION AND DECLINE

1. New England United Methodist Historical Society Mss., Zacariah Atwell Mudge (1813–1888), "Portraiture of Marshall Spring Rice (1800–1879)," a paper read at the annual meeting of the New England Methodist Historical Society, May 15, 1882.

2. See Richard J. Carwardine, "Methodists, Politics, and the Coming of the American Civil War," in *Methodism and the Shaping of American Culture,* ed. Nathan O. Hatch and John H. Wigger (Nashville: Kingswood, 2001), 309–42. Carwardine

states that "in 1868 Ulysses S. Grant remarked that there were three great parties in the United States: The Republican, the Democratic, and the Methodist Church."

3. See, for example, William Westfall, *Two Worlds: The Protestant Culture of Nineteenth-Century Ontario* (Montreal: McGill-Queen's University Press, 1989).

4. For a clear and accurate account of early Methodist ecclesiology and how it came into being see Richard P. Heitzenrater, *Wesley and the People Called Methodists* (Nashville: Abingdon, 1995). See Robert Currie, "A Micro-theory of Methodist Growth," *Proceedings of the Wesley Historical Society* 36 (1967): 65–73.

5. David M. Thompson, "The Churches and Society in Nineteenth-Century England: A Rural Perspective," *Studies in Church History* 8 (1972): 267–76.

6. To my knowledge no systematic work has been done on Methodist intermarriage and fertility rates, so the suggestion in this paragraph is based on impressions gleaned from Methodist archives in different parts of the North Atlantic region and on Albion Urdank's local study of Nailsworth in Gloucestershire, England, where he found unusually high fertility rates among evangelical nonconformists. He attributed this to a more optimistic worldview and a higher value on the "blessings" of children. For Canadian Methodism see the excellent tables in Neil Semple, *The Lord's Dominion: The History of Canadian Methodism* (Montreal: McGill-Queen's University Press, 1996), 178–210. The figures for the United States are taken from Russell E. Richey, Kenneth E. Rowe, and Jean Miller Schmidt, eds., *The Methodist Experience in America: A Sourcebook* (Nashville: Abingdon, 2000), 2:22.

7. Figures are taken from Peter Brierley, ed., *United Kingdom Christian Handbook: Religious Trends* (London: Harper Collins, 2000–2001). See also Robert Currie, Alan Gilbert, and Lee Horsley, *Churches and Churchgoers: Patterns of Church Growth in the British Isles Since 1700* (Oxford: Clarendon, 1977), 161–66. The American data were supplied by the General Board of Global Ministries of the United Methodist Church. I am grateful to Gregory Hastings and Samuel Johnson for access to their unpublished research paper titled "Old Cross, New Flame: A Portrait of New United Methodist Churches in Their Contemporary Sociological Context," Boston University School of Theology (1999).

8. See, for example, David Lowes Watson, *Class Leaders: Recovering a Tradition, and Forming Christian Disciples: The Role of Covenant Discipleship and Class Leaders in the Congregation* (Nashville: Discipleship Resources, 1991); and "Class Leaders and Class Meetings: Recovering a Methodist Tradition for a Changing Church," in *United Methodism in American Culture: Doctrines and Discipline*, ed. Dennis M. Campbell, William B. Lawrence, and Russell E. Richey (Nashville: Abingdon, 1999), 245–64. See also the many helpful articles in this book and the others in the series: *Connectionalism* (1997), and *The People(s) Called Methodist* (1998).

9. New England United Methodist Historical Society Manuscripts (NEUMHS Mss.), Howard Carey Dunham, "Methodists of Olden Times," read before the Society, November 19, 1888. See also Dunham, Semi-Centennial Address before the New England Conference (1888), typescript.

10. NEUMHS Mss., George McKendree Steele (1823–1902), "The Builders of Methodism in New England; centennial address delivered before the New England Annual Conference at Springfield" (1896). See also John William Hamilton (1845–1934), "Some things of the early Boston Methodism," the annual address before the New England Methodist Historical Society, in Wesleyan Hall, Boston (1909).

11. NEUMHS Mss., typescript, Frank Theodore Pomeroy (1852–1942), "Reminiscences."

12. Herbert Asbury, *Up from Methodism* (New York: Alfred A. Knopf, 1926), 173–74.

13. For a summary of the English part of this story see David Hempton, *Methodism and Politics in British Society, 1750–1850* (London: Hutchinson, 1984), 197–202. See also John Kent, *The Age of Disunity* (London: Epworth, 1966); W. R. Ward, *Religion in English Society, 1790–1850* (London: Batsford, 1972); and Benjamin Gregory, *Side Lights on the Conflicts of Methodism During the Second Quarter of the Nineteenth Century, 1827–1852* (London: Casell, 1898). For the American side see Richard Carwardine, "Trauma in Methodism: Property, Church Schism, and Sectional Polarization in America," in *God and Mammon: Protestants, Money, and the Market, 1790–1860,* ed. Mark A. Noll (New York: Oxford University Press, 2001), 195–216.

14. I am indebted to Professor Jeffrey Cox for this methodological comparison. See, for example, the important local study of a London borough by Jeffrey Cox, *The English Churches in a Secular Society: Lambeth, 1870–1930* (New York: Oxford University Press, 1982).

15. Alan Gilbert, *The Making of Post-Christian Britain: A History of the Secularization of Modern Society* (London: Longman, 1980). See also his influential book *Religion and Society in Industrial England: Church, Chapel, and Social Change, 1740–1914* (New York: Longman, 1976).

16. Peter Berger, *The Sacred Canopy: Elements of a Sociological Theory of Religion* (New York: Anchor, 1969), 150.

17. E. R. Wickham, *Church and Society in an Industrial City* (London: Lutterworth, 1957); K. S. Inglis, *The Churches and the Working Classes in Victorian England* (London: Routledge, 1963); Hugh McLeod, *Class and Religion in the Late Victorian City* (London: Croom Helm, 1974). For a more recent treatment see Theodore Koditschek, *Class Formation and Urban Industrial Society: Bradford, 1750–1850* (Cambridge: Cambridge University Press, 1990), 252–92. For a wider European analysis of the fate of religion in fast-growing cities see Hugh McLeod, ed., *European Religion in the Age of Great Cities, 1830–1930* (London: Routledge, 1995).

18. Geoff Robson, *Dark Satanic Mills? Religion and Irreligion in Birmingham and the Black Country* (Carlisle, England: Paternoster, 2002), 247–77; Brierley, ed., *United Kingdom Christian Handbook,* 2:13.

19. Harvey Cox, *The Secular City: Secularization and Urbanization in Theological Perspective* (New York: Macmillan, 1966), 1, 18.

20. Hugh McLeod, *Piety and Poverty: Working Class Religion in Berlin, London, and New York, 1870–1914* (New York: Holmes and Meier, 1996).

21. Harvey Cox, *Fire from Heaven: The Rise of Pentecostal Spirituality and the Reshaping of Religion in the Twenty-first Century* (Reading, Mass.: Addison-Wesley, 1995), 99–100.

22. Steve Bruce, ed., *Religion and Modernization: Sociologists and Historians Debate the Secularization Thesis* (Oxford: Clarendon, 1992), 8–30.

23. See John H. S. Kent, *Holding the Fort: Studies in Victorian Revivalism* (London: Epworth, 1978).

24. S. J. D. Green, *Religion in the Age of Decline: Organisation and Experience in Industrial Yorkshire, 1870–1920* (Cambridge: Cambridge University Press, 1996), 374–75, 384.

25. Ibid., 389–90. See also Cox, *The English Churches in a Secular Society*.

26. See Callum G. Brown, "Did Urbanization Secularize Britain?" *Urban History Yearbook* (1988): 1–14; Callum G. Brown, "A Revisionist Approach to Religious Change," in *Religion and Modernization*, ed. Bruce; Callum G. Brown, "The Mechanism of Religious Growth in Urban Societies," in *European Religion in the Age of Great Cities*, ed. Hugh McLeod (London: Routledge, 1995); and Callum G. Brown, *The Death of Christian Britain* (London: Routledge, 2001).

27. Many of these variables show up in Hugh McLeod, *Secularisation in Western Europe, 1848–1914* (New York: St. Martin's, 2000). See also Frances Lannon, *Privilege, Persecution, and Prophecy: The Catholic Church in Spain, 1875–1975* (Oxford: Clarendon, 1984); Ralph Gibson, *A Social History of French Catholicism, 1789–1914* (New York, 1989). For good studies of how religion could fuse with nationalism to create vibrant religious cultures see Jerzy Kloczowski, *A History of Polish Christianity* (Cambridge: Cambridge University Press, 2000); Piotr S. Wandycz, *The Lands of Partitioned Poland, 1795–1918* (Seattle: University of Washington Press, 1996); and Sean Connolly, *Religion and Society in Nineteenth-Century Ireland* (Dundalk: Dundalgan, 1985). For differential patterns in three nineteenth-century mega-cities see McLeod, *Piety and Poverty*. For other influential ways of looking at religion in nineteenth- and twentieth-century Europe see Sarah C. Williams, *Religious Belief and Popular Culture in Southwark, c. 1880–1939* (Oxford: Oxford University Press, 1999); S. J. Connolly, *Priests and People in Pre-Famine Ireland* (Dublin: Gill and Macmillan, 1982); Thomas Kselman, "The Varieties of Religious Experience in Urban France," in *European Religion*, ed. McLeod, 165–90; Lucien Hölscher, "Secularization and Urbanization in the Nineteenth Century," in *European Religion*, ed. McLeod, 263–88; Grace Davie, *Religion in Britain Since 1945: Believing Without Belonging* (Oxford: Blackwell, 1994); Carl Strikwerda, "The Rise of Catholic Social Movements in Nineteenth-Century Belgian Cities," in *European Religion*, ed. McLeod, 61–89. The most recent and authoritative treatment of the decline of Christianity in Europe is Hugh McLeod and Werner Ustorf, eds., *The Decline of Christendom in Western Europe* (Cambridge: Cambridge University Press, 2003).

28. William J. Callahan, *Church Politics and Society in Spain, 1750–1874* (Cambridge: Harvard University Press, 1984); S. J. Brown, *Thomas Chalmers and the Godly Commonwealth* (Oxford: Oxford University Press, 1982). See also the chapters by Callahan, Strikwerda, Otte, and Dixon in *European Religion in the Age of Great Cities*, ed. McLeod.

29. Roger Finke and Rodney Stark, *The Churching of America, 1776–1990: Winners and Losers in Our Religious Economy* (New Brunswick, N.J.: Rutgers University Press, 1992), 248. See also Mark A. Noll, *The Old Religion in a New World: The History of North American Christianity* (Grand Rapids, Mich.: William B. Eerdmans, 2002), 282–91, and Dean M. Kelley, *Why Conservative Churches are Growing: A Study in Sociology of Religion* (San Francisco: Harper and Row, 1977).

30. Hastings and Johnson, "Old Cross, New Flame," chapter 3.

## CHAPTER 9: CONCLUSION

1. The figures are official estimates based on the *Minutes of Conference* of the British churches (1908) and *The Methodist Year Book* in the United States (1908). See the tables in W. J. Townsend, H. B. Workman, and George Eayrs, eds., *A New History of Methodism*, vol. 2 (London: Hodder and Stoughton, 1909), facing page

532. Calculating the number of adherents from the number of church members is a notoriously hazardous business. I have chosen a multiple of four, which is higher than some estimates and much lower than others. The range is usually between 3:1 and 7:1.

2. For an excellent treatment of the theme of Methodism and work, including its historiographical complexity, see John Walsh, " 'The Bane of Industry'? Popular Evangelicalism and Work in the Eighteenth Century," *Studies in Church History* 37 (2002). The most articulate and influential articulation of this view is in E. P. Thompson, *The Making of the English Working Class* (Harmondsworth: Penguin, 1968), and E. P. Thompson, "Time, Work Discipline, and Industrial Capitalism," *Past and Present* 38 (1969): 86–89. For a recent treatment of Thompson's work on Methodism see David Hempton and John Walsh, "E. P. Thompson and Methodism," in *God and Mammon: Protestants, Money, and the Market, 1790–1860*, ed. Mark A. Noll (New York: Oxford University Press, 2001), 99–120.

3. See Marilyn J. Westerkamp, *Women and Religion in Early America, 1600– 1850* (London: Routledge, 1999).

4. I survey the shift in the attitudes of Roman Catholics to Methodism in *Methodism and Politics in British Society, 1750–1850* (Stanford: Stanford University Press, 1984), 31–42. For the respective poles of interpretation see Rev. Arthur O'Leary, *Miscellaneous Tracts,* 2nd ed. (Dublin, 1781), and W. J. Amherst, S.J., *The History of Catholic Emancipation, 1771–1820* (London, 1886), on one side, and the comments by Bishop Odd Hagen, Augustin Cardinal Bea, and Michael Hurley, S.J., in Hurley, *John Wesley's Letter to a Roman Catholic* (Belfast: Irish Methodist Publishing, 1968), on the other. For a more recent account of the relations between Roman Catholics and Methodists in the eighteenth century see David Butler, *Methodists and Papists: John Wesley and the Catholic Church in the Eighteenth Century* (London: Darton, Longman, and Todd, 1995). For an analysis of different views on Methodism's relationship to women's emancipation and empowerment see Westerkamp, *Women and Religion in Early America.*

5. See the essays in David Hempton, *The Religion of the People: Methodism and Popular Religion, c. 1750–1900* (London: Routledge, 1996).

6. Donald G. Mathews, "United Methodism and American Culture: Testimony, Voice, and the Public Sphere," in *The People(s) Called Methodist: Forms and Reforms of Their Life,* ed. William B. Lawrence, Dennis M. Campbell, and Russell E. Richey (Nashville: Abingdon, 1998), 284. Unfortunately there is no good modern biography of Francis Asbury, but one is in preparation by John H. Wigger. Dr. Wigger, in a splendid review of his forthcoming work at the University of Manchester, stated that Asbury's leadership of American Methodists was unique in American culture. Unlike most other American religious leaders he was not a charismatic communicator, nor a public intellectual, nor a domineering autocrat. Rather he built his supremacy on his personal piety, celibate life, organizational judgment, and sensitive-pragmatic approach to Methodism and American popular culture.

7. As with Francis Asbury, there is no good recent biography of Bunting. The standard nineteenth-century biography is by his son T. P. Bunting, *The Life of Jabez Bunting, D.D., with Notes of Contemporary Persons and Events* (London: T. Woolmer, 1887). Based on Professor W. R. Ward's transcripts of the Bunting correspondence I made an attempt to reconstruct his early life in "Jabez Bunting: The Formative

Years, 1794–1820," in *The Religion of the People,* 91–108. W. R. Ward has produced two excellent editions of Bunting's correspondence, *The Early Correspondence of Jabez Bunting, 1820–1829* (London: Royal Historical Society, 1972), and *Early Victorian Methodism: The Correspondence of Jabez Bunting, 1830–1858* (Oxford: Clarendon, 1976). For a more favorable view of Bunting than Ward's or mine see John Kent, *Jabez Bunting: The Last Wesleyan* (London: Epworth, 1955).

8. Leigh Eric Schmidt, *Hearing Things: Religion, Illusion, and the American Enlightenment* (Cambridge: Harvard University Press, 2000).

9. Mathews, "United Methodism and American Culture," 298.

10. Philip Jenkins, *The Next Christendom: The Coming of Global Christianity* (New York: Oxford University Press, 2002).

# Suggestions for Further Reading

Because the primary sources for this study are best followed through the notes, and since there are already in existence excellent bibliographies of secondary sources for Methodist studies throughout the North Atlantic region, what follows is a personal selection of the most important works on the Methodist tradition and its historical context under a number of different categories. This list is neither exhaustive nor completely defensible, but it should help guide those less familiar with the subject into some of the best and most influential work in what has become a very rich and distinguished historiographical tradition.

## MODERN EDITIONS OF SOURCES

Baker, Frank, ed. *The Bicentennial Edition of the Works of John Wesley*. 35 vols. projected. Nashville: Abingdon, 1984– .

Chilcote, Paul Wesley, ed. *Her Own Story: Autobiographical Portraits of Early Methodist Women*. Nashville: Kingswood, 2001.

Clark, Elmer T., J. Manning Potts, and Jacob S. Payton, eds. *The Journal and Letters of Francis Asbury*. Nashville: Abingdon, 1958.

Gaustad, Edwin S., ed. *A Documentary History of Religion in America*. 2 vols. Grand Rapids, Mich.: Eerdmans, 1982–83.

Heitzenrater, Richard. *The Elusive Mr. Wesley*. 2 vols. Nashville: Abingdon, 1984.

———, ed. *Diary of an Oxford Methodist: Benjamin Ingham, 1733–34*. Durham, N.C.: Duke University Press, 1985.

Outler, Albert C., ed. *John Wesley*. New York: Oxford University Press, 1964.

Richey, Russell, Kenneth E. Rowe, and Jean Miller Schmidt, eds. *The Methodist Experience in America: A Sourcebook*. Nashville: Abingdon, 2000.

Sernett, Milton C., ed. *African American Religious History: A Documentary Witness*. Durham, N.C.: Duke University Press, 1999.

Wesley, Susanna. *Susanna Wesley: The Complete Writings*. Ed. Charles Wallace, Jr. New York: Oxford University Press, 1997.

## BIBLIOGRAPHIES AND REFERENCE WORKS

Carroll, Bret E. *The Routledge Historical Atlas of Religion in America*. New York: Routledge, 2000.

Green, Richard. *The Works of John and Charles Wesley: A Bibliography.* London: Methodist Publishing House, 1906.

Lewis, Donald M. *The Blackwell Dictionary of Evangelical Biography.* 2 vols. Oxford: Blackwell, 1995.

Rowe, Kenneth E. *Black Methodism: An Introductory Guide to the Literature.* Madison, N.J.: General Commission on Archives and History, United Methodist Church, 1984.

———. *United Methodist Studies: Basic Bibliographies.* Nashville: Abingdon, 1992.

Vickers, John A., ed. *A Dictionary of Methodism in Britain and Ireland.* London: Epworth, 2000.

## COLLECTIONS OF ESSAYS

Davies, Rupert, and Gordon Rupp, eds. *A History of the Methodist Church in Great Britain.* 4 vols. London: Epworth, 1965–88.

Garnett, Jane, and Colin Matthew, eds. *Revival and Religion Since 1700.* London: Hambledon, 1993.

Hatch, Nathan O., and John H. Wigger, ed. *Methodism and the Shaping of American Culture.* Nashville: Kingswood, 2001.

Noll, Mark A., ed. *God and Mammon: Protestants, Money, and the Market, 1790–1860.* New York: Oxford University Press, 2002.

Richey, Russell E., Dennis M. Campbell, and William B. Lawrence, eds. *United Methodism and American Culture.* Nashville: Abingdon. Vol. 1, *Connectionalism* (1997); vol. 2, *The People(s) Called Methodist* (1998); vol. 3, *Doctrines and Discipline* (1999).

Richey, Russell E., Kenneth E. Rowe, and Jean Miller Schmidt, eds. *Perspectives on American Methodism: Interpretive Essays.* Nashville: Kingswood, 1993.

Robbins, Keith, ed. *Protestant Evangelicalism: Britain, Ireland, Germany, and America, c. 1750–c. 1950.* Oxford: Blackwell, 1990.

Ward, W. R. *Faith and Faction.* London: Epworth, 1993.

## ORIGINS

Campbell, Ted A. *The Religion of the Heart: A Study of European Religious Life in the Seventeenth and Eighteenth Centuries.* Columbia: University of South Carolina Press, 1991.

Ditchfield, G. M. *The Evangelical Revival.* London: UCL Press, 1998.

Dreyer, Frederick. *The Genesis of Methodism.* Cranbury, N.J.: Associated University Presses, 1999.

Erb, Peter C. *Pietists: Selected Writings.* London: SPCK, 1983.

Knox, R. A. *Enthusiasm: A Chapter in the History of Religion.* Oxford: Clarendon, 1950.

Noll, Mark A. *The Rise of Evangelicalism: The Age of Edwards, Whitefield, and the Wesleys.* Leicester: Inter-Varsity, 2004.

Podmore, Colin. *The Moravian Church in England, 1728–1760.* Oxford: Clarendon, 1998.

Walsh, John D. "Elie Halévy and the Birth of Methodism." *Transactions of the Royal Historical Society* 5th Series 25 (1975): 1–20.

———. " 'Methodism' and the Origins of English-Speaking Evangelicalism." In

*Evangelicalism: Comparative Studies of Popular Protestantism in North America, the British Isles, and Beyond, 1700–1990,* ed. Mark A. Noll, David W. Bebbington, and George A. Rawlyk. New York: Oxford University Press, 1994.

——. "Origins of the Evangelical Revival." In *Essays in Modern English Church History,* ed. J. D. Walsh and G. V. Bennett. London: A. & C. Black, 1966.

Ward, W. R. *Christianity Under the Ancien Régime, 1648–1789.* Cambridge: Cambridge University Press, 1999.

——. "Power and Piety: The Origins of Religious Revival in the Early Eighteenth Century." *Bulletin of the John Rylands University Library of Manchester* 63, no. 1 (1980): 231–52.

——. *The Protestant Evangelical Awakening.* Cambridge: Cambridge University Press, 1992.

## BIOGRAPHY

Abelove, Henry. *The Evangelist of Desire: John Wesley and the Methodists.* Stanford, Calif.: Stanford University Press, 1990.

Bunting, T. P. *The Life of Jabez Bunting, D.D.* London: T. Woolmer, 1858–87.

Green, V. H. H. *The Young Mr. Wesley: A Study of John Wesley and Oxford.* London: Edward Arnold, 1961.

Piette, Maximin. *John Wesley in the Evolution of Protestantism.* London: Sheed & Ward, 1938.

Rack, Henry D. *Reasonable Enthusiast: John Wesley and the Rise of Methodism.* London: Epworth, 1989.

Southey, Robert. *The Life of Wesley and the Rise and Progress of Methodism.* 2 vols. London: Humphrey Milford, 1925.

Stout, Harry S. *The Divine Dramatist: George Whitefield and the Rise of Modern Evangelicalism.* Grand Rapids, Mich.: Eerdmans, 1991.

Tyerman, Luke. *The Life and Times of the Rev. John Wesley, M.A., Founder of the Methodists.* 3 vols. London: Hodder and Stoughton, 1890.

Valentine, Simon Ross. *John Bennet and the Origins of Methodism and the Evangelical Revival in England.* Lanham, Md.: Scarecrow, 1997.

Vickers, John. *Thomas Coke: Apostle of Methodism.* London: Epworth, 1969.

Ward, W. R. *The Early Correspondence of Jabez Bunting, 1820–1829.* London: The Royal Historical Society, 1972.

——. *Early Victorian Methodism: The Correspondence of Jabez Bunting, 1830–1858.* Oxford: Clarendon, 1976.

## THEOLOGY, BELIEF, AND PRACTICE

Brown, Earl Kent. *Women in Mr. Wesley's Methodism.* Lewiston, N.Y.: Edwin Mellen, 1983.

Cell, George Croft. *The Rediscovery of John Wesley.* New York: Henry Holt, 1935.

Chilcote, Paul W. *John Wesley and the Women Preachers of Early Methodism.* Metuchen, N.J.: Scarecrow, 1991.

Dreyer, Frederick. "Faith and Experience in the Thought of John Wesley." *American Historical Review* 88 (1983): 12–30.

Hildebrandt, Franz. *From Luther to Wesley.* London: Lutterworth, 1951.

Holifield, E. Brooks. *Theology in America: Christian Thought from the Age of the Puritans to the Civil War.* New Haven: Yale University Press, 2003.

Kimbrough, S. T., Jr. *Charles Wesley: Poet and Theologian.* Nashville: Kingswood, 1992.

Maddox, Randy L. *Responsible Grace: John Wesley's Practical Theology.* Nashville: Kingswood, 1994. (Contains a comprehensive bibliography of works on Methodist theology.)

Noll, Mark A. *America's God: From Jonathan Edwards to Abraham Lincoln.* New York: Oxford University Press, 2002.

Rattenbury, J. E. *The Evangelical Doctrines of Charles Wesley's Hymns.* London: Epworth, 1941.

Tucker, Karen B. Westerfield. *American Methodist Worship.* New York: Oxford University Press, 2001.

Young, Carlton R. *Music of the Heart: John and Charles Wesley on Music and Musicians.* Carol Stream, Ill.: Hope, 1995.

## REGIONS

Almost all the historical writing on the Methodist tradition has been confined to single national traditions, with the notable exception of one work:

Townsend, W. J., H. B. Workman, and George Eayrs, eds. *A New History of Methodism.* London: Hodder and Stoughton, 1909.

### Canada

Rawlyk, George A. *The Canada Fire: Radical Evangelicalism in British North America, 1775–1812.* Montreal: McGill-Queen's University Press, 1994.

——. *Ravished by the Spirit: Religious Revivals, Baptists, and Henry Alline.* Montreal: McGill-Queen's University Press, 1984.

——. *Wrapped Up in God: A Study of Several Canadian Revivals and Revivalists.* Burlington, Ontario: Welch, 1988.

——, ed. *The Canadian Protestant Experience, 1760–1990.* Montreal: McGill-Queen's University Press, 1984.

Semple, Neil. *The Lord's Dominion: The History of Canadian Methodism.* Montreal: McGill-Queen's University Press, 1996.

Van Die, Marguerite. *An Evangelical Mind: Nathaniel Burwash and the Methodist Tradition in Canada, 1839–1918.* Montreal: McGill-Queen's University Press, 1989.

Westfall, William. *Two Worlds: The Protestant Culture of Nineteenth Century Ontario.* Montreal: McGill-Queen's University Press, 1989.

### England

Andrews, Stuart. *Methodism and Society.* London: Longman, 1970.

Baker, Frank. *John Wesley and the Church of England.* London: Epworth, 1970.

Baxter, John. "The Great Yorkshire Revival, 1792–1796: A Study of Mass Revival Among the Methodists." *A Sociological Yearbook of Religion in Britain* 7 (1974): 46–76.

Bebbington, D. W. *Evangelicalism in Modern Britain: A History from the 1730s to the 1980s.* London: Unwin Hyman, 1989.

Brown, Kenneth D. *A Social History of the Nonconformist Ministry in England and Wales, 1800–1930*. Oxford: Clarendon, 1988.

Currie, Robert. *Methodism Divided: A Study in the Sociology of Ecumenicalism*. London: Faber and Faber, 1968.

———. "A Micro-Theory of Methodist Growth." *Proceedings of the Wesley Historical Society* 36 (1967): 65–73.

Field, C. D. "The Social Structure of English Methodism, Eighteenth–Twentieth Centuries." *British Journal of Sociology* 28, no. 2 (1977): 199–225.

Gilbert, A. D. "Methodism, Dissent, and Political Stability in Early Industrial England." *Journal of Religious History* 10 (1978–79): 381–99.

———. *Religion and Society in Industrial England: Church, Chapel, and Social Change, 1740–1914*. London: Longman, 1978.

Gowland, D. A. *Methodist Secessions: The Origins of Free Methodism in Three Lancashire Towns*. Manchester: Manchester University Press, 1979.

Gregory, Benjamin. *Sidelights on the Conflicts of Methodism, 1827–1852*. London: Cassell, 1898.

Heitzenrater, Richard P. *Wesley and the People Called Methodists*. Nashville: Abingdon, 1995.

Hempton, David. *Methodism and Politics in British Society, 1750–1850*. Stanford: Stanford University Press, 1984.

———. *The Religion of the People: Methodism and Popular Religion, c. 1750–1900*. London: Routledge, 1996.

———. *Religion and Political Culture in Britain and Ireland: From the Glorious Revolution to the Decline of Empire*. Cambridge: Cambridge University Press, 1996.

Kent, John. *Holding the Fort: Studies in Victorian Revivalism*. London: Epworth, 1978.

———. *Wesley and the Wesleyans: Religion in Eighteenth-Century Britain*. Cambridge: Cambridge University Press, 2002.

Laqueur, T. W. *Religion and Respectability: Sunday Schools and Working Class Culture, 1780–1850*. New Haven: Yale University Press, 1976.

Lovegrove, Deryck W. *Established Church, Sectarian People: Itinerancy and the Transformation of English Dissent, 1780–1830*. Cambridge: Cambridge University Press, 1988.

Luker, David. "Revivalism in Theory and Practice: The Case of Cornish Methodism." *Journal of Ecclesiastical History* 37, no. 4 (1986): 603–19.

McLeod, Hugh. *Religion and Society in England, 1850–1914*. London: Macmillan, 1996.

Malmgreen, Gail. *Religion in the Lives of English Women, 1760–1830*. London: Croom Helm, 1986.

Moore, Robert. *Pit-Men, Preachers, and Politics: The Effects of Methodism in a Durham Mining Community*. Cambridge: Cambridge University Press, 1974.

Obelkevich, James. *Religion and Rural Society: South Lindsey, 1825–1875*. Oxford: Clarendon, 1976.

Olsen, Gerald Wayne. *Religion and Revolution in Early Industrial England: The Halévy Thesis and Its Critics*. Lanham, Md.: The University Press of America, 1990.

Perkin, Harold. *The Origins of Modern English Society, 1780–1880*. London: Routledge & Kegan Paul, 1969.

Rivers, Isobel. *Reason, Grace, and Sentiment: A Study of the Language of Religion and Ethics in England, 1660–1780*. Vol. 1, *Whichcote to Wesley*. Cambridge: Cambridge University Press, 1991.

Robson, Geoff. *Dark Satanic Mills? Religion and Irreligion in Birmingham and the Black Country*. Carlisle, U.K.: Paternoster, 2002.

Rupp, E. Gordon, *Religion in England, 1688–1791*. Oxford: Clarendon, 1986.

Scotland, Nigel. *Methodism and the Revolt of the Field*. Gloucester, U.K.: Alan Sutton, 1981.

Semmel, Bernard. *The Methodist Revolution*. London: Heinemann, 1974.

Shaw, Thomas. *A History of Cornish Methodism*. Truro, U.K.: D. Bradford Barton, 1967.

Smith, Mark. *Religion in Industrial Society: Oldham and Saddleworth, 1740–1865*. Oxford: Oxford University Press, 1994.

Snape, M. F. "Anti-Methodism in Eighteenth Century England: The Pendle Forest Riots of 1748." *Journal of Ecclesiastical History* 49, no. 2 (1998): 257–81.

Snell, K. D. M. *Church and Chapel in the North Midlands: Religious Observance in the Nineteenth Century*. Leicester: Leicester University Press, 1991.

Thompson, David. *Nonconformity in the Nineteenth Century*. London: Routledge & Kegan Paul, 1972.

Thompson, E. P. *The Making of the English Working Class*. Harmondsworth: Penguin, 1968.

———. "Patrician Society, Plebeian Culture." *Journal of Social History* 7, no. 4 (1974): 382–405.

Turner, John Munsey. *Conflict and Reconciliation: Studies in Methodism and Ecumenism in England, 1740–1982*. London: Epworth, 1985.

Valenze, Deborah M. *Prophetic Sons and Daughters: Female Preaching and Popular Religion in Industrial England*. Princeton: Princeton University Press, 1985.

Walsh, John. "Methodism and the Mob in the Eighteenth Century." *Studies in Church History* 8 (1972): 213–27.

Ward, W. R. "The Religion of the People and the Problem of Control, 1790–1830." *Studies in Church History* 8 (1972): 237–57.

———. *Religion and Society in England, 1790–1850*. London: Batsford, 1972.

Warner, Wellman J. *The Wesleyan Movement in the Industrial Revolution*. London: Longmans, Green, 1930.

Watts, Michael R. *The Dissenters*. Vol. 1, *From the Reformation to the French Revolution;* vol. 2, *The Expansion of Evangelical Nonconformity, 1791–1859*. Oxford: Clarendon, 1978–95.

Wearmouth, Robert. *Methodism and the Working-Class Movements of England, 1800–1850*. London: Epworth, 1937.

———. *Some Working-Class Movements of the Nineteenth Century*. London: Epworth, 1948.

Werner, Julia Stewart. *The Primitive Methodist Connexion: Its Background and Early History*. Madison: University of Wisconsin Press, 1984.

## Scotland

Brown, Callum G. *Religion and Society in Scotland Since 1707*. Edinburgh: Edinburgh University Press, 1997.

Hayes, A. J., and D. A. Gowland, eds. *Scottish Methodism in the Early Victorian Period.* Edinburgh: Edinburgh University Press, 1981.

Swift, Wesley F. *Methodism in Scotland.* London: Epworth, 1947.

Ward, W. R. "Scottish Methodism in the Age of Jabez Bunting." *Scottish Church History Society Records* 20 (1979): 47–63.

### Ireland

Crookshank, C. H. *History of Methodism in Ireland.* 3 vols. London: T. Woolmer, 1885–88.

Hempton, David. "Gideon Ouseley: Rural Revivalist, 1791–1839." *Studies in Church History* 25 (1988): 203–14.

——. "Methodism in Irish Society, 1770–1830." *Transactions of the Royal Historical Society* 5th Series 36 (1986): 117–42.

——. "The Methodist Crusade in Ireland." *Irish Historical Studies* 22, no. 85 (1980): 33–48.

Hempton, David, and Myrtle Hill. *Evangelical Protestantism in Ulster Society, 1740–1890.* London: Routledge, 1992.

Holmes, Janice. *Religious Revivals in Britain and Ireland.* Dublin: Irish Academic Press, 2000.

### Wales

Davies, E. T. *A New History of Wales: Religion and Society in the Nineteenth Century.* Llandybie, Wales: Dyfed, 1981.

——. *Religion in the Industrial Revolution in South Wales.* Cardiff: University of Wales Press, 1965.

Hempton, David. *Religion and Political Culture in Britain and Ireland.* Cambridge: Cambridge University Press, 1996.

Jenkins, G. H. *The Foundations of Modern Wales.* Oxford: Oxford University Press, 1987.

Jones, I. G., and David Williams. *The Religious Census of 1851: A Calendar of the Returns Relating to Wales.* 2 vols. Cardiff: University of Wales Press, 1976.

### United States (general)

Ahlstrom, Sydney E. *A Religious History of the American People.* New Haven: Yale University Press, 1972.

Andrews, Dee E. *The Methodists and Revolutionary America, 1760–1800: The Shaping of an Evangelical Culture.* Princeton: Princeton University Press, 2000.

Brekus, Catherine A. *Strangers and Pilgrims: Female Preaching in America, 1740–1845.* Chapel Hill: University of North Carolina Press, 1998.

Bucke, Emory S., et al. *The History of American Methodism.* 3 vols. Nashville: Abingdon, 1964.

Butler, Jon. *Awash in a Sea of Faith: Christianizing the American People.* Cambridge: Harvard University Press, 1990.

Carwardine, Richard. *Evangelicals and Politics in Antebellum America.* New Haven: Yale University Press, 1993.

——. "Methodists, Politics, and the Coming of the American Civil War." *Church History* 69 (Sept. 2000): 578–609.

Hatch, Nathan O. *The Democratization of American Christianity*. New Haven: Yale University Press, 1989.

——. "The Puzzle of American Methodism." *Church History* 63 (June 1994): 175–89.

Heyrman, Christine Leigh. *Southern Cross: The Beginnings of the Bible Belt*. New York: Alfred A. Knopf, 1998.

Howe, Daniel Walker. "The Evangelical Movement and Political Culture in the North During the Second Party System." *Journal of American History* 77 (March 1991): 1216–39.

Johnson, Paul. *A Shopkeeper's Millennium: Society and Revivals in Rochester, New York, 1815–1837*. New York: Hill & Wang, 1978.

Kirby, James E., Russell E. Richey, and Kenneth E. Rowe, *The Methodists*. Westport, Conn.: Praeger, 1998.

Long, Kathryn Teresa. *The Revival of 1857–1858: Interpreting an American Religious Awakening*. New York: Oxford University Press, 1998.

McEllhenney, John G., ed. *United Methodism in America*. Nashville: Abingdon, 1992.

Marini, Stephen. "Hymnody as History: Early Evangelical Hymns and the Recovery of American Popular Religion." *Church History* 71, no. 2 (2002): 273–307.

Mathews, Donald G. "United Methodism and American Culture: Testimony, Voice, and the Public Sphere." In *The People(s) Called Methodist*, ed. William B. Lawrence, Dennis M. Campbell, and Russell E. Richey. Nashville: Abingdon, 1998.

Moore, R. Laurence. *Selling God: American Religion in the Marketplace of Culture*. New York: Oxford University Press, 1994.

Noll, Mark A. *The Old Religion in a New World*. Grand Rapids, Mich.: Eerdmans, 2002.

Richey, Russell E. *Early American Methodism*. Bloomington: Indiana University Press, 1991.

Schmidt, Jean Miller. *Grace Sufficient: A History of Women in American Methodism, 1760–1939*. Nashville: Abingdon, 1999.

Schmidt, Leigh Eric. *Hearing Things: Religion, Illusion, and the American Enlightenment*. Cambridge: Harvard University Press, 2000.

Schneider, A. Gregory. *The Way of the Cross Leads Home: The Domestication of American Methodism*. Bloomington: Indiana University Press, 1993.

Sellers, Charles. *The Market Revolution: Jacksonian America, 1815–1846*. New York: Oxford University Press, 1991.

Stokes, Melvyn, and Stephen Conway. *The Market Revolution in America: Social, Political, and Religious Expressions, 1800–1880*. Charlottesville: University Press of Virginia, 1996.

Stout, Harry S., and D. G. Hart, eds. *New Directions in American Religious History*. New York: Oxford University Press, 1997.

Sutton, William R. *Journeymen for Jesus: Evangelical Artisans Confront Capitalism in Jacksonian Baltimore*. University Park: Pennsylvania University Press, 1998.

Taves, Ann. *Fits, Trances, and Visions: Experiencing Religion and Explaining Experience from Wesley to James*. Princeton: Princeton University Press, 1999.

Westerkamp, Marilyn J. *Women and Religion in Early America, 1600–1850*. London: Routledge, 1999.

Wigger, John H. *Taking Heaven by Storm: Methodism and the Rise of Popular Christianity in America*. New York: Oxford University Press, 1998.

## The American South

Frey, Sylvia R., and Betty Wood, *Come Shouting to Zion: African American Protestantism in the American South and British Caribbean to 1830*. Chapel Hill: University of North Carolina Press, 1998.

Lyerly, Cynthia Lynn. *Methodism and the Southern Mind, 1770–1810*. New York: Oxford University Press, 1998.

Mathews, Donald G. *Religion in the Old South*. Chicago: University of Chicago Press, 1977.

Raboteau, Albert J. *Slave Religion: "The Invisible Institution" in the Antebellum South*. New York: Oxford University Press, 1978.

## Transatlantic Region

Carwardine, Richard. *Trans-Atlantic Revivalism: Popular Evangelicalism in Britain and America, 1790–1865*. Westport, Conn.: Greenwood, 1978.

Noll, Mark A., David W. Bebbington, and George A. Rawlyk, eds. *Evangelicalism: Comparative Studies of Popular Protestantism in North America, the British Isles, and Beyond, 1700–1990*. New York: Oxford University Press, 1994.

O'Brien, Susan Durden. "A Transatlantic Community of Saints: The Great Awakening and the First Evangelical Networks, 1735–1755." *American Historical Review* 91 (Oct. 1986): 311–32.

Rawlyk, George A., and Mark A. Noll, eds. *Amazing Grace: Evangelicalism in Australia, Britain, Canada, and the United States*. Montreal: McGill-Queen's University Press, 1994.

Schmidt, Leigh Eric. *Holy Fairs: Scottish Communions and American Revivals in the Early Modern Period*. Princeton: Princeton University Press, 1989.

Westerkamp, Marilyn J. *Triumph of the Laity: Scots-Irish Piety and the Great Awakening, 1625–1760*. New York: Oxford University Press, 1988.

## MISSIONS

Barclay, Wade C. *History of Methodist Missions*. 6 vols. New York: Board of Missions and Church Extension of the Methodist Church, 1949– .

Findlay, G. G., and W. W. Holdsworth. *History of the Wesleyan Methodist Missionary Society*. London, 1921–24.

Koss, Stephen, "Wesleyanism and Empire." *Historical Journal* 18 (1975): 105–18.

Martin, R. H. "Missionary Competition Between Evangelical Dissenters and Wesleyan Methodists in the Early Nineteenth Century: A Footnote to the Founding of the Methodist Missionary Society." *Proceedings of the Wesley Historical Society* 42 (1979): 81–86.

Mason, J. C. S. *The Moravian Church and the Missionary Awakening in England, 1760–1800*. The Royal Historical Society: Boydell, 2001.

Piggin, Stuart. "Halévy Revisited: The Origins of the Wesleyan Methodist Missionary Society: An Examination of Semmel's Thesis." *The Journal of Imperial and Commonwealth History* 9, no. 1 (1980): 17–37.

Robert, Dana L. *American Women in Mission: A Social History of Their Thought and Practice*. Macon, Ga.: Mercer University Press, 1998.

Taggart, Norman W. *The Irish in World Methodism, 1760–1900*. London: Epworth, 1986.

## GROWTH AND DECLINE

Brierley, Peter, ed. *UK Christian Handbook: Religious Trends*, no. 2. London: Harper Collins, 2000–2001.

Brown, Callum G. *The Death of Christian Britain: Understanding Secularisation, 1800–2000*. London: Routledge, 2001.

Bruce, Steve, ed. *Religion and Modernization: Sociologists and Historians Debate the Secularization Thesis*. Oxford: Clarendon, 1992.

Cox, Jeffrey, *The English Churches in a Secular Society: Lambeth, 1870–1930*. New York: Oxford University Press, 1982.

Currie, Robert, Alan Gilbert, and Lee Horsley. *Churches and Churchgoers: Patterns of Church Growth in the British Isles Since 1700*. Oxford: Clarendon, 1977.

Finke, Roger, and Rodney Stark. *The Churching of America, 1776–1990: Winners and Losers in Our Religious Economy*. New Brunswick, N.J.: Rutgers University Press, 1992.

——. "How the Upstart Sects Won America, 1776–1850." *Journal for the Scientific Study of Religion* 28 (March 1989): 27–44.

Gilbert, A. D. *The Making of Post-Christian Britain: A History of the Secularization of Modern Society*. London: Longman, 1980.

Green, S. J. D. *Religion in an Age of Decline: Organisation and Experience in Industrial Yorkshire, 1870–1920*. Cambridge: Cambridge University Press, 1996.

Jenkins, Philip. *The Next Christendom: The Coming of Global Christianity*. New York: Oxford University Press, 2002.

McLeod, Hugh. "Class, Community, and Region: The Religious Geography of Nineteenth Century England." *Sociological Yearbook of Religion in Britain* 6 (1973).

Martin, David. *Pentecostalism: The World Their Parish*. Oxford: Blackwell, 2002.

Wacker, Grant. *Heaven Below: Early Pentecostals and American Culture*. Cambridge: Harvard University Press, 2001.

Williams, Sarah C. *Religious Belief and Popular Culture in Southwark, c. 1880–1939*. Oxford: Oxford University Press, 1999.

Wuthnow, Robert. *The Restructuring of American Religion: Society and Faith Since World War II*. Princeton: Princeton University Press, 1988.

Yeo, Stephen. *Religion and Voluntary Organisations in Crisis*. London: Croom Helm, 1976.

# Index